GOD LOVES JUSTICE

JESSICA NICHOLAS

GOD LOVES JUSTICE

A USER-FRIENDLY GUIDE TO BIBLICAL JUSTICE AND RIGHTEOUSNESS

Jessica Nicholas

S&E EDUCATIONAL PRESS

LOS ANGELES, CALIFORNIA

Copyright © 2017 by Jessica Nicholas

PUBLISHED BY:
S&E Educational Press
Los Angeles, California 90034

All rights reserved. No part of this publication may be reproduced, distributed, or transmitted in any form or by any means, including photocopying, recording, or other electronic or mechanical methods, without the prior written permission of the publisher, except in the case of brief quotations embodied in critical reviews and certain other noncommercial uses permitted by copyright law. For permission requests, email Book@Godlovesjustice.com.

Scripture quotations marked ESV are from the ESV® Bible (The Holy Bible, English Standard Version®), copyright © 2001 by Crossway, a publishing ministry of Good News Publishers. Used by permission. All rights reserved. Scripture quotations marked KJV are taken from the King James Version. Scripture quotations marked MSG are taken from THE MESSAGE, copyright © 1993, 1994, 1995, 1996, 2000, 2001, 2002 by Eugene H. Peterson. Used by permission of NavPress. All rights reserved. Represented by Tyndale House Publishers, Inc. Scripture quotations marked NASB are taken from the New American Standard Bible® (NASB), Copyright © 1960, 1962, 1963, 1968, 1971, 1972, 1973, 1975, 1977, 1995 by The Lockman Foundation. Used by permission. www.Lockman.org Scripture quotations marked NLT are taken from the Holy Bible, New Living Translation, copyright ©1996, 2004, 2007, 2013, 2015 by Tyndale House Foundation. Used by permission of Tyndale House Publishers, Inc., Carol Stream, Illinois 60188. All rights reserved. Scripture quotations marked GNT are taken from the Good News Translation in Today's English Version- Second Edition Copyright © 1992 by American Bible Society. Used by Permission.

GNT

ORDERING INFORMATION:

Quantity sales: Special discounts are available on quantity purchases by corporations, churches, nonprofits, and others. **For details, contact:**

BOOK@GODLOVESJUSTICE.COM
WWW.GODLOVESJUSTICE.COM

ISBN 13: 978-0-9989031-0-1
ISBN 10: 0-9989031-0-8
LIBRARY OF CONGRESS CONTROL NUMBER:
2017905685

EDITOR: ALLISON ARMERDING | WWW.ALLISONARMERDING.COM
COVER + INTERIOR DESIGN: SARA RIDKY | WWW.SARARIDKY.COM
AUTHOR PHOTO: SARAH SHEREVES PHOTOGRAPHY

DEDICATION

TO EDEN AND SHILOH.
May you inherit a world full of the justice and righteousness that God loves.

TABLE OF CONTENTS

	ACKNOWLEDGEMENTS	VII
	INTRODUCTION	IX
01	*What Do I Say That I Love?*	01
02	Defining Terms	09
03	*Mishpat:* Heaven's Design on Earth	19
04	*Sedeq:* Right Relationships, Right Life	33
05	Justice and Righteousness: The Foundation of God's Reign and God's People	43
06	Unified God: Just, Merciful, Righteous, and Kind	51
07	Does God Love the Poor?	59
08	Job: A Lifestyle of Justice and Righteousness	69
09	Amos: Justice and Righteousness in a Nation	85
10	Justice in the New Testament	105
11	The Liberating King	111
12	Victorious Justice	121
13	Sermon on the Mount: Righteousness in the Heart and in the World	133
14	Lawless Love	153
15	Justice & Righteousness in Everyday Kingdom Life	167
16	Conclusion: God of Hope	187
	APPENDIX: IMPLEMENTATION GUIDE	202
	ENDNOTES	209
	BIBLIOGRAPHY	222

ACKNOWLEDGEMENTS

-

"Commit your way to the Lord; trust in him, and he will act" (Psalm 35:7 ESV). Thank you first to God. You initiated, sustained, and completed this book. Without Your constant presence and support, this whole project would have been impossible.

Thanks to the David Hubbard Library at Fuller Theological Seminary for access to many of the resources used in this book.

To my miracle-working editor, Allison Armerding. You amaze me! I'm still in awe of how you managed to make the book feel cohesive. When I read the final draft, I see your fingerprints all over it. Thanks to Julie Guzzetta for making time to edit while adjusting to a new job. Your insights brought a whole new level of clarity to the book.

Thanks to Sheryl Hernandez, Jennifer Toledo, Bethany Stavros, Katie Hatcher, Jill Shook, and Paul Dabdoub for help making decisions and connecting me to the editors, theologians, artists, designers, etc. Your practical support was a lifeline during this whole process.

Thanks to the volunteers who read and gave feedback to the book. The quality of the book greatly improved because of the hours you gave to reading and providing feedback.

To my family, thank you! Kelly, thank you for your endless support and for being the bestest sister. Nathan, thank you for all of the business and practical advice. I'm so glad you're my big brother. Thank you to my parents, Bryan and Kim (the lover of door parts and the lover of all things gardening), for being constant examples of integrity, hard work, and generosity. You made so many sacrifices so that your kids could have better opportunities, and I am grateful to you both. Thank you, Aunt Crissy. You have no idea how much your kindness, humor, and love have shaped me, and helped me get through the process of writing this book. You've always made me feel like a success no matter what.

And finally, thank you Lance Jacobs: "The fruit of the righteous is a tree of life" (Proverbs 11:30a ESV). This book wouldn't have happened if it weren't for you. I have a feeling you won't believe me, so I'm putting it in writing. Whatever fruit comes from this book is the fruit of your life.

INTRODUCTION

I come from a family of door lovers. My grandpa and uncle are locksmiths and my dad is an expert in electronic door hardware. Yes, there are people out there who obsess about door hardware, and my family is full of them. As a kid, my dad took me to job sites if he needed an extra set of hands, wanted to show me inside an interesting building, or just wanted to impress his work clients with his blonde-haired daughter, complete with stick-on earrings, neon-laced shoes, and a cordless power drill in hand. That meant I got to see lots of grown-ups with lots of different kinds of jobs.

One of these visits exposed me to something new: the inner world of a cubicle-filled corporate office. I was on a ladder examining something at the top of a door when I turned to look out over the huge, open room in this generic office building where we were working. What I saw terrified me—an entire room full of adults dressed in casual career wear, crammed into row after row of cubicles looking like they hated their existence. Exhaustion, worry, and boredom wore clearly on their faces. I caught snatches of whispered conversations about things like weight loss and not wanting to be late on a mortgage payment. As the day wound down, I saw heads all over the room glancing compulsively at the clock, clearly desperate for the day to be over so they could leave.

I left that day in a stunned panic. *That* was going to be my life in twenty years? I had never felt the urge to live the typical "American dream"—get married, have a few kids, work a job, and then retire. But seeing this version of it up close made that dream seem more like a nightmare. If I didn't plan my life out, I too could end up crammed into a cubicle, obsessing over my weight and a hefty mortgage.

Thankfully as I grew up, I discovered that just because you have a desk job doesn't mean you aren't doing great, meaningful things with your life. I've put in plenty of years myself doing office work in the "real world." Working a job, learning skills, and supporting a family can be a meaningful, God-glorifying journey. But seeing that particular office certainly inspired in me an abiding fear of meaningless work.

Another very different type of experience that shaped me was being exposed at a young age to extreme poverty through my San Diego church. My door-loving father thought it would be fun for him and me to join the "clown ministry" at our church. Clowns are popular in Mexico, so we were always invited to go on the weeklong events my church hosted right over the border in some poor parts of Mexico.

Before these experiences, I had seen pictures and watched a news clip about poverty, so none of the sights and sounds surprised me. What really impacted me was the human side. Images and stories had given me an idea of life in poverty that was faraway and one-dimensional. Real exposure made poverty personal and relatable. I discovered that kids in the slums *also* liked candy and playing, my two favorite things. I played soccer with kids just like me, and I watched the shy ones hang onto their doting moms, who were just like mine. Girls whispered secrets to each other and giggled like my friends and me. Poverty began to feel human.

During one of those trips, a Mexican woman from a local church invited my parents and me to dinner in between meetings. My mom seemed strangely hesitant to accept, but the woman was so excited to host foreign guests that my mom said yes. When we walked into her house, the woman greeted us with a big pot of soup that had been slow-cooking all day. I had never had an opportunity to try Mexican food not cooked in a restaurant, so I gave an enthusiastic yes to everything she offered. A whole piece of chicken? Sure. Three pieces of bread? Of course my twelve-year-old stomach could hold that. When the host asked if I like corn, my mom quickly said, "Oh no, we don't like corn." I loudly corrected her: "No, I love corn!" The host took my bowl back to the kitchen, got me the biggest piece, and returned my bowl to me with a beaming smile.

My usually hungry parents seemed to be eating so little, but I didn't mind making up for them. When we left, I asked my parents why they

INTRODUCTION

had acted so weird. We were a corn-loving family—why hide that? My mom explained that the soup we ate was supposed to last that woman for the weekend, and she had fed us the full pot on a Friday. That meant she would likely be eating bread the rest of the weekend. The woman had been so genuinely happy to serve us dinner, it hadn't occurred to me that it could cost her so severely. That was the first time I felt what it was like to receive sacrificial generosity, and it came at the table of that woman.

Those real, person-to-person moments are what shaped my view of extreme poverty, gave it real names, and attached it to God-reflecting kindness and generosity. The poor people I met were hardworking, grateful, and kind, with lives full of challenges as well as rich in everyday joys. They experienced the same depth and range of emotions that I did. Who wouldn't want to help such wonderful people have safer, healthier lives?

That mix—seeing a mundane "American Dream" life against the dramatic poverty in Mexico—made it seem like my options for adulthood were wearing casual career wear in a cubicle or giving my life to something that really impacted my heart. That made my decision about how to spend my adult years easy. I wanted to give my life to something bigger—something to do with social justice. However, it took a while for me to settle on what that "something bigger" would look like. In my first year of college alone, I went from deciding to work for Doctors Without Borders (because of an emotionally moving episode of the show *ER*), to deciding to teach classical music to children in slums (because of an inspiring documentary), to deciding to become a human rights attorney (because of Gary Haugen's book *The Good News About Injustice*). The passion of each of those people was contagious. All it took was a few chapters of a book or a tearful video clip and I was ready to change career paths so I could do that great, wonderful thing they were doing. I wanted to hold on to the fantasy that I could "change the world," do every job, and reach every hurting person.

Though none of the social justice outlets I saw turned out to be places I could see myself landing in long-term, they did clarify one desire in my heart. I didn't want to do social justice alone. I wanted to be part of a church community that did justice together. Alone, I couldn't accomplish the growing list of jobs my heart wanted to do. But maybe if I was joined to the body of Christ, I could be integrated with millions of people who all had access to a limitless God. Together, we could accomplish what I longed to see.

Wonderfully, I have met many other Christians, especially from my generation, who are passionate about social justice. To many people, justice is attractive and exciting. While some people hear "social justice" and think of communists and hippies, more and more American evangelical Christians are connecting it with the gospel.

However, even though many people in this generation are excited about social justice, most of us can't articulate a clear definition of it or its theological basis. As I was getting involved in social justice projects, I assumed that eventually some pastor or Christian leader would sit me down and explain to me where justice appears in the Bible and then unpack the theology of biblical justice. But this never happened. The sermons I heard on justice were rare and most started with, "Webster's Dictionary defines *justice* as…" Instead of digging into what the Bible said, the speakers usually spent time criticizing all the terrible ways the secular world was doing social justice. Worst of all, many attached specific politics to social justice, making God seem like He could only be on the side of one American political party.

I came away from these sermons thinking that there had to be a theology of justice that went deeper than Webster's Dictionary. I couldn't have cared less about what politicians and philosophers said about justice—what did God say about it? How is it defined and demonstrated in the Bible? What are the biblical principles for living it out? I just wanted some plain, solid Bible teaching, unmixed with personal opinions and politics. While I found some wonderful books by Christians, I couldn't find a comprehensive Bible study on justice. Reading about justice in the Bible for myself felt too daunting. Surely a theologian or pastor with proper credentials should be the ones to put biblical justice into understandable terms for me—right?

It took years for me to finally listen to God's nudges and actually look at Scripture to see what He says about justice. Reading about these subjects in the Bible radically transformed me. After years of trying to cut through all the political and religious agendas driving social justice projects, I had finally discovered the secret formula. To get the

INTRODUCTION

best, most powerful, unbiased message about justice, I only needed to read the Bible.

After some not-so-gentle promptings from God, I decided to put together the "sit me down and explain biblical justice to me" resource that I would have wanted my eighteen-year-old self to have. I was frustrated when justice was talked about only in terms of politics, tired of cute stories and lessons like "volunteer at a soup kitchen," and stuck with so many questions about social justice and what God has to say about it. What I needed was an introductory resource that explained the foundation of biblical justice in clear, undiluted language. Though I realize that my experience isn't everyone's, I believe there are many people today who share the same questions and frustrations. I see this book as one of many resources on justice. Some church traditions have been teaching on social justice for generations, and thankfully, more and more evangelical leaders have been developing biblically based resources in recent years.

SOCIAL JUSTICE VS. JUSTICE AND RIGHTEOUSNESS

If the term "social justice" feels scary or too politically charged, don't worry. What we will be exploring in this book is the study of God's justice and righteousness in His own terms—not to gain support for a social agenda, but to know more about the God whom we love.

The beauty of this study is that it opens up infinite ways in which we as Christians can live out justice and righteousness. In our current culture, "doing" social justice seems limited to certain careers or to taking on large-scale systemic injustices. But what if you aren't called to start a nonprofit or become a social worker? The only remaining option, it seems, is to have a separate category of "justice" activities that we tack on to our busy lives—volunteering, protesting, watching documentaries for "awareness," going on a short-term service trip, or changing our shopping habits.

This way of thinking about justice has always seemed weird to me. As a Christian, I believe that I serve a really big God who makes all things possible, that I am supposed to live a life fully surrendered to

Him, that I am part of an unshakeable kingdom, and that I can live a life that makes an impact into eternity. Yet, when it comes to doing justice with my life, my options seemed limited to volunteering once a week and buying fair-trade coffee. Surely there is more to doing justice with the God of the impossible than that.

In the Bible, justice and righteousness are everywhere. They come first from the character of God and are an integral part of everything He does and how He rules. Justice and righteousness are the foundation of life for God's chosen nation, and how God's people follow His ways. Jesus brings justice to victory and executes righteousness. The kingdom of God is established and upheld with justice and righteousness, and they can have a lasting, permanent expression in every aspect of life on this planet. Justice and righteousness are not restricted to a short list of careers or hobbies, as social justice too often becomes in our world. They are a current, tangible part of the lives of all of God's people. We all get to be a unique expression of justice and righteousness in Christ's diverse body.

The biblical models of justice and righteousness give us the perfect cure to the reactionary cycle that the American church has a habit of falling into—reacting to the Social Gospel movement, to problems in capitalism, to feminism, and to the reaction to the reaction to social justice. Again and again, we turn our focus to what is wrong in the world around us and define our beliefs and practices in relationship to that. Every time we do this, we lose the opportunity to offer the world something truly different and redemptive. No matter where we currently are in our beliefs about social justice or where we land on the political spectrum, we can all move *toward* something: the justice and righteousness that God loves and Jesus lives out as expressed in Scripture.

And as we plant God's word in our lives, it will bear fruit. In Isaiah, God says that rain doesn't head back to heaven after it falls to earth without giving seed and food. And like the fruitful rain:

> so shall my word be that goes out from my mouth;
>   it shall not return to me empty,
> but it shall accomplish that which I purpose,
>   and shall succeed in the thing for which I sent it.
> (Isaiah 55:11 ESV)

INTRODUCTION

If we want to produce the real fruit of justice in our lives, then we need to plant God's word about justice. God's word will accomplish the full purpose God intends for us in the areas of justice and righteousness. The most fruitful message—one that will take root and grow in our lives—is found in the Bible.

People with an agenda will always try to manipulate justice for themselves. But when we as Christians continue to align ourselves with God's justice as revealed in Scripture, we won't pervert it with human reactions and selfishness. Instead, we will radically live it out in humility, generosity, and joy.

GOD LOVES JUSTICE

JESSICA NICHOLAS

WHAT DO I SAY I LOVE?

CHAPTER ONE

MY JOURNEY OF STUDYING God's heart for justice and righteousness began with a misguided mission to fix poverty. Many years ago, I picked up the idea that God had a special love for the poor. It's hard to remember where this idea started—it seemed as obvious as "the sky is blue"—but I'm pretty sure I came by it in church. While we didn't talk about poverty that much, every time sign-ups for a mission trip came around someone would make an announcement to the effect that we needed to show "God's love for the poor."

I came to assume that the poor belonged to a special category in God's eyes. Though the world usually forgot about them, He had an extra amount of love for the poor to make up for it. My mind took this reasoning one step further: if God loved the poor, then God must also hate the poverty that entrapped them. Because I wanted my love to match God's, it was obvious that I needed to share His love for the poor by stopping the poverty He hated.

Finally, I settled on a social justice career that lined up with this belief, which was working to end poverty. My undergraduate degree was done, so I began looking at going back to graduate school to get the kind of fancy academic credentials that make the world take you seriously. Before applying to graduate school and committing to take on a huge amount of student loans, however, I decided it was a good idea to do a test run. I took a month off of my office job in San Diego to go to a summer school session at the London School of Economics. My plan was to spend my time in one of the world's most dynamic cities locked in the LSE library reading all I could find on the best programs to fix poverty. Sure enough, during the hours I wasn't in class, I headed to the library and dug into all the best research on what helps stop cycles of systemic poverty.

Then one day as I was walking down a staircase in the library carrying a stack of books, God interrupted me with a simple question: "What do I say I love?"

I stopped right there in the middle of the stairs. *"What do You say that You love?"* The question forced my train of thought to jump tracks. My head was full of statistics, and God was asking me about His *feelings*. Why would He want me to think about His emotions when I should be thinking about important poverty stuff? I began searching my memory for a verse where God says what He loves. I felt sure I had read a verse somewhere saying that God loves the poor. But the only words that came back to me were these: "For I, the Lord, love justice" (Isaiah 61:8 NASB).

As I stood there stumped, a disturbing thought occurred to me. After a few decades in church, I felt so sure I knew the Bible well. But if I really didn't know what God says He loves, then maybe I didn't know the Bible as well as I thought. And if I couldn't answer a question so fundamental to all intimate relationships, then maybe I didn't know *God* as well as I thought. In all the years I had been saying that God loves the poor, I had never actually stopped to look at where in the Bible He said that. The belief had become such a guiding conviction in my life that I probably should have stopped to check it at some point. Obviously God loves everyone, the poor included. But does He ever specifically single out that one group and say that He has *more* love for them? In that moment, I knew what God was asking me to do—to actually look in the Bible at what He says He loves.

THE STUDY

Anytime God whispers a challenging question to me, I expect to

WHAT DO I SAY I LOVE?

be surprised by the answer, because He likes to change my thinking. I couldn't help trying to guess what I would find in the Bible about what God loves. I felt sure I would find a long list of the things God says He loves and that it would include sweet things like faithfulness, obedience, mercy, and grace. But of course, what I found surprised me far more than I had expected.

I decided to begin my search in the Old Testament. At the time God asked me the question, I had been reading a lot about poverty in the Old Testament, because there were so many practical rules about the poor when Israel was a nation. Growing up, I had mostly been taught to read the New Testament, which is unfortunately common for many modern Christians. Only later did I discover just how important it was for me to know the Old Testament, too. Without the Old Testament, we don't have the full picture of the biblical story. This is where God first introduces Himself, His design for the world, and His plan to make the world right again after sin entered it. Without it, the New Testament doesn't make sense.

The first step in my study was to sit cross-legged on the bed in my tiny rented London room with a strong cup of tea. The second step was to look up all the Hebrew words for "love" in the Old Testament. I then read every verse in which these words appeared, and recorded every time that either God says that He loves something, or someone says that God loves something.

There are multiple Hebrew words for love, but only one is used in reference to God loving something: the verb 'ahed, which appears in two forms.[1] The first form, 'ahaba, is used nine times—all of them referring to God's love for the people of Israel. The other form, 'ahab, is used twenty-eight times—nine times in reference to Israel, two times to immigrants to Israel, six times to leaders of Israel, once to Jerusalem, once to God's sanctuary, and once to King Cyrus, the Persian ruler God anointed to fight wars to deliver Israel from Babylon.

Twenty-nine out of thirty-seven times God says He loves something in the Old Testament, it is related to His chosen people, Israel.[2] That is easy to understand—He made a covenant with Israel and used the metaphor of marriage to describe their relationship.[3] Of course He loved them, their leaders, their immigrants, His sanctuary among them, and their cities.

But there are eight other times God says He loves something, and they reveal a surprising theme:

- For the Lord is righteous [*saddiq*]; He loves righteousness [*sedeqah*]. (Psalm 11:7a NASB)

- He loves righteousness [*sedeqah*] and justice [*mishpat*]. (Psalm 33:5a NASB)

- For the Lord loves justice [*mishpat*]. (Psalm 37:28a NASB)

- You have loved righteousness [*sedeq*] and hated wickedness. (Psalm 45:7a NASB)

- The strength of the King loves justice [*mishpat*]. (Psalm 99:4a NASB)

- The Lord loves the righteous [*saddiq*]. (Psalm 146:8b NASB)

- He loves one who pursues righteousness [*sedeqah*]. (Proverbs 15:9b NASB)

- For I the Lord love justice [*mishpat*]. (Isaiah 61:8a NASB)

What does God *say* He loves? He says He loves justice (*mishpat*) and righteousness (*sedeq*). The first time I looked at this list I didn't believe it, so I went back and double-checked. The results came back the same. As someone who had staked her future on loving the poor because of her belief in God's specific love for them, this information was profoundly disturbing.

After staring at the list for a while, my eyes didn't want to see it anymore, so I looked outside the window into a rainy garden. The gray sky didn't provide a good distraction from my mood. *How do I process this information?* I wondered. Out of everything God says He loves in the whole Old Testament, God singles out His chosen people, righteousness, and justice. This study shone a spotlight on two words that I absolutely couldn't say that I loved: justice and righteousness. To me, justice involved laws and courtrooms, and righteousness involved boring religious rules. Based on *my* understanding of justice and righteousness, a God who loved those things would look a lot like a rule-obsessed, emotionally detached ruler. But I knew God wasn't like that; therefore, something was wrong with my understanding.

My profound disturbance was real. This simple study was showing me that doing the thing I wanted to do most with my life—loving the poor through social justice—was missing a connection to a vital part of His heart. Despite being involved in social justice projects for nearly a decade, I had to admit that day in that tiny London bedroom that I couldn't say that I loved justice and righteousness—or even social justice.

At first, I thought there might be a way around this—another way of interpreting the study that wouldn't make me quite as disturbed. Maybe God had a different experience of love than I did. Or maybe He was saying something similar to what we mean when we say things like "I love pizza." Saying "I love" means we think pizza is fantastic, but our connection can be shallow. That would help me understand why God would say that He loved something to which I didn't attach the same emotion—maybe His experiences didn't involve any depth.

So I dug deeper into the meaning of the Hebrew word for love. The first time "love" appears in the Bible is when God tells Abraham to take his son Isaac, who he loves ['ahab], and sacrifice him (see Genesis 22:2). God asks Abraham to sacrifice the thing he values most in the world: his promised son. The level of sacrifice God asked of Abraham shows the level of love Abraham had to his son.

In the rest of the Old Testament, 'ahab is used to describe a lot of things, from the desire between the lovers in Song of Songs to a glutton's appetite.[4] One verse that gives a good picture of this love is when Israel was commanded, "You shall love ['ahad] the Lord your God with all your heart and with all your soul and with all your might" (Deuteronomy 6:5 ESV). Love is a deep and multifaceted experience involving emotions, intellect, will, spirit, affections, and actions. We can't assume God has the same experiences or "warm and fuzzy" feelings that we humans have. But we know that we are made in His image, and that love is a deep experience connected to every dimension of body, soul, and spirit.

As I read more about the justice and righteousness God loved, it became clear that His emotions toward them were different than mine. This verse from Jeremiah hit me particularly hard:

"but let him who boasts boast in this, that he understands and knows me, that I am the LORD who practices steadfast love, justice [*mishpat*], and righteousness [*sedeqah*] in the earth. For in these things I delight, declares the LORD" (Jeremiah 9:24 ESV)

To know and understand God is to know that He does justice and righteousness. Equally important, God tells us what motivates Him to do what He does: "…in these things I delight." This is huge. Delight is God's *why* behind the justice, righteousness, and steadfast love He practices. It's not out of frustration or obligation, but *delight*.

The biblical story is the full display of God's love for justice and righteousness.

No, I could not find any way around it. The biblical story is the full display of God's love for justice and righteousness. And that love is passionate, full of delight, anchored in faithfulness, and a part of everything God does. The realization that I did not share His love for them was painful. In all the years I had done great, important-sounding projects, I had missed His heart. How could I not know what He loved? It was a clear moment of correction, although I understood that it wasn't because I was doing anything wrong. God wasn't disciplining me because social justice work was terrible and He wanted me to stop. Rather, there was a part of His heart He wanted to share with me, which I had missed. His goal was to bring me closer to His heart so everything I was working for could come from a place of deep relational connection.

By the time I left London, I had made a decision: if God loves justice and righteousness, I wanted to be able to say that I loved them, too. Simply doing social justice because it felt right wasn't enough. To understand God is to know His delight toward justice and righteousness, and I wanted to know Him better. That would take some work. But when you really love someone, you want to know what's important to them. Understanding what they love and why they love it, connects you to their heart. I started to see this journey of learning about God's love for justice and righteousness as just that—an opportunity to know Him better and connect with His heart.

THE INVITATION

To all the trained theologians throwing up red flags about this study already, I get it. Overly-simplified word studies aren't how to build theology. I am not suggesting that my simple Hebrew word study forms the foundation of the theology of what God loves. When I did this same study in the New Testament, I found a longer list of the things that God says He loves.

However, God's question to me revealed a part of Him I did not know or understand and challenged my assumptions about what I thought the Bible said about poverty and justice. By inviting me to pursue His heart, God lifted the restraints that had caused me to hesitate in looking deeper into Scripture about social justice. The invitation was simple: to explore the justice and righteousness that God loves.

> *By inviting me to pursue His heart, God lifted the restraints that had caused me to hesitate in looking deeper into Scripture about social justice.*

My goal is to extend the same invitation to you in the pages ahead. Whatever your current political opinions are, keep them. All I want to do is to challenge you to go deep into what God says He loves and allow God's love for these things to transform your heart so you too can love what He loves.

DEFINING TERMS

CHAPTER TWO

MY "SOCIAL JUSTICE" RÉSUMÉ is a good one. At nineteen, I joined a social justice ministry through a Christian fellowship on my college campus and went on to lead it for a few years. We held Bible studies, organized fundraisers, and planned awareness events for our 400-member student fellowship. At the same time, I got involved in a long list of student social justice projects and ended up, at twenty-two, accidentally starting a nonprofit organization working with Mayan students in Guatemala. We do real-world-outside-of-college social justice work to improve the long-term health of the community by investing in the next generation of indigenous leaders. After college, I did a Christian social justice internship through a church-nonprofit partnership that gave me exposure to Christ-centered projects around the world.

I don't list all this to impress you, but to show that out of anyone, I should have been able to give a precise, detailed definition for this thing to which I gave so much of my time. If anyone should have known what social justice was, it was me. But for around a decade, I had an embarrassing secret: I couldn't define the thing that I was working so hard for. Sure, I knew "social justice" projects involved working for things it seemed like God would like: a healthier world, freedom for all people, etc. Even without a clear definition, it seemed to me that it must be something good.

For years, I kept holding my breath, waiting for someone to ask that very question and uncover my secret—that I, a big "social justice" person, couldn't tell you what social justice actually was. But funny enough, no one ever asked me that question, and I finally figured out why. Most were in the same boat—excited about social justice, assuming everyone around them knew what it was, but never able to tell you exactly what it was.

At one point during the time I was living with my shameful secret, I watched a video lecture on human rights given at a workshop. Early on in the presentation, the lecturer said, "The way I define social justice is 'how you show up in the world.'" She paused for effect like a teacher introducing something new, then repeated what she had just said slowly enough for her audience to write down her definition: "Social justice is defined as '*how…you…show…up…in…the…world.*'"

Wait…*what?* That phrase is so weird. It didn't seem to mean anything. And who let her make a definition so precise that others were supposed to write it down and repeat it?

Later, I wondered whether I could find others presenting their own opinions about social justice as fact. After a quick Internet search, I came up with a list of around ten definitions that were wildly different from each other—from ambiguous phrases like the one the woman gave, to complicated academic definitions, to angry, condemning definitions basically claiming that social justice would destroy the whole world.

Every single person and organization felt passionately that their definition of social justice was the correct, authoritative one. This left me wondering—what does social justice mean exactly, and who gets to decide? Depending on your personal experiences, you probably have a precise opinion about a phrase that has an ambiguous meaning in our culture. Whatever deeply held understanding you have based on your background is more real to you than any dictionary's definition. When I started the study on justice and righteousness, it became clear that it was time to learn more about the backstory of the term "social justice," try to discover why there isn't a single definition, and maybe find out why people are divided over it.

DEFINING TERMS

WHAT IS SOCIAL JUSTICE?

I am going to take a moment to summarize what I learned, because I think it will help to clarify why we are going to explore biblical justice and righteousness, instead of social justice.

Since social justice is often associated with liberal movements, the source of the term surprised me: a 19th-century, politically conservative, Italian Jesuit priest named Luigi Taparelli D'Azeglio. He coined the term "social justice" at a seemingly unusual time—during debates about whether Italy should unify into a single nation or stay divided into smaller kingdoms. Taparelli's writings about social justice during this time talk about how people are *not* equal. He believed that people were equal in value, but unequal in their capabilities. Some people are naturally smarter, stronger, and better; therefore, they should be the ones in charge. If that sounds like the opposite of what social justice means now, you're right. What many now would see as inequality and injustice, Taparelli said was actually "social justice."[1] His idea was that social justice was justice between individual people; but individuals aren't equal, so how you govern a nation should reflect their inequality. The most just way to rule is simply to let the better people have the power, because that would result in justice in that society. He was very politically conservative for his time. In fact, a collection of his essays were published under the title of *Tyrannous Liberty,* which argued against what he saw as liberal political and economic ideas coming out of the Protestant Reformation.

After his death, many of Taparelli's teachings remained influential in the Catholic church. His new term, "social justice" even stuck, although his exact ideas didn't stay connected to it. Within a few decades, "social justice" had become an official part of Catholic doctrine. By the time it did, however, the term had come to mean something different—applying not just to the government, but to everything from economics to sex, and to promoting change over tradition.

Discussions in the church around ideas of social justice became more popular at this time because the 19th century was full of dramatic change. New forms of democratic governments formed, giving new power to ordinary citizens. The Industrial Revolution in England raised a lot of questions about who should get the benefits from the new advances in technology, health care, work, and so on. If the resources existed for people to live healthier lives with a better standard of living, then who should get it? Should only the rich reap the benefits while letting the poor keep working their lives away just because they were poor? And if a nation wanted to give access to these new advantages, how would they do that? These new forms of government and advances in technology brought up a lot of questions, and the church looked to the Bible to address these in different ways.

Even though the term "social justice" originated from the Catholic side of the church, the Protestant side also addressed the questions brought up by these major changes in the world. In the U.S., the Social Gospel movement, which applied Christian values to solve social problems, gained popularity. People saw terrible things—like kids being forced to work and families crammed into unhealthy slums—and wanted to apply the gospel to these real-world issues. While the Social Gospel promoted good things for the poor and vulnerable, many church leaders have criticized it for having weak theology and for focusing too much on making this temporary earth more comfortable instead of getting souls into heaven. Unfortunately, a lasting legacy from that movement has been that evangelical Christians think they have to choose between social justice and the gospel. Many sincere, Jesus-following Christians have never heard the Scriptural foundations of social justice taught, so they reject everything related to "social justice" with the good intention of following the Bible.

However, the church also has a rich legacy of movements that have successfully combined social justice with evangelizing the pure gospel. The Salvation Army, for example, was started by William and Catherine Booth in London's East End at a time when the area looked like a Victorian slum. While most of the traditional churches at the time saw the addicts, criminals, prostitutes, and street kids in the East End as hopeless, the Booths saw an army. The Booths paired passionate evangelism with practical projects to help the poor. For most of their converts, the gospel brought massive change in their lives. Because of this, many devoted themselves wholeheartedly to spreading the gospel by singing and preaching in the streets to testify to the transforming power of God. At the same time, they offered practical help like rehab houses and feeding programs. The impact of the Salvation Army was enormous. A survey of churchgoers in 1882 London found that on a weeknight, 17,000 were worshiping in Salvation Army services, compared to 11,000 in all of the other churches *combined*.[2] The movement spread all over the world, and the Salvation Army continues to be one of the biggest charities on earth.

William Booth's groundbreaking book, *The Darkest England and the Way Out* (published in 1890), laid out a strategy for applying the gospel and Christian work ethic to solve social problems, including the role that the government should play. In fact, the book became influential in forming England's modern welfare state. That's right—one of the most effective evangelists in history, who helped bring millions to Christ, also helped shape England's social welfare state.

Along with the church using "social justice," secular thinkers and philosophers began to adopt the term. Since World War II, it has been tied to the more socialist meanings we have today.[3] From the origins of a religious, conservative philosopher, "social justice" has evolved to mean something that is mostly secular and liberal. This is why many modern evangelicals associate "social justice" with secular politics and therefore struggle to align themselves with it. Some of the actions that can connect to social justice (like helping orphans or fighting corruption) are good, but the term is so politically charged that it makes many back away out of fear and confusion.

This history lesson showed me two important things. First, it reminded me that though social justice is being rediscovered in my generation and evangelical Christianity, it's not new to the Christian church as a whole. Certain traditions and denominations have strong histories of social justice, even if they don't call it that, which continue today. Those of us who were raised in churches that viewed social justice as too secular and political, actually have a rich history of Christian social justice from which to draw.

The second thing is that the basic definition of social justice is broad and simple, and thus makes room for it to mean different things to different people. The Oxford American Dictionary says that social justice is "justice in terms of the distribution of wealth, opportunities, and privileges within society." People with widely different philosophies have been able to use the term "social justice" because they agree on this definition, but disagree on what social justice looks like. If four people from four different political backgrounds adopted this definition of social justice, each would do the "distribution of wealth, opportunities, and privileges within society" in a different way. And each perspective would likely say that the way the others are doing it is unjust.

The term itself doesn't provide the values or principles of justice—or a way to do it. In order to find those, we must look elsewhere. The world offers many ideas about social justice and how to do it, and without understanding clear biblical truth, most Christians feel like they have to work with one of the world's existing ideas. This is why it is essential to get aligned with the biblical definition and models of doing justice, because they line us up with God's values and truth. We need the Bible to find a unifying, God-centered, and gospel-centered expression of justice and righteousness that Christians can live out.

We need the Bible to find a unifying, God-centered, and gospel-centered expression of justice and righteousness that Christians can live out.

JUSTICE

In the next chapter, we're going to look closer at the Hebrew word, *mishpat*. Before looking at its definition, I think it's helpful to give you a general overview of how the Hebrew view of justice is different from our English-speaking, Western view.

Western views of justice are primarily focused on *how things should be done*—laws, rules, and what should happen when laws are broken. In Hebrew thought, justice is focused on *what life should be like*.[4] Justice in the Hebrew world was concerned not just with laws, but with enhancing all human life, especially the social world. That meant justice applied to all relationships—between a ruler and his subjects, between the weak members of a community and the strong, and between institutions of the nation of Israel and citizens.

The Hebrew word that sums up "what life should be like" is *shalom*.

That word usually shows up as "peace" in our English Bibles, but the meaning in Hebrew is more than simply the lack of conflict. *Shalom* comes from a root word that means "to be complete" or "to be sound."[5] *Shalom* is a peace that comes from everything being complete and whole, so it can be translated also as "security," "well-being," or "prosperity."[6] The purpose of justice in Hebrew society was to restore and sustain *shalom*.[7] In particular, those with the least amount of power needed special protection. This is why the Old Testament contains many reminders that Israel must do justice to the poor, widow, immigrant, and orphan. And "doing justice" meant not only not doing wrong, but also actively doing right and restoring what is broken.[8]

Another major difference between justice in the Bible and our modern views of justice is that in our world, justice has to be *enforced* by institutions like the police force, courts systems, and prisons. This gives rise to the impression that doing justice is the responsibility of only a few people. If something is broken and it's not our fault, then we commonly assume we don't have to do anything to fix it. In the biblical world, however, justice was done by everyone and was everyone's responsibility. Because of that, justice was *taught,* not merely enforced.[9] People took ownership of the *shalom* and wholeness of their community, and if something was wrong, they worked to right it, even if it wasn't their fault. When you look at the Law given by God to Israel, especially in the book of Deuteronomy, you can see how this education looked. The laws are not given line by line in a strict code; they are backed up with teaching and encouragement.[10] God intended the entire culture of Israel to learn and teach how to do justice in a way that shaped their hearts as well as their behavior.

RIGHTEOUSNESS

The other words we will look at are "righteous" and "righteousness." I would never have connected these words to justice or social justice, until I saw the connection in the Bible. Most of us associate "righteousness" with personal morality, and we often define that by what a person *doesn't* do.

Like *mishpat*, the Hebrew word for righteousness, *sedeq*, doesn't line up with our common English understanding. Biblical righteousness has much more to do with social morality and justice and is foundational to relationship. It is demonstrated through positive, constructive action, not merely refraining from destructive behavior.

CHANGING PICTURES

When I used my Western lens to look at God's love for justice and righteousness, the picture I saw was scary. It looked like God enjoyed making rules and punishing me if I broke them—which meant of course that He could only love *me* when I wasn't doing bad things. As I started to learn more about biblical justice and righteousness, my picture changed from an angry, faraway, law-obsessed King to a loving Creator who would go to any length to restore relationship with His sons and daughters and to make the world right again.

DIFFERENCES IN WESTERN & HEBREW VIEWS OF JUSTICE	
WESTERN	HEBREW
Justice is static, idealistic, and codified.	Justice is dynamic, realistic, and creative.
Justice is focused on *how things should be done*: making laws and enforcing them.	Justice is focused on what *life* should be like: creating *shalom* and enhancing all human life.
Justice is the responsibility of and done by a few.	Justice is the responsibility of and done by *everyone*.
Justice belongs in the public, legal parts of the world.	Justice belongs in all parts of a culture.
Justice is *enforced*—by public agencies like the police department, courts, or lawyers.	Justice is *taught*—to everyone.
Justice shapes behavior.	Justice shapes hearts.
Justice is not doing wrong.	Justice is actively doing right and restoring what is broken.

DEFINING TERMS

STUDY QUESTIONS

Off the top of your head, what are some definitions of social justice you have heard?

What are some of the good ways that social justice has been done that you think reflect biblical values?

What are some of the negative ways that social justice has been done that you think are against biblical values?

What are some of the ways your culture has shaped the way you think about justice? Righteousness?

MISHPAT: HEAVEN'S DESIGN ON EARTH

CHAPTER THREE

JUSTICE IS A MAJOR theme of the Bible—a fact that unfortunately frightens and confuses a lot of people. Part of the reason for that is that Old Testament verses about this theme sound disturbing when translated into English:

> "All His ways are judgment [*mishpat*]." (Deuteronomy 32:4 KJV)
>
> "The Lord loves judgment [*mishpat*]." (Psalm 37:28a KJV)
>
> "He has set up His throne for judgment [*mishpat*]." (Psalm 9:7a NASB)

God loves *judgment*, His ways are *judgment*, and His throne is set up for *judgment*. Doesn't that sound kind of unsettling? But God isn't saying that He loves the English word "justice" or "judgment." He is saying He loves something else: *mishpat* (pronounced *mish-pat*).

Mishpat shows up *425 times* in the Old Testament, in 31 of the 39 books.[1] In comparison, hell is mentioned 31 times and angels 103 times. While most American Christians would immediately recognize the importance of those topics, justice is often lost. One reason is that *mishpat,* one of the most essential Hebrew words to understand the topic, is translated into a whole range of words, including "justice," "judgment," "law," "plans," and "rights." It is also hard for us to see it when it is in the many passages that describe the non-legal parts of justice, because again, for us, justice primarily belongs in legal systems.[2]

STARTING AT THE ROOT

The best place to start learning about *mishpat* is its root: the verb *shaphat*, which is usually translated "to judge or govern." That kind of sounds boring, like people sitting around handing out punishments or debating laws. But *shaphat* gets interesting when you look at the impact of this kind of judging.[3] *Shaphat* is not about using raw power for the sake of power, like some politicians may do. In many places, *shaphat* is used to describe the prosperity brought by the king's leadership.[4] The power to *shaphat* is focused on creating the right outcome. That outcome looks like freedom and restoration. One way to say it is that *shaphat* is "an active, saving rearranging of broken relationships. In the context of justice, this means to save from oppression, to liberate, and to rescue."[5] In the Bible, "judging" shelters and defends the least protected people, like orphans and the poor, from those who try to hurt them. When *shaphat* is translated as to "do justice," the poor and oppressed are the ones most often receiving that justice.[6] After the Israelites were brought into the Promised Land, God established judges as their leaders. The reason God gave them judges was so that they would be saved and delivered from their enemies (see Judges 2:16-18). God calls His leaders to carry out this kind of judgment for His people—to free the oppressed and bring prosperity to the land.[7]

God Himself is described as our Judge, Lawgiver, and King: "For the LORD is our judge [*shaphat*]; the LORD is our lawgiver; the LORD is our king; he will save us" (Isaiah 33:22 ESV). When God is our ruler—when He sets the laws and makes the decisions—it leads to us being saved. When God *judges,* it means that the poor and the oppressed are saved and set free.

In Psalm 98, there is a happy picture of all creation being told to "break forth into joyous song and sing praises!" (Psalm 98:4b ESV). Rivers are clapping, seas are roaring, all the earth's residents are singing, and the reason is this: God is coming to *shaphat* the earth (Psalm 98:7-9). The news of God coming as Judge makes all of creation so happy that they break out into an ecstatic worship party. That picture shows just how wonderful God's justice is.

MULTIPLE MEANINGS[8]

From the root *shaphat*, this powerful way of leading, we get *mishpat*. The word has many dimensions of meaning depending on the context.[9] Here are some of the ways *mishpat* is defined:

Mishpat **is an attribute of God.** True justice is rooted in God (see Isaiah 30:18, Malachi 2:17, Proverbs 29:26). *Mishpat* is not just something that God does; it is who He is. God is the originator and protector of *mishpat,* and everything He does shows His just character. *Mishpat* flows from Him. When we act justly, we are not following some made-up, meaningless human law; we are reflecting God's character to the world. God loves and does *mishpat,* and He therefore expects His people to mirror that.[10]

Mishpat **is right order.**[11] Theologian Bruce Waltke powerfully sums up *misphat* as "to establish the heavenly norm or pattern on earth."[12] When God created the world, He had an intention for *what life should be like* for His creation. His whole creation should be full of *shalom*—whole and complete, full of thriving life and right relationships. "Right order" sounds kind of boring, but think about it. When you look at the order God created in the physical world—in our bodies, galaxies, ecosystems, and more— you see a structure that invites and sustains life. When something is out of order in the physical world, disease and death take hold. God's intention for His creation is *shalom,* so how He orders the world and the ways He commands His people to live together establishe and sustain *shalom*. *Mishpat* can be summarized as honoring and expressing God's intended order for His creation.[13] In His chosen people, that order is reflected in all parts of their nation—relationships, families, legal systems, and even religious practices—everything needed for people and the physical world to holistically flourish. It isn't about enforcing a made-up, bureaucratic system of justice in the world; it's about honoring and protecting the life-giving, divine order of God. That means bringing the freedom-filled culture of heaven to earth in a practical way.

Mishpat is the design for God's physical dwelling place.[14] *Mishpat* can mean plan or design.[15] In three places, *mishpat* refers to the plan used to create a space for God's presence to dwell on earth: The tabernacle of Moses (Exodus 26:30), Solomon's temple (1 Kings 6:38), and the temple prophesied in Ezekiel (Ezekiel 42:11). In each, God gave a blueprint for how to build His house on earth, a practical plan for His people to follow for a physical space to host His presence. This definition doesn't imply that if we have the right order in a building, then God will come. But it does give a beautiful image of the power of *mishpat*.

Mishpat describes legal order and individual rights. Legal order is an important way to build and keep structure and stability in a nation.[16] The legal dimensions of *mishpat* are the easiest to understand, probably because "judgment" and "justice" have a legal tone in English. *Mishpat* commonly shows up in legal terms and can mean a case, verdict, right, commandment, decision, entitlement, or sentence (see Exodus 21:1, 24:3; Leviticus 18:4-5, 24:22, 26:46; Numbers 27:5, 35:29; Deuteronomy 4:8, 17:9, 18:3; 1 Kings 8:59; Psalm 9:4, 35:23, 140:12).[17] *Mishpat* is expressed when someone is given what is due to them, whether their God-given rights, or punishment when they've broken the law.[18] Justice is anchored in the value for right relationship with both God and people, so even the legal parts of justice are built on a foundation of valuing relationships.

Laws and commandments show up in the Old Testament as the plural *mishpatim*. These rules made sure that justice was expressed in every part of Israel's culture. When people needed clear, specific instructions about how to behave in certain parts of their world—economic, religious, or social—the *mishpatim* gave them guidance.[19] Many of these laws establish the God-given rights of each individual. Respecting the rights of others is respecting God's order for human society—a way of practically showing God's value for relationships. Denying someone his or her rights mocks God and is a sin against both God *and* man.[20]

Even when expressed in a static law, justice is still a response to

God's character, words, and actions.[21] In many modern governments like the United States, the law rules our government. But in Old Testament times, even when a nation had a law the government centered around a person—for instance, a king. In Israel's case, their government centered around God, their ultimate King and Judge.[22] Their *mishpat* started from their connection to God, while conforming to His laws and customs came second to that as an expression of relationship with Him. For Israel, that meant *mishpat* was active and revolutionary because it flowed first from God, not impersonal rules.[23]

Mishpat means "custom," "manner," or "routine."[24] [25] *Mishpat* is used to describe the custom of a god or king. For example, when Israel was scoping out the Promised Land, they found people living there "after the manner [*mishpat*] of the Sidonians" (Judges 18:7 NASB). Other gods had their *mishpat,* customs and ways of living that people could imitate and follow. Israel didn't follow a random, impersonal form of justice. The *mishpat* of Israel, again, came from their relationship with God and ordered their entire way of life.[26] This is important when we look at how God's justice connects to other parts of His character, like mercy and grace.

Every person has a choice of how they will respond to *mishpat* (see chart).

MISHPAT CAN BE:[27]	
Loved: Ps. 33:5, 37:28, 99:4; Isa. 61:8)	**Hated:** Job 34:17
Done: Gen. 18:19, Deut. 10:18, 1 Kings 10:9)	**Rejected:** Eze. 20:13
Sought out: Isa. 1:17, 16:5	**Loathed:** Mic. 3:9
Spoken: Ps. 37:30, Jer. 12:1	**Not understood:** Prov. 28:5
Established: Isa. 42:4, Amos 5:15	**Mocked:** Prov. 19:28
Brought forth: Isa. 42:1	**Perverted:** Job 8:3, Hab. 1:4
Understood: Prov. 2:9	**Violated:** Ecc. 5:8
Chosen: Job 34:4	**Turned into poison:** Amos 6:12
Preserved: Isa. 56:1	
Guarded: Hos. 12:6	
Taught: Ps. 119:108	
Known: Mic. 3:1, Ecc. 8:5	

PUNISHMENT & DELIVERANCE

We are going to stop and look at one dimension of the meaning of *mishpat* that I think is the hardest for us Western-minded folks to understand. *Mishpat* does more than distinguish right from wrong—it takes revolutionary action to stop injustice and restore the damage done by it.[28] Punishment might be needed as part of that process of righting wrongs. However, when viewed through the lens of *mishpat*, punishment is seen positively. It is not viewed as an end in itself, but as the necessary means for bringing restoration, deliverance, and salvation.[29] Freedom for the oppressed, not punishment of the perpetrator, is the more important result of judgment.[30] Whenever *mishpat* requires punishment, the purpose is to set things right again.[31] Jewish rabbi and philosopher, Eliezer Berkovits, explains it this way:

> The purpose of judgment is to save the innocent from injustice. The idea is so deeply anchored in biblical thought that "to judge" becomes the equivalent of "to save." Of the terrible anger of God, the psalmist says: "You caused the sentence to be heard from heaven; the earth feared, and was still. When God arose *to judgment, to save* all the humble of the earth." God judges in order to save....If salvation is to go forth, judgment is to be instituted. And indeed from numerous passages in the Bible the idea that the function of the judge is to save....The commandment to judge is the responsibility to deliver.[32]

Berkovits also says:

> *Mishpat* is done not that justice prevail, but that life prevail...Thus, while *mishpat* may be grim, it will always be an act of saving and deliverance...It is a principle of preservation; the restoration of a disturbed balance which is needed because life has become unbalanced.[33]

It's out of love and compassion for the suffering that God brings *mishpat*. God judges because He cannot stand the effects of sin, evil, and injustice on people's lives—both the perpetrators and the victims. Sometimes that process of bringing deliverance and restoration involves strong correction, but *even when* mishpat *is harsh, it is for the purpose of deliverance.*[34]

Berkovits uses the following passage from Jeremiah as a key example of how God saves Israel through correction:

> For I am with you, says the Eternal, to save you;
> For I will make a full end of all the nations which I have scattered you,
> But I will not make a full end of you;
> For I will correct you in *mishpat*,
> And will not utterly destroy you.
> (Jeremiah 30:11 Berkovits' translation)

God corrected His people with *mishpat* because His purpose was saving them, not destroying them. Earlier in Jeremiah, the prophet asks God to correct him, but distinguishes between justice and anger: "Correct me, O Lord, but with justice [*mishpat*]; Not with Your anger, or You will bring me to nothing" (Jeremiah 10:24 NASB). *Mishpat* and anger are distinct and different. When God corrects in justice, He is bringing salvation. Even when God punishes in the Old Testament, His justice is never equated with vengeance.[35]

On the surface, God's extreme emotions can seem frightening. But think of God's love and hatred as two sides of the same coin. How would you react to the news that something unjust and painful happened to the person you love most? Your love for them is expressed in your anger toward what hurt them.

The idea of a "Judgment Day" sounds terrifying to some, but to the victims of injustice it sounds like hope. If you were unjustly locked away in prison, and you had a court date to present all the evidence showing your innocence and guaranteeing your release, then that "judgment day" would be wonderful. In this case, facing a judge means freedom from your oppression.

God's justice is satisfied when there is restoration.[36] Many human justice systems focus on punishing what's wrong, while God's justice focuses on reconciling and healing. His justice will go to incredible lengths to right wrongs, so that all His people (especially the most destitute and oppressed) can enjoy life as He created it to be. Punishment is needed, not to emotionally satisfy God's desire to inflict pain on people who break the rules, but so that *shalom* and wholeness can return to His children about whom He cares so deeply.[37] This way of seeing justice, punishment, and restoration is an especially important connection to make when we look at how God's justice is expressed in the New Testament through Jesus.

God's justice is satisfied when there is restoration.

While we're on this subject of punishment, it's helpful to know that there are other Hebrew words for justice or judgment— the most common ones are *din* and *shephet/shephot*. *Din* refers only to legal matters.[38] *Shephet/shephot* is a less common word and is tied to sentencing and inflicting punishment.[39] As English readers, we miss the distinctions between *din, shephet,* and *mishpat* because they are all translated "judgment" or "justice." If you aren't careful to look at which Hebrew word is being used in a verse, it could suggest that God's love of justice includes other things that "justice" is linked to, like cannibalism between family members (*shephet* in Ezekiel 5:10) or punishments with swords (*din* in Job 19:29). God doesn't say that He loves *shephet* or *din*; He says that He loves *mishpat*.

Learning the meaning of *mishpat* changed how I saw a justice-loving God. God loves *mishpat*. *Mishpat* is anchored in His character. God's *mishpat* is focused on bringing order where there is chaos, life where there is death, and salvation where there is destruction. He loves establishing heavenly patterns on earth and setting the oppressed free from the oppressor.

SOLOMON: DOING MISHPAT

Now that we've seen how beautiful God's *mishpat* is, the next question is this: What would it look like to *do mishpat*? The verbs paired most often with *mishpat* are action-oriented: to "do," "execute," and "keep."[40] In Israel, *mishpat* was dynamic, causing change and making wrongs right again.[41] The following story from the life of Solomon gives us a great example of how to express *mishpat* in action.

Soon after Solomon became king, God appeared to him in a dream, saying that He would give Solomon anything he requested. Solomon asked for wisdom to rule his people well. According to God, that was a great request:

> The LORD was pleased that Solomon had asked for wisdom. So God replied, "Because you have asked for wisdom in governing my people with justice [*mishpat*] and have not asked for a long life or wealth or the death of your enemies—I will give you what you asked for! I will give you a wise and understanding heart such as no one else has had or ever will have! (1 Kings 3:10-12 NLT)

Why was God pleased that Solomon asked for wisdom? *Because it meant that Solomon would have the wisdom to govern his people with* mishpat. Solomon could have asked for a better law or more help in governing, but instead, he asked for wisdom, knowing that it was what was needed most to administer *mishpat*.

The first time we see Solomon using the gift of wisdom to bring justice is recorded in 1 Kings 3. Two women appear before Solomon, both claiming the same infant as their own. Kings were generally only consulted to judge hard cases, so we know that Solomon was hearing this case because it was complicated.[42] Here is the account:

> One day two prostitutes came and presented themselves before King Solomon. One of them said, "Your Majesty, this woman and I live in the same house, and I gave birth to a baby boy at home while she was there. Two days after my child was born, she also gave birth to a baby boy. Only the two of us were there in

the house—no one else was present. Then one night she accidentally rolled over on her baby and smothered it. She got up during the night, took my son from my side while I was asleep, and carried him to her bed; then she put the dead child in my bed. The next morning, when I woke up and was going to nurse my baby, I saw that it was dead. I looked at it more closely and saw that it was not my child."
But the other woman said, "No! The living child is mine, and the dead one is yours!"
The first woman answered back, "No! The dead child is yours, and the living one is mine!"
And so they argued before the king. (1 Kings 3:16-22 GNT)

You can just picture how dramatic this was—two desperate women arguing about a baby in front of the most important political leader in the nation. There were no witnesses who could give testimony and no DNA tests to prove who was right. Solomon needed a creative solution to find the right mother. He decided on a simple test:

> Then King Solomon said, "Each of you claims that the living child is hers and that the dead child belongs to the other one." He sent for a sword, and when it was brought, he said, "Cut the living child in two and give each woman half of it." (1 Kings 3:23-25 GNT)

To our ears, Solomon's test sounds shocking, almost brutal. This isn't the way most of us would think to bring justice in this situation. But look at what happened next:

> The real mother, her heart full of love for her son, said to the king, "Please, Your Majesty, don't kill the child! Give it to her!"
> But the other woman said, "Don't give it to either of us; go on and cut it in two."

> Then Solomon said, "Don't kill the child! Give it to the first woman—she is its real mother." (1 Kings 3:26-27 GNT)

Solomon knew that the real mother would not have cared about where her child was, as long as it was alive. He came up with a brilliant way to get the true mother to provide her own proof to back her claim.

The whole nation took notice of this case:

> And all Israel heard of the judgment [*mishpat*] that the king had rendered [*shaphat*], and they stood in awe of the king, because they perceived that **the wisdom of God was in him to do justice [*mishpat*]**. (1 Kings 3:28 ESV, emphasis mine)

The result of Solomon "doing *mishpat*" was the restoration of a relationship between a mother and her child. And notice what was missing: punishment. The mother who had stolen the other woman's child in her grief and guilt was not prosecuted. Remember, God's justice is higher than merely punishing someone who has committed an injustice—He desires to restore everything that was lost.

God's justice is higher than merely punishing someone who has committed an injustice—He desires to restore everything that was lost.

GOD LOVES *MISHPAT*

For many of us, justice is something that is static, idealistic, and codified. In contrast, *mishpat* is dynamic, realistic, and creative.[43] Commonly in our culture, justice belongs to certain people, professions, or activities. In Israel, everyone was taught *mishpat* and understood that it was to be structured into every aspect of society—even down to mundane parts like the weights and measures merchants used in business transactions (see Proverbs 11:1). And while we often view justice as belonging to the public, secular realm, in Israel, *mishpat* was a religious activity as much as it was legal.[44]

From the beginning, God's *mishpat* has been transformational[45]—restoring the world back to right again and covenantal—restoring our relationships with Him and others.[46] This is the *mishpat* God loves and calls us to love.

UNDERSTANDING *MISHPAT*

FACTS:

- Appears 425 times in the Old Testament.
- Is active and revolutionary because it starts with and flows from God
- Parallels salvation and deliverance
- Justice is satisfied when there is restoration
- If *mishpat* requires punishment, it is so that life can prevail
- God's judgment is focused on reconciling and healing what is wrong to make it right

DEFINITIONS:

Mishpat can be defined multiple ways.
- "To establish the heavenly norm or pattern on earth"
- Honoring and expressing God's intended order for His creation
- Plan or design
- Legal order and individual rights
- "Custom," "manner," or "routine"

KEY TAKEAWAY:

God's *mishpat* is **transformational**—restoring the world back to right again—and **covenantal**—restoring our relationships with Him and others. It brings order where there is chaos, life where there is death, and salvation where there is destruction.

MISHPAT: **HEAVEN'S DESIGN ON EARTH**

STUDY QUESTIONS

Is *mishpat* different from your own understanding of justice? If yes, then how?

What do you think doing mishpat in your own life today would look like?

What would it be like facing a judge who you knew was doing everything possible to bring you freedom and salvation?

In Solomon's example of doing mishpat, what would it look like to do justice in similar ways in the world today?

SEDEQ: RIGHT RELATIONSHIPS, RIGHT LIFE

CHAPTER FOUR

GROWING UP IN MY church, "righteousness" meant that I had to make *not sinning* my constant and highest goal. There was a long list of stuff you couldn't do: try drugs, get drunk, have sex, cuss, or listen to unholy pop music. Righteous living felt boring, but I did it because I was afraid of God's wrath if I didn't do it well enough.

I remember going to a church youth group sleepover when I was around twelve. One of the older kids wanted to watch a PG-13 movie. All the others were okay with it, and I didn't want to be the only uncool one, so I didn't protest. On the inside, however, I was panicking. Someone had told me that righteousness meant I couldn't watch PG-13 movies at the tender age of twelve, so it felt wrong. But I couldn't tell anyone, because I also needed to keep my social reputation intact for my upcoming teen years. My solution was to try to fall asleep at the beginning of the movie. It worked! I slept through the whole movie. The kids teased me for going to sleep too early, but at least my reputation was intact. I was so proud of my righteous decision. Successful righteous living in my world was defined by what you didn't do with your life.

Beyond that, "righteousness" only appeared in my world in confusing sermons on the book of Romans. When I got older, I decided it was time in my Christian growth process to finally learn about righteousness for myself. But it only took about a day of trying to tackle the subject to convince me to stop. I learned enough to see that theologians with really fancy degrees spent lots of energy arguing over small word choices in the definition or the use of righteousness in a particular verse. If righteousness was such a complicated subject for theologians, how was an average Christian like me supposed to understand it?

To be honest, when I first started this study of justice and righteousness, I wasn't excited about looking into righteousness. Justice was interesting at least, because I could see how it was attached to social justice. But really, God loves *righteousness*? The way righteousness appeared in my world was definitely not something I could love. It was either a barrier keeping PG-13 movies out of my life or a philosophical idea that really smart theologians spent their lives arguing over. The small amount of time in which I had tried to read up on righteousness made me feel so intimidated that I never wanted to look again. But I'm glad I pushed past my reluctance to start looking at the biblical meaning of righteousness. Starting in the Old Testament actually helped me understand the New Testament parts I had found so confusing. The real meaning is so much better than I thought.

THE ROOT OF *SEDEQ*

Let's start with the Hebrew root word, *sadaq*. The basic meaning is to be straight or to conform to a standard.[1] From this root, there are three derivative terms:

- *Sedeq* (pronounced *se-dek*): the masculine noun form, used 119 times
- *Sedeqah* (pronounced *se-de-ka*): the feminine noun form, used 157 times
- *Saddiq* (pronounced *sa-deek*): the adjective, used 206 times.[2]

Sedeq and *sedeqah* are the masculine and feminine form of the same word and have the same meaning.³ For the sake of clarity, I'm going to use "*sedeq*" instead of going back and forth between the words. If *sedeqah* is used in a verse, I will specifically state the word. Otherwise, you'll just see it as *sedeq*.

WHAT IS *SEDEQ*?

Sedeq is most often translated "righteousness," but it's also translated "justice," "equity," "honesty," "deliverance," "integrity," and "victory."⁴ The meaning is broader than the way most English speakers think of "righteousness." Here are some of the dimensions to the definition of *sedeq*:

Sedeq is an attribute of God. Righteousness is not a man-made idea. Like *mishpat*, it is anchored in God Himself. *Sedeq* is *who* He is, not just how He acts (see Jeremiah 23:6, Ezra 9:15, Psalm 4:1).

Sedeq is relational. The heart of righteousness is relationship. It is essential to understand the demands of our relationship with God and others. Fulfilling the demands of each unique relationship is righteousness.⁵ These demands aren't only legal. In a community, relationships are also dependent on qualities you can't legislate, like kindness and loyalty.⁶ It also means that when someone is living "righteously," they have a good relationship toward the poor and needy (see Deuteronomy 24:13, Job 29:12-15).⁷ Righteous people are in tune with the needs of others and never take advantage of them, even if they could get away with it.

Sedeq is a standard. The word is used to describe accurate weights and measures (see Leviticus 19:36, Deuteronomy 25:15), and also describes the correct standard in judgment (see Leviticus 19:15, Deuteronomy 1:16). Everyone had to follow the same, unchanging standard, no matter how much or how little money someone had.⁸

Righteous people follow God's ways, His standard for life. A common way that English-speaking Christians think about righteousness in the Old Testament is that it means following rules. And that is one dimension of it. Observing the order and commandments that God establishes is considered righteousness (see Deuteronomy 6:25).⁹ God's people could joyfully embrace His laws, because they brought life into their world: "The law of the LORD is perfect, reviving the soul" (Psalm

19:7 ESV).[10] His commands express the right standard for life and relationship, so following His ways leads to healthy community and the opportunity for everyone to flourish.[11] Staying inside the boundaries He set up was beneficial for everyone. Righteousness can also mean being free from guilt.[12]

Sedeq is saving action. Righteousness is God's will to save His people put into action.[13] In the Old Testament, *sedeq* can mean "saving action." It parallels deliverance, victory, and salvation.[14] The previous definitions described righteousness in terms of relating to God's standards—doing things His way understanding that His ways lead to life. But righteousness is not just about our relationship with God's *standard*; it's about our relationship with *Him*.[15] This is why *sedeq* is almost synonymous with deliverance, because it describes the action that God takes to save, deliver, and restore His people to Himself. When God intervenes to save His people, it is an expression of His righteousness.[16] This dimension of the definition of *sedeq* is prominent in Psalms and Isaiah.[17] When God's righteousness invades for the sake of the oppressed, His salvation comes.[18]

My idea that righteousness meant you disengage and separate from the "terrible, sinful world" was so wrong. Instead of using His righteousness as an excuse to distance Himself from people, God's righteousness means that He comes so close that He can save His people.

Instead of using His righteousness as an excuse to distance Himself from people, God's righteousness means that He comes so close that He can save His people.

God's righteousness is a gift, not a punishment.[19] It might seem that righteousness means you have to *live up* to God's standards, like when you are in school and have to do everything right in order to get a good grade. But a better way to think of righteousness is *living inside* God's intended order. Yes, He sets standards and expects His people to follow His ways. But their purpose isn't to punish you. The welfare of you, your community, and the world are central to living righteousness. The Creator of the universe knows what we need to do to stay healthy, balanced, and free within the design of His creation. This is His how-to guide for living our healthiest, most relationally rich and happy life. Staying inside His boundary lines is ultimately for our own benefit. When we go outside them, we are hurting ourselves and others.

THE LIFE OF THE *SADDIQ*

The Lord loves righteousness (*sedeq*), and He also loves the righteous (*saddiq*): "The Lord loves the righteous [*saddiq*]" (Psalm 146:8b NASB). What does it look like to live a righteous life? The Bible provides us with many examples of righteous people and descriptions of what a righteous lifestyle looks like. From these examples and descriptions, we can find principles that make righteousness less vague and more applicable. Let's take a look at two people who are specifically listed as righteous in the Bible.

The first person ever mentioned as being righteous in Scripture is Noah. What characterized Noah's life? He walked blamelessly with God at a time when humanity was known for being evil (see Genesis 6:9-12). But what really made him unique was his radical obedience to God's crazy command—to make a giant boat on dry land when no one had ever seen rain before (see Genesis 6:13-22). Because of that, the human race and animal life were saved.

Abraham is another person called out as righteous in the Old Testament. Like Noah, Abraham's life was characterized by radical faith and obedience. God told Abraham to leave his homeland and move to an unknown land with the promise that he would start a nation, and that all the nations in the world would be blessed through him (see Genesis 12:1-3). After Abraham obeyed this command and came to the land of Canaan, God promised the childless Abraham that he would have a son even though he and his wife Sarah were too old to conceive. The Bible says, "And he believed the Lord, and he counted it to him as righteousness [*sedeqah*]" (Genesis 15:6 ESV). The nation through which God birthed His redemptive plan for all of humanity started because of one man's simple faith.

Notice that both Noah and Abraham were called righteous not because they were morally perfect, but because they risked everything to protect their relationship with God and honor His authority in their lives. That is the character of the *saddiq*.

Other righteous men and women have shaped history, leaving legacies that still impact us today. These people were not boring—they were exciting, dynamic leaders characterized by their wholehearted loyalty to God and willingness to take huge steps of faith that didn't make sense to the world around them. Living out a righteous life for them meant patterning their lives after God's life-giving order, which made them stand out against the violent, evil people who surrounded them. They shifted the history of the world and played an important part in God's redemptive plan for humanity.

CHARACTERISTICS OF THE *SADDIQ*

Psalms and Proverbs give some great illustrations of what the righteous, *saddiq,* are like—often highlighting how different their lives are compared to the wicked. The *saddiq* are known to…

> **…take shelter in God:** "Let the righteous one rejoice in the Lord and take refuge in him!" (Psalm 64:10a ESV)
>
> **…praise God:** "Glad songs of salvation are in the tents of the righteous." (Psalm 118:15 ESV)
>
> **…find security in God:** "The name of the Lord is a strong tower; the righteous runs into it and is safe." (Proverbs 18:10 NASB)
>
> **…be generous:** "The wicked borrows and does not pay back, but the righteous is gracious and gives." (Psalm 37:21 NASB)
>
> **…live in integrity:** "The righteous who walks in his integrity—blessed are his children after him!" (Proverbs 20:7 ESV)
>
> **…enjoy doing *mishpat*:** "When justice [*mishpat*] is done, it is a joy to the righteous but terror to evildoers." (Proverbs 21:15 ESV)
>
> **….be generous:** "The righteous gives and does not hold back." (Proverbs 21:26b NASB/ESV)
>
> **…not give up:** "for the righteous falls seven times and rises again, but the wicked stumble in times of calamity." (Proverbs 24:16 ESV)

…be bold: "The wicked flee when no one is pursuing, but the righteous are bold as a lion." (Proverbs 28:1 ESV)

…think justly: "The thoughts of the righteous are just [*mishpat*], but the counsels of the wicked are deceitful." (Proverbs 12:5 NASB)

…be teachable: "Teach the righteous, and they will learn even more." (Proverbs 9:9 NLT)

…have longevity: "The wicked are overthrown and are no more, but the house of the righteous will stand." (Proverbs 12:7 ESV)

…care about the poor: "The righteous is concerned for the rights of the poor, the wicked does not understand such concern." (Proverbs 29:7 NASB)

…speak wisdom and justice: "The mouth of the righteous utters wisdom, and his tongue speaks justice [*mishpat*]." (Psalm 37:30 ESV)

…have mouths flowing with wisdom: "The mouth of the righteous flows with wisdom, but the perverted tongue will be cut out." (Proverbs 10:31 NASB)

…be unshakeable: "For the righteous will never be moved…" (Psalm 112:6a ESV)

…leave a legacy: "[the righteous] will be remembered forever." (Psalm 112:6b ESV)

…think before speaking: "The heart of the righteous ponders how to answer, but the mouth of the wicked pours out evil things." (Proverbs 15:28 ESV)

…say life-giving words: "The mouth of the righteous is a fountain of life, but the mouth of the wicked conceals violence." (Proverbs 10:11 ESV)

Psalm 112 also offers a beautiful picture of a righteous person. It starts out by saying that the righteous person is "blessed." In English, that sounds like God gives a reward to someone who follows the rules. But in Hebrew, *'asre*—"blessed"—can also be translated as "fortunate" or "happy." The idea is that the life of the '*asre* person is happy and fortunate, and they deserve to be congratulated.[20] *Happiness* is a mark of the righteous—not frustration, boredom, or a judgmental attitude. God isn't sitting up in heaven, giving out blessings to the righteous like a teacher giving out candy to the best-behaved kids in class. Rather, the lifestyle of righteousness attracts and keeps happiness and blessing.

The list of what righteousness does is a list of things that most people would want: it delivers from death (see Proverbs 11:4); gives life (see Proverbs 12:28); exalts a nation (see Proverbs 14:34); establishes the king's throne (see Proverbs 16:12); and brings blessings (see Psalm 106:3), rewards (see Proverbs 11:18), and peace (see Isaiah 32:17).[21] I thought that righteous people were the types that liked rules for the sake of rules. But really, righteous people love things like people, relationship, happiness, connection, holistic prosperity, and community. I also thought that righteousness was about what you didn't do, but I had that exactly backwards. What's important in a righteous lifestyle is what you *do*, rather than what you *don't do*. If you had asked me years ago what a righteous life looks like, it would have been something like following a lot of rules and pointing out when others aren't. But I've had to admit that's not actually biblical. Righteous people fulfill God's commands and work for the wholeness and justice of their community.[22] A self-righteous attitude has nothing to do with truly living out righteousness. Rather, a righteous lifestyle is defined by good things, which makes it very attractive and anything but boring.

SEDEQ: RIGHT RELATIONSHIPS, RIGHT LIFE

UNDERSTANDING *SEDEQ*

FACTS:

- Comes from the root word *sadaq,* which means to be straight or to conform to a standard.
- From the root come three closely related words:
  - The two nouns "righteousness," *sedeq* (pronounced *se-dek*), which appears 119 times, and *sedeqah* (pronounced *se-de-ka*), which appears 157 times
  - The adjective "righteous," *saddiq* (pronounced *sa-deek*), which appears 206 times
- *Sedeq* and *sedeqah* are most often translated "righteousness," but they are also translated "justice," "equity," "honesty," "deliverance," "integrity," and "victory."
- At the heart of *sedeq* is relationships—our relationship with God and with others

DEFINITIONS:

Sedeq can be defined in multiple ways.

- A standard set the same for everyone
- Following and keeping God's ways, His standard for life
- "Saving action," God's will to save His people in action

What are righteous people, the *saddiq*, like?

Righteous people follow God's ways and His standard for life. Living a righteous life is marked by what you do, rather than what you don't do. The righteous lifestyle attracts and keeps happiness and blessing.

KEY TAKEAWAY:

Think of righteousness as living *inside of*, instead of *up to*, God's standard for the right life. The welfare of you, your community, and your relationship with God are central to living righteousness.

STUDY QUESTIONS

Who in your world do you see modeling righteousness well? What are they like?

What would it look like to express righteousness in your relationships, especially in relationships with the poor and vulnerable?

Look at the list of what the righteous do. Which ones are you already doing? Which ones are you lacking?

JUSTICE & RIGHTEOUSNESS: THE FOUNDATION OF GOD'S REIGN & GOD'S PEOPLE

CHAPTER FIVE

NOW THAT WE'VE LOOKED at what justice and righteousness mean in Hebrew, there's one last part of our word study we need to do: what does it mean when they appear together? Not only do *mishpat* and *sedeq* show up frequently by themselves; they also are used as a word pair around 80 times in Scripture,[1] including Psalm 33:5, which says that God "loves *sedeqah* and *mishpat*." It's important to look at this phrase, because when the words appear together, they create a different meaning.[2] In Hebrew, sometimes two independent words joined together with "and" express one concept[3]—a bit like phrases such as "fire and brimstone" or "assault and battery" in English. Sometimes they appear side by side, and sometimes they appear in parallel verses.[4]

JUSTICE AND RIGHTEOUSNESS

In order to see this one concept of "justice and righteousness," we need to go back to the beginning—to the context of God's *shalom*-filled design for the world.[5] After finishing each part of creation, God declared it "good." The structure God put into His creation allowed everything in it, including humans, to prosper. Before sin entered the world and distorted everything, everyone had the opportunity to holistically thrive, enjoying the goodness He created.

Doing "justice and righteousness" means honoring and expressing God's intended order and His ways for life. That means doing things that lead to wholeness, freedom, and prosperity for people and His physical world.

Doing "justice and righteousness" doesn't mean becoming judgmental, law-obsessed rule-followers, but rather loving the things that lead to life and actively righting the wrongs that keep people from experiencing life as God created it to be. When God does "justice and righteousness," it brings liberation and freedom.[6] Likewise, when people do "justice and righteousness" it protects and nourishes their freedom instead of constraining it. This is why He expects His people to pattern their lives after His ways, because He wants them to experience the free, thriving life full of *shalom* in all their world and relationships.[7]

Doing "justice and righteousness" means loving the things that lead to life and actively righting the wrongs that keep people from experiencing life as God created it to be.

I realize this sounds broad and brings up a lot of questions about what doing justice and righteousness looks like practically. The best way to learn what it means is to watch what it looks like expressed in the life of Israel—something you will see illustrated by the stories in the coming chapters.

There are some scholars who say that when justice and righteousness appear together, the meaning is "social justice."[8] I can understand why. "*Mishpat* and *sedeq*" often looks like things we would think of as social justice—practical help for the poor, promoting integrity and good governance, and holding people accountable when they take advantage of the vulnerable. But as we have seen, "social justice" is not clearly defined. Tying such an important God-centered biblical idea to an English phrase that people all define differently makes it open to being manipulated. For that reason, I won't define "*mishpat* and *sedeq*"

JUSTICE & RIGHTEOUSNESS: **THE FOUNDATION OF GOD'S REIGN**

as social justice.

There is also the problem that even when we have a definition of social justice, it doesn't tell you how to do it. In our culture, what "social justice" looks like is vague, while in Hebrew culture "*mishpat* and *sedeq*" were concrete and understandable.[9] The biblical models we will look at show that it's a reality that comes from God's heart for people and is expressed in everyday actions. Every practical expression of biblical justice and righteousness is rooted in God Himself, and the examples of it in the Old Testament express His clear intention for *what life should be like*. This is where our focus will stay, on biblical justice and righteousness instead of biblical social justice.

THE FOUNDATION OF HIS THRONE

Even before sin distorted the world, justice and righteousness have been foundational to God's own rule over creation. One of my favorite illustrations for this is found in Psalms:

> Clouds and thick darkness are all around him;
> righteousness [*sedeq*] and justice [*mishpat*] are the
> foundation of his throne. (Psalm 97:2 ESV; see also
> Psalm 89:14)

During Old Testament times, a throne was a symbol of royal authority. The very seat of God's authority rests on a foundation of "justice and righteousness." Describing justice and righteousness as the base of God's throne gives a picture of how God Himself rules and keeps His authority established. Everything He does is *from* that place, so His entire rule is colored with "justice and righteousness." As Rabbi Heschel puts it: "['Justice and righteousness' are] not one of His ways, but in all of His ways."[10] Understanding and knowing God—who He is, what He values, how He acts, and what brings Him delight—is to know what a priority "justice and righteousness" are to Him.

Everything God does is from that place, so His entire rule is colored with "justice and righteousness."

That image of God's throne is a great illustration for us as well. God's personal, passionate concern for justice and righteousness was the starting place for His people to build them into every part of their culture.[11] The place we should all live from is "justice and righteousness." Everything we do, from the way we raise our families to the way we run our businesses to our own relationships with the vulnerable, should reflect "justice and righteousness."

"Justice and righteousness" was never meant to be the work of only one person, or one part of society. It should be the foundation of how everyone stewards their lives, as well as an integral, normal part of all of society. Every aspect of this world needs God's "justice and righteousness."

THE FOUNDATION OF HIS PEOPLE & KINGDOM

Let's look at a quick overview of how important "*mishpat* and *sedeq*" were throughout the history of Israel.[12] The first time "justice and righteousness" appear in the Bible is when God says that He won't hide from Abraham what He plans on doing in Sodom and Gomorrah:

> The Lord said, "Shall I hide from Abraham what I am about to do, seeing that Abraham shall surely become a great and mighty nation, and all the nations of the earth shall be blessed in him? For I have chosen him, that he may command his children and his household after him to keep the way of the Lord by doing righteousness [*sedeqah*] and justice [*mishpat*], so that the Lord may bring to Abraham what he has promised him." (Genesis 18:17-19 ESV)

The significance of this is easy to miss. Abraham was chosen by God to establish His plan of redemption for the whole earth through his family line. Abraham's blessing would be significant for every nation.[13] How was Abraham going to keep the way of the Lord? By doing "*sedeqah* and *mishpat*" and teaching his descendants to do the same. This put "justice and righteousness" front and center in the culture and identity of the family line carrying God's redemptive plan for humanity.[14]

JUSTICE & RIGHTEOUSNESS: **THE FOUNDATION OF GOD'S REIGN**

From that first promise to Abraham, we can follow the importance of "justice and righteousness" throughout the history of Israel, which we will look at more in the following chapters. And the foundation of "justice and righteousness" does not end in the Old Testament. Rather, Jesus makes them foundational to the kingdom to which we now belong. The Old Testament prophecies also show a powerful picture of how the Messiah (Jesus) will ultimately fulfill God's redemptive plan by executing "*mishpat* and *sedeq*" (see Jeremiah 23:5, 33:15) and establishing and upholding His everlasting kingdom with "*mishpat* and *sedeq*" (see Isaiah 9:7). In Acts 17:31, we are told that Jesus will "judge the world in righteousness" (see also 1 Peter 2:23, Revelation 19:11). The Biblical story shows that of justice and righteousness continue to be central, relevant parts of our modern Christian lives.

JUSTICE & RIGHTEOUSNESS ARE WHAT:

- **God loves** (Ps. 11:7, 33:5, 37:28, 45:7, 99:4, 146:8; Pro. 15:9; Isa. 61:8; Heb. 1:9)
- **God delights in** (Jer. 9:23-24)
- **He expects His nation to do** (Deut. 16:20, Prov. 21:3, Isa. 56:1, Mic. 6:8, Amos 5:24)
- **He expects His leaders to do** (Deut. 16:18, 2 Sam. 8:15, 1 Kings 10:9; Ps. 72; Jer. 7:5, 22:3, 15-16)
- **Jesus will do** (Ps. 72, Isa. 11:1-5, Jer. 23:5-6, 33:15-16)
- **Will be permanent when the Holy Spirit comes** (Isa. 32: 15-18)

JUSTICE & RIGHTEOUSNESS ARE FOUNDATIONAL TO:

- **God's reign** (Ps. 89:14, 97:2, 98; Acts 17:31; 1 Peter 2:23; Rev 19:11)
- **God's chosen people** (Gen. 18:19)
- **Jesus' kingdom and reign** (Isa. 9:7, 16:5, 42:1-4; Ps. 72; Rom. 14:17)

THE JUSTICE & RIGHTEOUSNESS THAT HE LOVES

God loves "justice and righteousness." He delights in it and actively works to establish it. When we look at God, we see justice and righteousness expressed along with mercy, grace, steadfast love, and all His other attributes. The picture of this God as revealed in Scripture is not a God who loves to punish people, but a God who loves things like this:

- Relationship
- When we are completely loyal to Him
- Freeing the oppressor from the oppressed
- When we pattern our lives after His life-giving order
- Deliverance, salvation, and victory
- Creating a heavenly norm on earth
- When people are given their rights
- Restoring what's been lost, stolen, or broken
- Environments where everyone can live in their fullness
- Good, unselfish governance
- Laws that reflect the value and dignity of the weak and poor
- Rescuing the poor and defenseless

What a powerful picture of our God! God loves justice and righteousness not because He loves rules, but because He loves people. Justice and righteousness are an essential part of who He is and how He acts. True justice and righteousness flow from our Creator, not from man-made laws to police our behavior. He wants us to live in the world the way He designed it to be enjoyed. His design has boundaries, yes, but living within these boundaries does not constrict our freedom; it expands it.

God wants justice to manifest on the earth. He wants the oppressed, the poor, and the vulnerable to receive justice. Our just and righteous God actively works to restore His order in the world, righting wrongs and pursuing relationship. He desires to have a full, right relationship with everyone (see 1 Timothy 2:4). Desiring to see justice and righteousness in the world is a reflection of God's heart. As those made in God's image, justice and righteousness should be an integral, normal part of our lives just as they are for Him.

JUSTICE & RIGHTEOUSNESS: **THE FOUNDATION OF GOD'S REIGN**

STUDY QUESTIONS

What would it look like if everyone lived their lives from a place of justice and righteousness, so it was expressed in all parts of the world?

Do you feel like you can say that you love justice and righteousness? Why or why not?

When you think about how God originally designed us to experience life—the way that life *should* be—what do you think of? What are ways that you can contribute to that happening in the world?

UNIFIED GOD: JUST, MERCIFUL, RIGHTEOUS, & KIND

CHAPTER SIX

FOR MOST OF MY life, my best solution for understanding that God was both merciful and just was to picture God as temperamental. The Jews had the angry version of God and we Christians have the nice one. He was angry and rule-driven in the Old Testament, but He's become a sweet old Abba in the New—full of grace and mercy. Jesus changed everything—including God's character. Jesus' death meant God could go from justice/judgment mode to mercy/grace mode. When justice was connected to rules and punishment in my mind, it didn't make sense that God could be both just by enforcing the rules, and merciful by forgiving and pardoning those who break them. Only one or the other seemed possible. If both justice and mercy were at work at the same time, then one would undermine the other.

Because many of us Westerners think justice is all about laws and punishments, we often struggle to reconcile God's justice with the other qualities of His character—compassion, mercy, kindness, and love. But the more we study *mishpat* and *sedeq*, the more we see that God's justice and righteousness harmonize perfectly and work in unity with these other qualities. As we study God's justice, it is important to see this harmony and unity in God's attributes and imitate His fullness of each.

GRACE AND MERCY

My picture of a temperamental God was so wrong. Jews have always understood God to be full of kindness, mercy, and grace. When God first introduces Himself to Moses, He describes Himself as "a God merciful and gracious, slow to anger, and abounding in steadfast love and faithfulness" (Exodus 34:6b ESV). The Psalms (which Christians still like to quote today) paint a picture a God who is loving, kind, strong, merciful, and compassionate. And Christians have a God of justice who will bring in a Judgment Day where we will stand before Him and account for our lives. God is consistent in His mercy and justice in both the Old Testament and the New.

So how can we start to understand God's mercy and justice coexisting in Him? One rabbi in the Jewish Talmud uses this illustration:

> It may be likened to a king who had empty vessels. The king said, "If I put hot water into them they will crack; if I put icy cold water into them they will contract." What did the king do? He mixed the hot with the cold and poured the mixture into the vessels, and they endured. Similarly said the Holy One, blessed be He, "If I create the world only with the attribute of mercy, sins will multiply beyond all bounds; if I create it only with the attribute of justice, how can the world last? Behold, I will create it with both attributes; would that it might endure!"[1]

We try to create balance by making it one or the other—either God is just or merciful. But God creates balance by being and doing both. They are each needed for the world to function—each playing an essential role that complements the other. Over and over again in the Old Testament, God's justice and righteousness work in parallel to His forgive-

UNIFIED GOD: JUST, MERCIFUL, RIGHTEOUS, & KIND

ness, grace, love, kindness, deliverance—not in opposition to them.[2]

Remember that *mishpat* can refer to a characteristic of a person or a king.[3] The character of God perfectly integrates justice with mercy. When we reflect the manner, order, or custom of God, we are reflecting His *mishpat*—one that works in harmony with His other qualities.

The character of God perfectly integrates justice with mercy.

God's mercy is such an intricate part of how He acts that it is included when He does *mishpat*:

> Therefore the Lord waits to be gracious [*chanan*]
>   to you, and therefore he exalts himself to show
>   mercy [*raham*] to you.
> For the Lord is a God of justice [*mishpat*]; blessed
>   are all those who wait for him. (Isaiah 30:18 ESV)

God is gracious and shows mercy to Israel *because* "the Lord is a God of *mishpat*." What does it mean that God wants to be gracious towards them? *Chanan* means to be gracious or show favor to someone.[4] It's a heartfelt response to someone in need.[5] Israel didn't deserve this response, but God freely gave it. Grace is the basis of God's relationship with man.[6] The word "mercy" here, *raham*, means to have mercy, be compassionate, or love deeply. It's closely related to the Hebrew word for "womb," showing the depth of the emotion.[7] Think of the profound love a mother experiences for her child—that's what God's mercy is like.

So this God of *mishpat* is gracious and shows mercy. His response to need is deep and heartfelt. Mercy and grace are never at odds with His justice and righteousness. In Jewish thought, mercy and justice work together in unity.[8] If mercy lacks justice, or justice lacks mercy, neither is complete.

Scripture also connects God's justice and righteousness with His steadfast love:

> He loves righteousness [*sedeqah*] and justice [*mishpat*];

> The earth is full of the steadfast love [*hesed*] of the LORD. (Psalm 33:5 ESV)

> "I am the Lord who practices steadfast love [*hesed*], justice [*mishpat*] and righteousness [*sedeqah*] in earth." (Jeremiah 9:24b NASB)

God does these three things—justice, righteousness, and steadfast love—all together. The Hebrew word for "steadfast love," *hesed,* is important. *Hesed* is the foundation of God's covenant with Israel.[9] The sense *hesed* carries is love, devotion, faithfulness, or loyalty. It is abundant and eternal.[10] What I love about this is that it describes God's covenant commitment to Israel as marked with kindness, loyalty, and love—not frustration and anger. Israel received a unique experience of God's mercy, kindness, and compassion because of their covenant with Him.

The foundation of God's throne is another picture of how these qualities join together:

> Righteousness [*sedeq*] and justice [*mishpat*] are the foundation of Your throne; Steadfast love [*hesed*] and faithfulness go before You. (Psalm 89:14 ESV)

All of these qualities characterize God's reign. God is not divided, with part of Him showing *hesed* and the other part exercising justice and righteousness. He never stops showing steadfast kindness when He does justice and righteousness, or vice versa.

These qualities characterizing Israel's relationship with God continue to be an integral part of our relationship with God as Christians. In Hosea, we find a picture of how these define God's covenant—first with Israel, and now with us as the bride of Christ:[11]

> And I will betroth you to me forever. I will betroth you to me in righteousness [*sedeq*] and in justice [*mishpat*], in steadfast love [*hesed*], and in mercy [*racham*]. (Hosea 2:19 ESV)

UNIFIED GOD: JUST, MERCIFUL, RIGHTEOUS, & KIND

God chooses His bride and commits Himself to her in justice, righteousness, steadfast love, and mercy. In perfect compassion, He saves His bride and reveals righteousness to the world.[12] The covenant we have as the bride of Christ includes all of these qualities joined together.

So how do all of these work together side by side? We see it in the way God responds to the conditions of His children with mercy and compassion. He is so quick to forgive and extend grace, because that is what is needed to stay in relationship with us. And His justice governs how His children should live in order to thrive within the bounds of His design for life. His justice acts to transform whatever is in the way for *shalom*. His righteousness is His radical commitment to relationship, which means He will save His people if they need it. He demonstrates how to live in a way to stay faithful to relationships. All of these together give an astounding picture of a God who wants a relationship with His children and His intention for all of life to grow and prosper. Think of these attributes as working together toward the same goal of life, restoration, and relationship. One doesn't undermine the others but rather complements and completes the others, each playing a role in the same purpose.

Think of these attributes as working together toward the same goal of life, restoration, and relationship.

COMMANDED IN ISRAEL

God expects His chosen people to express these qualities together, just as He does. The nation of Israel was commanded to do all, not some:

> Observe kindness [*hesed*] and justice [*mishpat*],
> And wait for your God continually. (Hosea 12:6b NASB)

The prophet Zechariah delivered a similar message:

> Dispense true justice [*mishpat*] and practice kindness [*hesed*] and compassion [*rahamim*] each to his

brother. (Zechariah 7:9b NASB)

We are created in the image of God, who is compassionate and kind and just and righteous. When the world sees justice being done by God's people, it should be full of kindness and compassion. The famous "Micah Mandate" summarizes this perfectly:

> He has told you, O man, what is good;
> And what does the Lord require of you
> But to do justice [*mishpat*], to love kindness [*hesed*],
> And to walk humbly with your God?
> (Micah 6:8 NASB)

Doing *mishpat* requires a heart of kindness and an attitude of humility. Any relationship requires many qualities working together to keep connection and intimacy. Our relationship with God needs justice, righteousness, mercy, steadfast love, loyalty, and commitment. We need the same qualities in order to live in community with one another as God's children.

GOD'S JUSTICE

Clearly our God of *mishpat* doesn't have a problem being just, gracious, and merciful. Justice without mercy (or mercy without justice) is actually a perverted version of both qualities. When we think about this just God, we should remember that He is not only just, He is also merciful and compassionate. Living out *mishpat* should show a tangible expression of God's mercy, kindness, and steadfast love.

UNIFIED GOD: **JUST, MERCIFUL, RIGHTEOUS, & KIND**

STUDY QUESTIONS

How have you seen God be just and merciful in the Bible?

Now that you've learned about justice *[mishpat]* and righteousness *[sedeq],* how do you think those could work in parallel with grace, mercy, and compassion in the world?

What would it look like for you to reflect mercy, compassion, grace, justice, and righteousness in your life?

DOES GOD LOVE THE POOR?
CHAPTER SEVEN

NOW THAT WE'VE LOOKED at the justice and righteousness God says He loves, let's go back to that question God first asked me: "What do I say that I love?"

It seemed automatic to answer that He loved the poor, probably because I had heard it thrown around in Christian circles my whole life. I had never really thought about it until God asked me what He says He loves. In fact, when He first whispered the question to me, I felt almost offended. Did His question suggest that He really didn't love the poor?

When I finally looked to see what God says that He loves in the Bible, I found that I had indeed been wrong. Nowhere in the Old or New Testament does God say specifically that He loves the poor *more than* anyone else. Then it hit me: *If God said that He loves the poor, then that would mean having less money makes you more lovable.* But God's love for us is not dependent on anything temporary. Money itself isn't evil, so having less of it doesn't make you better in His eyes. Loving money and using it to hurt people is the problem, which both the rich and the poor can do.

Yes, God loves the poor. But He loves everyone, and so should we. Being rich or poor doesn't tell you about someone's life, just about how much money they have. Plenty of wicked, corrupt, depressed people have lots of money. Plenty of godly, happy, powerful people have little money. The amount of money someone has doesn't tell you a lot of important things, like whether they are happy, have a good family, are kind and generous, work hard, feel loved, or are rich in spiritual resources. We make so many judgments about the poor and rich, when all we really know about them is the size of their bank account. The rich can be judged just as negatively as the poor, which isn't right either.

MADE IN HIS IMAGE

While God doesn't love the poor more than anyone else, the justice and righteousness God loves *do* have a strong connection to the poor. To understand this connection, we have to understand that justice and righteousness are the order of life as God created it to be: relationally rich and full of goodness. And the people least likely to experience that in the world are the ones with the least amount of power and resources.

The experience of poverty is far more than not having money in your pocket. In the Old Testament, the poor are the ones without fathers or husbands to protect them, the new immigrants who are open to exploitation and suspicion, and those without land to give them stability or resources to give them power. These experiences create extreme vulnerability and can degrade a person's sense of value, dignity, and power. Those deeper experiences fall short of God's standard of *shalom*—the peace and wholeness He designed for His creation. This is why God called Israel to have so much concern for the poor. Rabbi Jonathan Sacks describes Israel's mandate to care about poverty in their nation this way: "Poverty not merely deprives; it *humiliates,* and a good society will not allow humiliation."[1]

The Bible never says that the poor get an extra amount of God's love, but it does emphasize that they are made in the image of God. Because of that, they deserve to live in the fullness of life God designed for every human being. In Proverbs, for example, God identifies Himself as the Maker of the poor:

DOES GOD LOVE THE POOR?

Whoever is generous to the poor lends to the Lord,
   and he will repay him for his deed. (Proverbs 19:17 ESV, emphasis mine)

Whoever mocks the poor insults his Maker;
   he who is glad at calamity will not go unpunished. (Proverbs 17:5 ESV, emphasis mine)

Whoever oppresses a poor man insults his Maker,
   but he who is generous to the needy honors him. (Proverbs 14:31 ESV, emphasis mine)

The theme is clear: our actions toward the poor reflect our attitude toward God Himself. Oppressing or mocking the poor personally offends the One who gives them their value. When we think of it this way, it's crazy even to think about taking advantage of a poor or vulnerable person for our own gain, much less mock them (see also Proverbs 22:2, Job 34:19).

Our actions toward the poor reflect our attitude toward God Himself.

We are to see the image of the Almighty God in all people, no matter what value our culture says they have. God made all of us with the capacity to be powerful, creative, loving, strong, and spiritual; so, when we look at any person, we should see that they have a unique strength to bring into the world.

In recognizing that we all have the same Maker, we recognize that we all have the ability to be spiritual and powerful. Seeing the rich as automatically less spiritual just because they have more money is just as bad as seeing the poor as less human just because they have less money. Yes, it is easier to get your heart stuck in some of the trappings that go along with having material wealth—greed, materialism, pride, and arrogance—which the Bible condemns. But the Bible never condemns money itself. There have been and continue to be plenty of godly, hardworking, justice-loving, and generous rich people. When our identity and value are not rooted in money, then rich and poor alike can unite with a common identity as children of God.

THE LEAST OF THESE

The New Testament parallels this theme in Jesus' famous teaching on how we are to treat the "least of these":

> "'For I was hungry, and you fed me. I was thirsty, and you gave me a drink. I was a stranger, and you invited me into your home. I was naked, and you gave me clothing. I was sick, and you cared for me. I was in prison, and you visited me.'
> "Then these righteous ones will reply, 'Lord, when did we ever see you hungry and feed you? Or thirsty and give you something to drink? Or a stranger and show you hospitality? Or naked and give you clothing? When did we ever see you sick or in prison and visit you?'
> "And the King will say, 'I tell you the truth, when you did it to one of the least of these my brothers and sisters, you were doing it to me!'" (Matthew 25:35-40 NLT)

Jesus takes our treatment of the "invisible" people in society personally. Our relationships with the hungry, the foreigner, the needy, the imprisoned, and the sick are an expression of our relationship with Jesus. Most sobering of all, He says that our treatment of these "least" is what qualifies or disqualifies us to "inherit the kingdom" (Matthew 25:34). Our faith in Christ should massively change how we see and treat the people society hides and devalues the most.

The story of St. Martin of Tours illustrates the point of Jesus' parable beautifully. The story goes that Martin, a young Roman soldier, came across a half-naked beggar one cold night. Martin tore his uniform cloak in two and gave half to the beggar. That night, he saw Jesus wearing his cloak in a dream, surrounded by angels. Jesus told the angels, "Do you know who gave me this cloak? My servant, Martin, gave it to me."[2] When we give to the vulnerable and marginalized in this world, we love Jesus in a way that we will never be able to love Him in eternity.

UNDERSTANDING THE CAUSES OF POVERTY

When I teach on justice and poverty, I find that American Christians generally have two basic beliefs about the causes of poverty. The first is the "teach a man to fish" belief. As the popular saying goes, "If you give a man a fish, he eats for a day. But if you teach a man to fish, he will eat for a lifetime." Many think that people are poor because they lack the skills to take care of their own needs, and that the way to solve their problem is to give them training. The other belief is simply that the poor are poor because they are lazy. If they worked harder, they wouldn't be poor.

Yes, a person can be poor because they don't know how to fish or don't work hard at fishing. But a lot of the poor in the world know how to fish and work hard at it, yet they face other obstacles preventing them from getting out of poverty. They don't own the rights to the land around the fishing lake. Or the government won't issue them a fishing license. Or they have a physical disability that prevents them from fishing and need another way to provide for themselves. Or there is no market to sell all the fish they catch. Or they have an addiction that stops them from fishing. Or a company is polluting the water and killing off all their fish. To fix these other problems, you need a totally different solution to get people to "fish for themselves."

The Bible isn't simplistic about the causes of poverty or the diverse circumstances in which the "poor" live. There are *nine* Hebrew words for the poor and poverty.[3] (Some of these words show up together in word pairs like "poor and needy" or "weak and needy."[4]) These words describe a variety of people: peasant farmers, day laborers, debt slaves, beggars, everyday people living in villages, and those lacking political power. The fact that so many words are used to describe these people and their reality should tell us that "the poor" are a diverse group and deserve to be treated as such.[5] All over the Old Testament prophetic books, poverty is talked about in terms of power and social structures. There are intense descriptions about the suffering that the poor experience due to injustice caused or allowed by the powerful in the nation. We will look at one of these examples in detail in Chapter 9.

It's absolutely true that the Bible affirms the value of hard work (and excellent craftsmanship in your work),[6] and lists laziness as one of the causes of poverty. The book of Proverbs, just like any good parent, warns us that if we have opportunities and choose to sit around and do nothing, we will end up poor. But Proverbs lists many other things that can lead to poverty and hunger: lack of preparation for the future (6:6-11), lack of generosity (11:24), ignoring discipline (13:18), lack of *mishpat* (13:23), "mere talk" (14:23), loving sleep (20:13), loving pleasure (21:17), oppressing the poor to get wealth (22:16), being a drunk and glutton (23:21), not working your land (24:30-34), or chasing fantasies (28:19). Poverty is a destination many roads can lead to. Just because someone ended up there doesn't mean they all took the same path.

I've heard American Christians quote the apostle Paul's words—"Whoever refuses to work is not allowed to eat" (2 Thessalonians 3:10b GNT)—to support the belief that the poor are poor because they don't work hard enough. But Paul was not referring to the poor in this verse. He was addressing irresponsible busybodies in the church, who refused to work but liked meddling in other people's business (3:11). These busybodies were behaving in a way contrary to the model he and the missionaries to Thessalonica had set—to work hard so that they wouldn't be a financial burden to the church (3:6-9).[7] The specific command—*if anyone wants to eat, then they need to work for it*[8]—was given to a specific church to solve a specific problem. Paul didn't even give it as a command to all of the churches he had authority over, and he wasn't making a comment about all the hungry people in the city.[9] Paul was correcting the problem of irresponsible busybodies bringing chaos into the church, not lazy poor people living off of the hard work of others. I actually think today we need to flip this verse and ask why so many poor people are working and still can't afford to eat?

Injustice can produce the same impact as laziness—creating poverty and making people desperate and dependent on others to meet their needs. Random chance, like a natural disaster or a drought, can also lead to poverty and need. We live in a world where sin has distorted *every-*

thing. For a healthy nation and economy, you need hardworking people to steward the earth. And because life is unpredictable and sin can create poverty, you also need ways to meet needs and stop injustice so that everyone in the nation can have the opportunity to prosper and thrive.

The idea behind "teach a man to fish" is good. Getting to the root of poverty is needed otherwise you'll always have to work to meet needs. However, it oversimplifies the solution and tends to give those who aren't poor a superiority complex. People are poor for many reasons, most of which are complicated. Many need more complex help, help that involves multiple groups working together to establish justice and give the poor opportunities to use their own strengths to improve their lives. An entire nation will benefit from the skills and talents of the poor being expressed instead of locked away because of poverty.

Many Christians also use the phrase "taking care of the poor." We have to be careful how we think of that, though, too. It can make it seem like the poor are helpless and the rest of the world needs to carry the burden of their needs. What other category of people do we "take care of"? Pets, kids, the elderly—generally people who are unable to care for themselves. I don't think that phrase is helpful, and it never appears in the Bible. A lot of the poor are powerful and capable of taking care of themselves when they are given justice and good opportunities.

God never gives a vague statement about "caring for" the poor. His actions toward them are concrete and specific. If you want to know where to start with how to practically "care for" the poor, try mirroring one of God's own actions (see chart).

GOD DESCRIBES HIS PERSONAL RELATIONSHIP TO THE POOR, OPPRESSED & VULNERABLE, INCLUDING CONCRETE ACTIONS HE DOES FOR THEM:

God ensures that orphans and widows receive justice: *Deut. 10:18*	God provides for the needy: *Ps. 68:10*
God gives the poor hope by saving and protecting them: *Job 5:15-16*	God helps orphans and widows: *Ps. 146:9*
	God keeps the boundaries of the widows intact: *Prov. 15:25*

God secures justice for the poor: *Ps. 140:12*	God personally defends the weak and poor: *Prov. 22:22-23*
God heard and responded to Israel when they cried out because of oppression from the Egyptians: *Deut. 26:6-9*	God stands up for the poor who are being oppressed by the powerful: *Isa. 3:14-15*
God raises up the poor: *1 Sam. 2:8*	God defends the rights of the helpless: *Isa. 11:4*
God is a refuge for the oppressed: *Ps. 9:9*	God brings the poor into safety: *Isa. 14:30*
God never forgets the needy: *Ps. 9: 17-18*	God will deliver the oppressed when they cry out: *Isa. 19:20*
God rescues the poor from violence: *Ps. 12:5*	God is a shelter for the poor and needy: *Isa. 25:4*
God protects the oppressed: *Ps. 14:6*	God will answer the hurt and needy Himself: *Isa. 41:17*
God rescues and protects the helpless: *Ps. 35:10*	God protects the immigrant: *Ps. 146:9*
God keeps the poor and needy in His thoughts: *Ps. 40:17*	God rescues the needy from the wicked: *Jer. 20:13*
God acts as a father to the fatherless and the defender of widows: *Ps. 68:5*	God personally defends the poor and weak from His heavenly court: *Ps. 82*
God gives the immigrant food and clothing: *Deut. 10:18-19*	

The process of establishing justice is something in which everyone, rich and poor, can participate. Instead of "taking care" of the poor, we need to make them feel seen, heard, respected, and treated as equal. They should be actively integrated into all parts of a nation. The more we explore justice and righteousness in the Bible, the more we will see how to live out this perspective—in individual lives, in a nation, and in the New Testament church.

GETTING TO THE "WHY"

Caring about the lives of the poor isn't rooted in earthly politics but in the heart of God. Why should we care about justice for the weakest in a society? On one level, we should care because God cares and it aligns our values with God's. But as we do this, we will discover the deeper levels of "why" for doing justice for the poor.

First, doing justice to the poor promotes justice in all of society. Martin Luther King, Jr., captured the logic of biblical justice in his statement, "Injustice anywhere is a threat to justice everywhere."[10] The level of justice available to the most vulnerable is the measure of justice set for that entire nation. If justice is only available for those who can afford it, then the level of justice for the whole nation is set at zero. When the poor are exploited and not given justice, then the stability of the ground we all stand on is shaken (see Psalm 82:5).

Second, doing justice to the poor honors God's design for us to be His family. Israel was called to be a nation of brothers and sisters. No matter how much each individual had, they were supposed to respect and show love to each other. In a family, if one child is being hurt and abused, then everyone is impacted. If a family treats some members well and others poorly, it is dysfunctional. The fact that most of them are well-treated doesn't matter. The level of justice for the weakest member of the family determines whether the family as a unit is functional or dysfunctional. Ensuring justice for all makes the entire family unit strong.

The poor don't have a special relationship to God's love, but they do have a special relationship to His justice. The way that God's people love the poor and do justice should reflect this, demonstrating biblically-based values, attitudes, and commands.

STUDY QUESTIONS

Do you see your nation or church community stereotyping and judging the poor and the rich? If so, what are ways you can keep those influences from impacting your heart?

What are ways that you could contribute to the *shalom* of the poor in your own community?

Look at the chart of verses that describe God's relationship with the poor. What would it look like if Christians reflected that relationship?

JOB:
A LIFESTYLE OF JUSTICE
& RIGHTEOUSNESS

CHAPTER EIGHT

NOW THAT WE SEE how essential *mishpat* and *sedeq* are to God and how the poor fit into them, we are going examine what it looked like for Israel to live these out. God's justice and righteousness are meant to be lived, done, and expressed in the world—both in our individual lives and integrated throughout culture. For our purposes, we are going to look at two stories that give a good overview of what justice and righteousness look like practically—one that will show us what they look like for an individual, and one that will show us what they look like for a nation. We'll begin with the individual story in this chapter and dive into the national story in the next.

If you have heard the story of Job, you are likely to associate him with words like "pain and suffering" rather than "justice and righteousness." But tucked away in the book of Job is a clear, powerful description of what living out justice and righteousness in Hebrew culture looked like.

Job was a wealthy and influential person, and as I studied justice in the Bible, I was surprised to find that his life demonstrated justice and righteousness. In my world, the models for living "social justice" involved giving away worldly power and resources. Going into a career like finance or politics meant you risked "selling out" and becoming as unjust as everyone else after a while. It's hard to sell out if you become an education justice lawyer or sell all your possessions to live with the poor. But in the Bible, the people most expected to live out justice and righteousness were those with the most power, wealth, and influence. Therefore, the Old Testament models include the top leaders with the most authority—kings, prophets, priests, judges, and governors.[1]

JOB'S STORY

In case you aren't familiar with the book of Job, I'm going to give you a quick recap of Job's story.

The book of Job begins by describing Job as a devoted spiritual leader and father. He was both a virtuous man—"blameless and upright, and one who feared God and shunned evil" (Job 1:1 ESV)—and extremely prosperous man—"the greatest of all the people of the east" (Job 1:3 ESV).

After this description, the scene shifts to the court of heaven, where God initiates a conversation with the Accuser, Satan. God says, "Have you noticed my servant Job? He is the finest man in all the earth. He is blameless—a man of complete integrity. He fears God and stays away from evil" (Job 1:8 NLT).

Satan, the ultimate cynic, replies, "Yes, but Job has good reason to fear God. You have always put a wall of protection around him and his home and his property. You have made him prosper in everything he does. Look how rich he is! But reach out and take away everything he has, and he will surely curse you to your face!" (Job 1:9-11 NLT).

In response to Satan's accusation that Job only serves God conditionally because God blesses him, God tells Satan that he is allowed to do anything to Job, except touch his health. Soon after, news reaches Job that he has lost his children and wealth. Yet even in the midst of shattering grief, Job still praises God and does not sin or curse God as Satan had predicted.

God and Satan talk again. God points out Job's virtue once more,

JOB: A LIFESTYLE OF JUSTICE & RIGHTEOUSNESS

and Satan again mocks Him, arguing that if Job lost his health, he would cease to worship God. God gives permission for Satan to touch Job's health but prohibits him from taking his life. Satan then afflicts Job with a terrible disease that covers his body in painful boils. At this point, even Job's wife says, "Are you still trying to maintain your integrity? Curse God and die" (Job 2:9 NLT). But even in total misery, Job refuses.

Soon, three of Job's friends, Eliphaz, Bildad, and Zophar, hear of Job's misfortune, and come to be with him. They all try to make sense of the situation and what should be done about it. However, much of the extended conversation between Job and his friends involves Job defending himself from their accusations. All three friends insist that Job must have done something to deserve his wretched state, and they urge him to repent and to appeal to God for forgiveness. In the end, God shows up and responds to Job directly. He teaches Job a lesson about His sovereignty, rebukes Job's friends, and ultimately restores Job's health, family, and wealth beyond what they had been before Satan attacked him. God "blessed Job in the second half of his life even more than in the beginning" (Job 42:12a NLT). There is a redemptive ending to it all.

A JUSTICE HERO

This is an unusual set-up for a justice story: A person loses everything for no real reason, and then sits around talking with his friends and God. Theologians have many different interpretations of the story of Job, most of which focus on explaining how God both allows and redeems our suffering. Some say that you can't apply this story to us today, because Jesus changes everything about how God works in our lives. I'm going to leave the theology of suffering to them.

What we're going to examine is Job's lifestyle of justice and righteousness. In the book, Job and his friends try to make sense of the chaos that has taken over his life. Because they can't understand why terrible things could happen to a good person, Job's friends are convinced that Job has some hidden sin that has invited all of this destruction. They make all sorts of accusations against Job trying to find a cause-and-effect. In response, Job defends himself with a description of what his life looked like before everything was taken away. Tucked away in his response is a vivid picture of a lifestyle of justice and righteousness, which Job lived every day. (In fact, the prophet Ezekiel lists Job, along with Noah and Daniel, as one of the most righteous [*sedeqah*] people who ever lived—see Ezekiel 14:14, 14:20.) And because he was wealthy and influential, his account lets us in on how it looks for someone powerful to touch an entire community through justice and righteousness.

Job's recollection of his former life begins in Job 29. The first thing he says he misses is God's favor and friendship, "when his lamp shone upon my head" and "when the friendship of God was upon my tent" (Job 29:2-5 ESV). Job's *friendship* with God was the source from which everything in his life flowed. When direct connection to God is the source of your life, it helps you get lined up with His heart, values, and priorities.

When direct connection to God is the source of your life, it helps you get lined up with His heart, values, and priorities

---

Job then describes how people used to react to him when he walked through the city:

> When I went out to the gate of the city,
>   when I prepared my seat in the square,
> the young men saw me and withdrew,
>   and the aged rose and stood;
> the princes refrained from talking
>   and laid their hand on their mouth;
> the voice of the nobles was hushed,
>   and their tongue stuck to the roof of their mouth.
> When the ear heard, it called me blessed,
>   and when the eye saw, it approved…
> (Job 29:7-11 ESV)

This would have been a pretty dramatic scene to witness. As Job passed them, princes and nobles became speechless. Younger men got out of his way. The *elderly* rose out of respect for *him,* rather than expecting him to rise for them. These are all visual signs that Job was held in highest esteem by everyone in town.

Job goes on to describe *why* he received such honor, and it's a little surprising:

> When the ear heard, it called me blessed,
>   and when the eye saw, it approved,
> **_because_** I delivered the poor who cried for help,
>   and the fatherless who had none to help him.
> The blessing of him who was about to perish came upon me,
>   and I caused the widow's heart to sing for joy.
> I put on righteousness [*sedeq*], and it clothed me;
>   my justice [*mishpat*] was like a robe and a turban.
> I was eyes to the blind
>   and feet to the lame.
> I was a father to the needy,
>   and I searched out the cause of him whom I did not know.
> I broke the fangs of the unrighteous
>   and made him drop his prey from his teeth.
> (Job 29:11-17 ESV, emphasis mine)

According to Job, he didn't receive all of that honor from important people because of his worldly wealth or title.[2] People honored him for the acts of justice he performed—for his compassion for the poor, fatherless, and widows. His lifestyle of justice and righteousness was what left people speechless.[3]

Let's break this passage down and examine these acts in more detail. First, Job says, "I delivered the poor who cried for help and the fatherless who had none to help him." Job is disputing Eliphaz's accusation that he oppressed the poor (see Job 22:5-9), saying that instead of oppressing the poor and the orphaned, he heard their cry and saved them.

Why is this description so important? It reflects God's own attitude toward the poor. God hears the cry of the poor and delivers them (see Psalm 35:10, 69:33, 82:4), and so does Job. In Psalm 72, Solomon describes how an ideal leader should rule. He states that they should defend the cause of the poor, deliver the needy and their children, and show compassion for the weak (see Psalm 72:4, 12-14).[4] The prophets often lamented that Israel's rulers were ignoring the rights of the poor, not giving them *mishpat,* and oppressing them (see Isaiah 3:15, 10:1; Amos 2:6, 4:1; Ezekiel 22:29, Micah 3:1-4). But Job's actions proved him to be a model leader for the weak and vulnerable.

Next, Job says, "The blessing of him who was about to perish came upon me." Innocent people were suffering and on the brink of death. In reaction to seeing their suffering, Job stepped in and saved them, naturally earning their thanks and blessing.[5] If you were dying and someone saved your life, you would probably thank God for them for the rest of your life. Job had a string of people who owed him their lives, and they blessed him for it.

Job then says that he "caused the widow's heart to sing for joy." He had a reputation for helping widows with practical needs, defending their cause, and punishing those who tried to take advantage of them. But his help had such a profound effect that it healed their hearts—hearts likely broken by loss, poverty, and social exclusion—and brought them to a place of joy.[6] The Hebrew word for "to sing for joy" is *ranan,* meaning "to emit a tremulous and stridulous sound" or "to lift up joyful outcries."[7] Imagine living in such a way that you make the hearts of those devastated by tragic loss cry out with joy. Remember, when God first created the world, He wanted all of His creation to prosper, not just survive. Doing justice and righteousness should not just help people back to the level of survival but to the place where they can thrive in body, soul, and spirit. Righteous and just living has an active, not passive, attitude toward the *hearts* of the weak and suffering.[8]

Righteous and just living has an active, not passive, attitude toward the hearts of the weak and suffering.

Job's next line is a metaphor: "I put on righteousness, and it clothed me; my justice was like a robe and a turban." Everyone (well, almost everyone) has to wear clothes every day, no matter how you feel. Your mood doesn't dictate whether you wear clothes. When Job says he was clothed in righteousness, he meant he constantly lived righteousness. Job wore righteousness from the time he woke up to the time he went to sleep, no matter if he felt like it or not. In Hebrew, the verse literally says,

"I habited myself in *sedeq* and it habited itself in me."[9] Righteousness lived in both his internal and external worlds. His external actions were linked to his internal world, permanently clothed in *sedeq*.[10] The "robe and turban" Job mentions are his outer garments—the clothing most visible to everyone else.[11] That's what *mishpat* was to Job. In the same way that others could see Job's robe and turban, they could see his justice. The turban was a *kefije;* a head covering made from a thick cotton cloth and tied up with a camel's hair cord.[12] In his day, the turban and robe were the prominent characteristics of a high priest's clothing.[13] So his *mishpat* was his uniform that set him apart, like the priest's garment. When you see someone wear a uniform, like a soldier or doctor, you don't have to know them personally to understand what they do. Job's "uniform" of *mishpat* commanded respect from those who saw him.

Job then says, "I was eyes to the blind and feet to the lame." Where there was a need, he filled it.[14] The small, practical needs in their lives were seen, known, and met. Such acts of service are often tedious and unglamorous and don't always feel like they have a significant impact. Job was present in the full spectrum of the lives of the vulnerable, from the life-and-death moments to the daily, routine ones.[15][16]

"I was a father to the needy and I searched out the cause of him whom I did not know," Job continues. This tells us something powerful about his attitude. As I mentioned in the last chapter, there are multiple Hebrew words for the poor and needy. The word used here, *ebyon*, means that the poor were exploited by the more powerful.[17] Job didn't approach those being exploited as if he were a lawyer or a distant, charitable patron, but as a father. He went way beyond just giving resources; rather, he cared about and defended them from a more intimate place.

Take a minute and think of one of your own children. If you don't have children, imagine a child about whom you care deeply. Connect to your feelings of love and affection for that child. Now imagine that this child is caught up in one of a million scenarios of injustice going on in the world today. They are trafficked and forced to work as a prostitute. An army comes and kidnaps them, forcing them to fight in a war they don't understand. They are a teen stuck alone in a group foster home, turning to drugs because they think there is not a person in the world who cares about them. A corrupt official arrests them for a crime they didn't commit and leaves them to rot in prison for a decade. What would you do? Throw your hands up and say, "Not my problem. I'm not being unjust, so injustice isn't my responsibility"? No. You would be relentless. When fathers and mothers see their children hurting or caught up in injustices bigger than themselves, they won't stop until justice comes.

The most powerful weapons against injustice are the hearts of mothers and fathers, because their heart's desire is to see every child healthy and thriving.

The most powerful weapons against injustice are the hearts of mothers and fathers, because their heart's desire is to see every child healthy and thriving. How much would it change the lives of the weak and needy if we adopted the attitude of a father or mother toward them, instead of the attitude of a distant benefactor? Benefactors like to give checks and then hear reports on the results of their donations. Fathers and mothers are present in the process of restoration. So many people in this world just need someone to care for them like family, not as a special project or mission trip. This is how we demonstrate the Father's heart for them. Yes, God is our Lord and King, but He is also our Father. His Fatherhood and His Kingship are two perspectives on the same relationship.[18] To understand God's perspective on justice, we have to understand His Father's heart for every individual person, especially the poor and the victims of injustice. When God sees injustice, His response isn't as a faraway ruler, who wants to maintain order. Rather, he is a loving Father, who wants healing and restoration to come when His children are ignored or hurt.

The second portion of the verse connects to the first: "I *searched out the cause of him whom I did not know*" (emphasis mine). How easy is it to take the attitude "Out of sight, out of mind" or "Not my problem"? But even those who were strangers to Job still mattered to him. He was active in the causes of those for whom he had no direct responsibility. He cared that they got justice. In Job's day, the poor often did not have protection, so Job willingly advocated for the friendless who didn't have someone to take up their cause.[19] He gave them something precious: his attention.[20]

Job then says, "I broke the fangs of the unrighteous and made him drop his prey from his teeth." Job is comparing the unrighteous to a predatory animal. "Fangs" represent the weapons they use to harm and destroy the weak. Job protected the innocent by disarming the weapons of the unrighteous. The Good News Translation says it this way, "I destroyed the power of cruel men and rescued their victims." Job did more than just bandage up the victims of injustice; he dealt with the perpetrators and removed them as a threat. Job was an instrument in God's hand to break their jaw.[21]

In the world today, there is a great need for "fang-breaking"—for God's people to stand up and disarm those who are causing innocent people to die in the jaws of injustice. Of course, as we know from the New Testament, these enemies are ultimately not just physical, but spiritual: "For we do not wrestle against flesh and blood, but against the rulers, against the authorities, against the cosmic powers over this present darkness, against the spiritual forces of evil in the heavenly places" (Ephesians 6:12 ESV). Spiritual darkness enslaves both the victims and perpetrators of injustice. When we disarm forces of darkness, we offer God's invitation for everyone to receive redemption and reconciliation.

JOB 29 TODAY

When you break this passage down, it creates a powerful description of what a just and righteous life looks like. Don't you think Job is an awesome justice hero? When I get to the end of my life, I want to be able to say these same sorts of things about myself.

Obviously, the way you and I will live out any of these aspects will look different than it did for Job. His situation and ours are different in a few key ways. For one, Job was an extremely rich man. He wasn't responsible for cooking dinner every night, working a nine-to-five job, or putting his kids to bed. I don't know how you could live the life he did without a whole team of servants to juggle all the everyday logistics that take up most people's time and energy. Therefore, we shouldn't look at Job's life as a to-do list that makes us feel guilty for everything we aren't doing but as a holistic picture that shows what kind of actions can come from a heart set on justice and righteousness.

Another difference is that Job likely lived his entire life in the same community and would have had a simple, straightforward career path. Many of us, in contrast, live with a lot of change, whether it is in our careers, schools, cities, or spiritual communities. Navigating changes in life seasons and priorities will mean that living justice and righteousness will look different from one time to the next. However, we can live according to the same principles and carry the same heart in every situation or season. We just have to ask God to show us what it looks like to live them out in our given circumstances.

JOB 31

Job's description of his lifestyle of justice and righteousness continues in Chapter 31. He explains that he also refuses to lust (v. 1), lie (v. 5), trust in his wealth (v. 24-25), worship idols (v. 26-28), take pleasure in seeing his enemies in pain (v. 29-30), or care about the negative opinion of others (v. 33-34). He is committed to keeping his heart clean of materialism, bitterness, pride, and shame.[22] Job makes it clear that his spiritual and moral purity and his integrity were essential to his lifestyle of justice and righteousness. The modern world is often arguing that it doesn't matter whether a person has integrity in private, as long as they are doing good works in public. But Job's public demonstrations of justice and righteousness flow directly from his pure heart.

While Job's spiritual and moral purity are important, I want to continue to highlight the justice and righteousness parts of Job's lifestyle addressed in this passage, because they generally don't get a lot of attention.[23] For this purpose, let's zoom in on the two categories of sin Job discusses in verses 13-22—injustice toward servants and injustice towards the poor, widows, and orphans.

We saw verses 13-15 in the last chapter:

> "If I have been unfair to my male or female servants
>   when they brought their complaints to me,
> how could I face God?
>   What could I say when he questioned me?
> For God created both me and my servants.
>   He created us both in the womb.
> (Job 31:13-15 NLT)

JOB: A LIFESTYLE OF JUSTICE & RIGHTEOUSNESS

Masters in Job's time had a lot of power and control over their servants. With his position, Job could easily have ignored his servants' rights or dismissed them, and no one would have known or cared. Yet, Job recognized that he must give justice to his servants, because "he created us both in the womb." The source of their life is the same; therefore Job is accountable to their Maker. As humans, we may say that he can get away with injustice because of his wealth, but God sees it all, so Job lives by God's standard instead.[24]

Job then lists various types of wrongs against the poor, widows, and orphans that he has been careful not to commit:

> "If I have withheld anything that the poor desired,
>   or have caused the eyes of the widow to fail,
> or have eaten my morsel alone,
>   and the fatherless has not eaten of it
> (for from my youth the fatherless grew up with me as with a father,
>   and from my mother's womb I guided the widow),
> if I have seen anyone perish for lack of clothing,
>   or the needy without covering,
> if his body has not blessed me,
>   and if he was not warmed with the fleece of my sheep,
> if I have raised my hand against the fatherless,
>   because I saw my help in the gate,
> then let my shoulder blade fall from my shoulder,
>   and let my arm be broken from its socket.
> For I was in terror of calamity from God,
>   and I could not have faced his majesty.
> (Job 31:16-23 ESV)

The first part of this passage continues Job's rebuttal to his companion Eliphaz, who had made some heavy accusations—that Job stripped clothes from the naked and refused to share water with the exhausted or food with the hungry (see Job 22:6-7). Job's answer is that he has never withheld anything from the poor.[25] He goes on to say that he never "caused the eyes of the widow to fail," a metaphor for despair or grief.

A similar expression is used in Job 11:20, where the phrase is translated, "to cause despair," and in Psalm 69:3, where eyes grow dim because of crying. Job says that he never made a widow despair; but instead, always gave them a reason to hope.[26]

"Have I been stingy with my food and refused to share it with orphans?" (NLT) is Job's next rhetorical question. Job wasn't just generous with food—he was generous with *his* food. One of the wealthiest and most prominent people in the town shared his food with some of the most vulnerable and invisible. That's a great picture. God blessed Job with a lot of resources, and orphans were able to participate in God's blessing by eating from Job's table like family.[27]

Job continues this thought: "From my youth the fatherless grew up with me as with a father, and from my mother's womb I guided the widow..." He uses the hyperbole "from my mother's womb" to make a point.[28] Job is saying that caring for the vulnerable became a habit for him when he was very young.[29] This is a great lesson for us to train children in the habit of caring for the needy early in life, so that it is natural for them as they grow up.

Job then adds, "If I have seen anyone perish for lack of clothing, or the needy without covering, if his body has not blessed me, and if he was not warmed with the fleece of my sheep..." The verse in Hebrew poetically says that the poor's "warmed hips" blessed him for covering them.[30] In Job chapter 1, the description of Job's wealth mentions that he had over 7,000 sheep. What God had blessed him with, he used to care for the needs of others.[31] His wealth did not cause him to develop an entitled attitude—acting as though his wealth "rightfully" belonged to him because he worked for it. He saw his resources as belonging to God, and he was able to demonstrate God's heart for people with the blessings God had given him.

He saw his resources as belonging to God, and he was able to demonstrate God's heart for people with the blessings God had given him.

Job's next statement is, "If I have raised my hand against the fatherless, because I saw my help in the gate, then let my shoulder blade fall from my shoulder, and let my arm be broken from its socket." The phrase "raised my hand against the fatherless" means "to shake the hand at someone in a threating gesture."[32] Job is saying that he never used his power to threaten or hurt the poor and weak. He recognized that having a lot of power meant he was in a position to easily exploit people. If you have the ability to hurt people because of your money or influence, then you need to take it seriously and be careful not to do so.

"I saw my help in the gate" meant that Job had powerful friends who stood in positions of authority in the city gate, which was where legal cases were decided. The town officials knew Job, and if he wanted, he could have gotten them to look the other way if he did something wrong. The Good News Translation says, "If I have ever cheated an orphan, knowing I could win in court…"[33] Job said he would rather have his arm be removed from his body than for it to be used as an instrument of intimidation or exploitation, and he tells us why in the next sentence: "For I was in terror of calamity from God, and I could not have faced his majesty." Job reiterates that he is accountable to God, not to any human law.[34] Even if his powerful friends could have gotten him off the hook for hurting someone weaker, he knew God would be the one to defend those he had harmed.

Remembering that God holds you accountable to a higher standard of justice (one that protects the value of every human life no matter their social status) is essential to living out a just and righteous life. There is a lot you can probably get away with in human legal systems. But you will someday stand before the Creator of the person you took advantage of, and what do you want Him to say?

JOB 31 TODAY

When put into context with a little translation help, the story of Job gives us an incredible gift. Job is a picture of a wealthy, influential person who lived out a lifestyle of justice and righteousness. Job didn't just have great ideas or a nice attitude. He wanted to see people thrive—especially those easiest to slip through the cracks. To do that, he actively used his own resources and power to make it happen. Job shows us that living justice and righteousness doesn't require selling everything and living among the poor. He is a biblical model that justice and righteousness can resemble the selfless stewarding of power and resources.

Whether or not you or I ever have material wealth like Job's, we can train ourselves not to live a limited life. As Christians, we should be confident and passionate in responding to areas of need and injustice, because we know we are backed by our limitless Father and His kingdom. It's hard to be generous or respond to needs in this world if you feel like you are poor. Our decisions should be shaped by the wealth and resources we have as children of God instead of any perceived limitations in our material circumstances.

Job's life demonstrates definitively that justice and righteousness must be lived out in our practical actions. If you ever start talking about poverty at a dinner party (or on social media), you will discover that almost everyone has an opinion about what should be done to help the poor and needy. The poor should be given more welfare, less welfare, no welfare, or an alternative to welfare. Food banks, the UN, and the government should do more to solve the root causes of hunger. But out of all these opinionated people sitting on the sidelines with their ideas, how many of them are actually doing something? It seems like our culture has equated having an opinion about how the poor should be helped with actually loving them. What I love about Job is that he models what anyone from any political or cultural background can be doing to help the poor. His example leaves all of us free to have our own opinions about how to care for the vulnerable—as long as we all use our own lives and resources to be part of the solution to the problems closest to us.

WHAT A JOB 29 AND 31 SELF-DESCRIPTION MIGHT SOUND LIKE TODAY...

People respect and honor me because of the way I live my life. God's own heart toward the weak and poor is shown through my own attitude and actions. I hear the cries of the

poor because my ear is turned toward them. When I hear their pain, I act to deliver them. When I see their needs, I move to meet them. When I see someone who doesn't have a person to fight for them, I step in and fight. When I see an innocent person imprisoned, I won't stop until they are free. I love justice so much that I want everyone to get it, not just those whom I know. The earthly authority, resources, and power I have been given to show God's heart for people and for justice and righteousness.

I see the people my culture usually forgets about or ignores. The way I act gives opportunity for God to bring emotional restoration and healing to the hearts of those who are traumatized, grieving and suffering. Joy is brought to their hearts, which have experienced so much pain. *If a child doesn't have a parent, I love being able to step in and fill that role. My heart sees every child of God like a child of mine.*

Justice and righteousness live inside of me, and I wear them as constantly as I wear my everyday clothes. They distinguish me like a uniform of honor. My heart toward the vulnerable and suffering is like that of a parent. How could I let my children be caught up in injustice? *I hate when innocent victims are caught up in injustice.* When I see injustice happening, I act to stop it at its source so it can't hurt anyone else.

I will have nothing to do with the excuse of apathy. I will not wipe my hands clean and plug my ears from the cries of the hurting just because I am not the one causing harm. I recognize that God calls Himself their Father, so I will make the injustice that is hurting them my problem.

When people have needs, it makes me excited to be able to meet them. I am blessed with great resources so that I can bless others. Widows have a reason to hope because of how I live my life. I know that no matter what I think I can get away with in a human justice system, God Himself will hold me accountable for my actions. I would rather my arms be ripped away from my body than to use them to harm those weaker than I.

From childhood, I have personally cared about the needy, so it's been a lifelong habit. *I teach children how important it is*

> *to look at and care for the poor, orphans, and widows.* Generosity is my norm. The poor get to share in God's blessing on my life by joining me at my own table. I don't just have an opinion about how the poor should receive care; I use my own food and resources to do something.

STUDY QUESTIONS

When you look at the description of Job's life, what are some of the qualities that you want said about how you live your own life? How can you start building those habits?

What are the "fangs of the unrighteous" that you see in the world—people hurting innocent victims over and over?

What resources, talents, and skills has God blessed you with? How are you using them to bless people?

AMOS: JUSTICE & RIGHTEOUSNESS IN A NATION

CHAPTER NINE

WHAT WOULD IT LOOK like to have justice and righteousness established in a nation? God loves justice and righteousness, and He expected His chosen nation, Israel, to reflect this in every aspect of their social and cultural life. Everything from their government and leadership to business laws and practices, to family life, religious culture, and care for the poor and vulnerable was supposed to practically demonstrate that. He not only intended this for Israel's own good, but also so that His people would serve as a model of *misphat* and *sedeq* to surrounding nations.

Unfortunately, Israel failed to practice justice and righteousness far more often than they succeeded.[1] In response to Israel's disobedience, God frequently raised up prophets to call His people back to His covenant standard of justice and righteousness. The good part for us is that the prophetic books of the Old Testament give modern readers clear descriptions of what injustice and sin look like when they impact a whole nation, as well as clear expressions of the justice and righteousness God expected of His people. In this chapter, we are going to look at the prophet Amos and what was happening in Israel during his time. But first I'll give you some backstory.

KINGS AND PROPHETS

Since before the days of the first kings of Israel, God used prophets to confront His chosen people. The prophet Samuel was among the first. When Israel demanded that God give them a king, Samuel warned the nation that they wouldn't like the ways [*mishpat*] of human kings. He explained that kings would tax them, use their children for the military and labor, and take their land—basically enslaving them and everything they owned (see 1 Samuel 8:11-18). The nation still insisted that they wanted a king like other nations, someone who could rule them and lead them into battle. God's response was simple: "Do what they want and give them a king" (1 Samuel 8:22 GNT). Israel made the decision despite knowing that human kings could be cruel, and God honored their choice.

However, even though God gave them a king, He also gave specific instructions for how Israel's kings should honor their role. The Mosaic Law has a section about how the king was supposed to rule and conduct himself:

> The king is not to have many wives, because this would make him turn away from the Lord; and he is not to make himself rich with silver and gold. He is to keep this book [the Law] near him and read from it all his life, so that he will learn to honor the Lord and to obey faithfully everything that is commanded in it. This will keep him from thinking that he is better than other Israelites and from disobeying the Lord's commands in any way. (Deuteronomy 17:17-20 GNT)

Even though the natural bent of human kings is to be exploitative and selfish, God wanted something different. He wanted the king of Israel to remember that the power of his position was given by God and should be used for the good of everyone in the nation. While political officials often use their position to make their own lives more comfortable, God's model for leadership stopped the king from gaining personal wealth and required him to stay humble and connected to his fellow man. Keeping a copy of God's Law close to him to study it for his entire life would help him cultivate humility while staying connected to God. He was to be a true public servant.

From the beginning, Israel's leaders were given authority by God so they could establish and keep God's order—His justice and righteousness.[2] A job description for the ideal king is found in Psalm 72:

> He rescues the poor who call to him,
> and those who are needy and neglected.
> He has pity on the weak and poor;
> he saves the lives of those in need.
> He rescues them from oppression and violence;
> their lives are precious to him.
> (Psalm 72:12-14 GNT)

This description is clear: the priority of the king's power should be delivering the oppressed and being personally connected to the most poor and invisible in the nation.[3] The passage gets specific with a list of actions the king takes. He delivers the needy when they call, saves the lives of the poor, and redeems their lives from oppression and violence. The reason he did all this was simple: "their lives are precious to him" (vs 14). He protected them because they were so valuable to him, not out of legal obligation. When he liberated people from oppression, he restored the nation back to the divine order God had established for their nation.[4] Again, oppressing the poor is wrong not merely because it breaks the Law but because it keeps someone from experiencing the free, *shalom*-filled life God designed.[5] To build a culture of justice and righteousness, you need to know how to integrate the people least likely to experience it. For Israel that meant the fatherless, the widows, the immigrants, and the poor.

I think part of the power in this picture is seen once we consider what the alternatives could have been. The description could have included that the king built the biggest walls and most extravagant buildings or that he met with the coolest, most innovative, and important people in the land. But instead, the primary expression and test of his kingship was his attitude toward the weakest and most invisible. Properly using power looks like helping the most powerless by creating a world full of *shalom*, justice, and righteousness for everyone to enjoy.

Verse 14 introduces a significant image: the king as the redeemer (Hebrew: *go'el*) of the poor from oppression and violence. In the nation of Israel, there were laws about how someone who lost something could get it back. If someone lost their land, a close relative could buy it back due to their position as *go'el*—the "kinsman redeemer."[6] This description of the ideal king as the *go'el* of the poor and oppressed meant he was supposed to see himself as their family relative. This, of course, is what God does with His authority. He acts as our kinsman redeemer, going to extreme lengths to deliver us when we are at our most weak and needy. This is why He expects the same of His leaders. The model wasn't a high-and-mighty king surrounded by lowly servants but brothers and sisters who care about each other and use their God-given power to contribute to the *shalom* of the nation.

The God whose throne rests on justice and righteousness expected His appointed leaders to rule from the same foundation and held them accountable for the standard they were setting in the nation. Central to ruling with *mishpat* and *sedeq* were two basic principles. The first principle was mutual support—treating everyone fairly and with kindness.[7] The second principle was protecting the most defenseless and the weakest members of the society.[8] For the values of mutual support and protection of the weak to remain vibrant in the culture, leaders had to actively promote them. Those with the most power were held to the highest standard because their decisions directly impacted the nation. It wasn't enough to do good work in public; they were also expected to keep integrity in their hearts and private lives (see Psalm 101). If they allowed corruption, bribery, exploitation, and injustice, then the whole nation would be affected. Thus, all the people in authority—from the king of Israel to community elders—were expected to live *mishpat* and *sedeq* (see Deuteronomy 16:18). They were called to embody it in their actions, decisions, and lifestyle.[9]

Other passages show a similar picture of what God expected of kings. When the prophet Jeremiah confronts the evil king Jehoiakim, he describes how the king uses injustice to build a luxurious palace and declares that: "But a beautiful cedar palace does not make a great king!" (Jeremiah 22:15a NLT). Jeremiah goes on to compare Jehoiakim to the good king, Josiah, describing what Josiah did as:

> he was just [*mishpat*] and right [*sedeqah*] in all his dealings.
>   That is why God blessed him.
> He gave justice and help to the poor and needy,
>   and everything went well for him.
> Isn't that what it means to know me?"
>   says the Lord. (Jeremiah 22:15b-16 NLT)

God's response to Josiah's righteous and just leadership is significant: *"Isn't that what it means to know me?"* As a king, the way to demonstrate that you know God is giving justice to the poor and needy (see also Proverbs 29:14, 31:4-9; Daniel 4:27).

As a king, the way to demonstrate that you know
God is giving justice to the poor and needy.

A DESTABILIZING PRESENCE

Again, the prophetic office was created to keep Israel's kings accountable to God's standard, putting kings and prophets in a tense, but necessary relationship.[10] Prophets played an active role in national affairs[11]—not as reformers but as confrontational voices reminding the king and the nation how far they had fallen away from Israel's true faith and calling.[12] Prophets held the moral power to keep the king's military power in check.[13] If society in Israel had become unjust or unfaithful, the prophets were supposed to become, in the words of theologian Walter Brueggeman, "a destabilizing presence."[14]

When injustice and sin takes over a nation, it's easy for everyone to go with the flow and act like these things are normal. It's precisely in those times—when sin becomes accepted as okay and the weak and vulnerable are silently suffering—that someone needs to step in and say that what everyone has accepted as normal is actually wrong. They have to destabilize the unjust reality in the nation and make everyone uncomfortable with what is going on.

ENTER AMOS

Here's where Amos comes into Israel's story. He lived during the period in Israel's history in which the nation was divided into two kingdoms: Judah and Israel. Amos was a simple shepherd and farmer from Judah who received a call from God to prophesy to the kingdom of Israel.

Amos plays this "destabilizing" role with his prophetic message. At this time in the history of the kingdoms of Israel and Judah, things looked pretty stable on the surface. The two kingdoms had been enjoying economic prosperity, as well as relative peace with each other and with their neighboring nations.[15] Religious activities had also been increasing with people bringing more animal sacrifices to shrines.[16] Into this comfortable, seemingly blessed and virtuous environment, God dropped a simple shepherd with a very uncomfortable message. Israel was not doing *mishpat* and *sedeq*. The corrective words of the prophet powerfully convey God's passion for His people to honor His standard for the sake of their own survival as a nation.

The book of Amos gives us a picture of a nation that is out of divine order. Israel's leaders had long been distant in their relationships with God and with the poor in their nation. Whenever Israel's king demonstrated justice and righteousness toward the weak and poor, the entire order of the nation stayed in balance.[17] However, when the weak and the poor were being crushed, oppressed, or ignored, the balance of the whole nation was off, creating instability in every part of society. As Rabbi Jonathan Sacks puts it, "The message of the Hebrew Bible is that civilizations survive not by strength but by how they respond to the weak; not by wealth but by how they care for the poor; not by power but by their concern for the powerless. What renders a culture invulnerable is the compassion it shows to the vulnerable."[18] Amos was sent to help the people see where their nation was falling short and invite them to change their course.

AMOS: JUSTICE & RIGHTEOUSNESS IN A NATION

ECONOMIC INJUSTICE

Amos starts his prophetic message by listing the things God is upset about in eight different nations, progressively building up to his main target—the kingdom of Israel.[19] Pay special attention to the dramatic language he uses in his final message[20]:

> The LORD says, "The people of Israel have sinned again and again, and for this I will certainly punish them. They sell into slavery honest people who cannot pay their debts, the poor who cannot repay even the price of a pair of sandals. They trample down the weak and helpless and push the poor out of the way. A man and his father have intercourse with the same slave woman, and so profane my holy name. At every place of worship people sleep on clothing that they have taken from the poor as security for debts. In the temple of their God they drink wine which they have taken from those who owe them money." (Amos 2:6-8 GNT)

Instead of laying out a logical, scientific observation of the nation with a report of specific laws that needed to be changed, the prophets used poetic imagery—extreme images and metaphors intended to make a profound, emotional impact on the person hearing them. This can make it hard for a modern reader to understand, because we are so far removed from the everyday life of the ancient world from which these images came.[21] But the goal of this rhetorical approach was to disrupt people's everyday world by exposing how their "normal" was actually outrageous.[22]

The point of Amos' imagery is that Israel's façade of prosperity was hiding a high level of social and economic injustice. The rich were getting richer while the poor became poorer, and the power imbalance made it easy to take advantage of the weak and vulnerable.[23] In this passage, he gives four specific examples of injustice, each of which represents a whole category of injustices that were taking place in Israel.

First, Amos says that the Israelites "sell into slavery honest people who cannot pay their debts, the poor who cannot repay even the price of a pair of sandals." This scenario exposes the fact that the banking and justice systems in Israel were colluding in the unjust exploitation of the poor. When poor, honest people defaulted on petty loans—no bigger than the price of a pair of sandals—moneylenders in Israel were selling them into slavery.[24] In order to do this, they were bribing judges to condemn these innocent poor.[25][26]

Next, Amos says, Israel "[tramples] down the weak and helpless and [pushes] the poor out of the way." The exact translation from the Hebrew is not totally clear. The NASB says, "These who pant after the very dust of the earth on the head of the helpless," which suggests a picture of wealthy landowners who are so greedy that they wanted everything from the poor, including the dust on their heads. The ESV says, "Those who trample the head of the poor into the dust of the earth"—a clear image of the poor being crushed and forced to live in miserable conditions.[27] Either way, the phrase indicates that the poor were being forcefully oppressed and exploited by the wealthy, and the wealthy were enjoying it. The next phrase—"push the poor out of the way"—meant that the needy were being bullied by the more powerful, who were keeping the afflicted from getting justice.[28][29]

For Israel's third infraction, Amos says, "A man and his father have intercourse with the same slave woman, and so profane my holy name." Israel had a serious problem with sexual immorality and sexual exploitation.[30] A father and a son sleeping with the same woman was considered a major sin, similar to incest.[31] But in this case, the woman was a slave or household servant. Amos is describing a scenario in which a servant is being sexually abused by two powerful members of the home where she is employed. A better translation is, "not only the son, but even the father, goes after the servant girl."[32] This continues the theme of the weak being abused by the powerful. The double offense is that two men are both violating God's Law for sexuality, as well as abusing a vulnerable woman.

Israel's fourth offense is this: "At every place of worship people sleep on clothing that they have taken from the poor as security for debts. In the temple of their God they drink wine which they have taken from those who owe them money." The Mosaic Law stated that lenders were to return all "garments taken in pledge" to their owners by sunset, because for the poor, a cloak was often their only protection against the cold of night (see Exodus 22:26, Deuteronomy 24:12). Instead of returning these items to the poor as God instructed, lenders were illegally keeping and using them. And where was all of this taking place? In the house of God. The space that was supposed to be set aside to worship and honor God was being used as a site to exploit people. The passage about wine is citing a parallel offense. People sometimes had to pay fines to the temple. Apparently, the rich and powerful were using this money for extravagant drunken parties.[33] The powerful were lying down on cloaks the Law said they couldn't take and enjoying themselves at the expense of the poor.

Taken together, these four offenses paint a clear picture: Some of Israel was living the high life at the expense of the poor and needy.[34] Despite being blessed by God, they had loose morals and no concern for the vulnerable in their own nation.[35] For this reason, God declared that He would punish Israel. These were not just crimes against people; they were crimes against God.[36]

In the next verses, God intensifies His rebuke by reminding Israel that they were "the whole family that I brought up out of the land of Egypt" (Amos 3:1 ESV). When God called Israel out as a nation, they were slaves in Egypt. *They* were poor, vulnerable, exploited by those in power, and completely powerless to change their situation. Instead of leaving them in bondage, God liberated them, walked with them for forty years through a desert, and gave them a homeland (see Amos 2:9-12).

God's gracious and powerful actions stand in stark contrast to Israel's cruel treatment of their poor brothers and sisters.[37] They had apparently forgotten that the way He had treated their ancestors from the beginning should have been the standard for how they treated one another. Their political aim as a nation was supposed to be defined by what God had graciously done for them—freeing them when they were oppressed.[38] His saving justice set the model for Israel. When the eternal, all-knowing, all-powerful Creator God personally ensures that you are liberated from oppression, how much more terrible is it to decide to go back to oppressing your own poor brothers and sisters?

COWS OF BASHAN

As Amos' corrective word to Israel continues, he turns his attention to the women of the nation. Though men had most of the power in their society and were responsible for how they were abusing the public power, women had their share in the injustice, too.[39]

Amos addresses the women with:

> "Hear this word, you cows of Bashan,
>   who are on the mountain of Samaria,
> who oppress the poor, who crush the needy,
>   who say to your husbands, 'Bring, that we may drink!' (Amos 4:1 ESV)

Bashan was a lush area in Israel, known for its excellent cattle.[40] The "cows of Bashan" is a sarcastic name for the well-kept women in Israel, who pressured their husbands to do whatever it took to maintain their lavish, pampered lifestyles. Amos accuses them of oppressing the poor and crushing the needy. The Hebrew word for "oppress," *asaq*, is sometimes translated "exploit." It means economic abuse—someone with power who is wrongly using that power to get more wealth by hurting those with less. Holding back wages (Deuteronomy 24:14-15), charging interest on loans (Ezekiel 22:12), and other shady business practices fall into the category of *asaq*.[41] Such exploitation was always a one-way relationship. The rich could "*asaq*" the poor, but the poor could not "*asaq*" the rich. While the wealthy could be robbed, they could not be oppressed like the poor and vulnerable.[42] Here, *asaq* is put together with *ratsats*—to "crush." The poor are not only taken advantage of, they are trampled. This choice of words implicates the wives of those men accused of trampling the poor in Amos 2. Though the women may not have directly participated in the public injustices in the courts or the temple, they nagged their husbands for more, and their husbands in turn went out and exploited the poor in order to fulfill their wives' demands.[43]

INJUSTICE IN BUSINESS

In Amos 8, the prophet turns his attention to Israel's merchants and

AMOS: JUSTICE & RIGHTEOUSNESS IN A NATION

addresses some of their terrible business practices.[44] God expected Israel's businesses to uphold a standard of justice and righteousness along with everyone else. Businesses and their leaders played an important role in culture and economy. Depending on the practices they adopted, they could hurt and take advantage of people, or they could create opportunities, innovations, and good order. Building wealth wasn't wrong, but it was meant to be based on hard work, trusting God, integrity, and respecting the rights of the poor.

In this passage, God is not happy about how these merchants are conducting their business:

> Listen to this, you that trample on the needy and try to destroy the poor of the country. You say to yourselves, "We can hardly wait for the holy days to be over so that we can sell our grain. When will the Sabbath end, so that we can start selling again? Then we can overcharge, use false measures, and fix the scales to cheat our customers. We can sell worthless wheat at a high price. We'll find someone poor who can't pay his debts, not even the price of a pair of sandals, and we'll buy him as a slave." The LORD, the God of Israel, has sworn, "I will never forget their evil deeds." (Amos 8:4-7 GNT)

Amos is calling out these merchants who are hurting the poor. He starts by showing how their hearts and minds were consumed by a desire to make as much money as possible, no matter the cost to themselves and others.[45] The holy days were supposed to be days of rest, connection, and enjoyment of God's creation. But these businesspeople were so completely consumed by their greed that they couldn't stop to rest, connect, or enjoy anything. They viewed this sacred time as a nuisance. The Sabbath rest would have been very important to the poor, who worked hard for a living. The Sabbath was part of God's divine order that was to protect the nation from a destructive, greed-driven work economy—both employers and employees. But these merchants despised that these were human beings with human needs who needed time off, too.[46]

Amos cites three specific ways these profit-consumed merchants were cheating their customers: overcharging, using wrong measures, and altering scales. Overcharging was a big deal. Prices were supposed to be accurate, honest, and fair to all customers (see Leviticus 25:14, 19:11, 19:13). That meant you couldn't lie, deceive, steal, or take advantage of the person you were doing a deal with. You could make a profit, but had to do so without cheating anyone.

Weights and measures may not seem too exciting in today's world, but they were an essential part of trade in Israel. These scales needed to be a standard size and weight, because they measured the food and goods for sale and customers needed to guarantee that they were getting the full amount they had paid for. Merchants could cheat their customers by tampering with them. When God gave the Israelites rules about their business practices, He made sure that they used fair, just measures (see Leviticus 19:36, Deuteronomy 25:13).

Proverbs twice describes God's own attitude toward unjust measurements:

> The Lord detests the use of dishonest scales,
> but he delights in accurate weights. (Proverbs 11:1 ESV)

> Unequal weights are an abomination to the Lord,
> and false scales are not good. (Proverbs 20:23 ESV)

God *detests* unjust measurements. They are an *abomination* to Him. But when accurate weights are used, He feels *delighted*. I would think the God of the universe had more important things to do than getting emotionally caught up in Israel's scales and weights. But remember that God is a God of justice, so He delights in it. An expression of His justice in the everyday doings of Israel's world is exciting.

Amos also mentions that the merchants were selling "worthless wheat." This meant they were mixing the chaff of the wheat (the part that is inedible and supposed to be thrown out) in with the good wheat and selling it to desperately hungry people. They were using the poor to profit on *food waste*, an example of how much greed distorted their relationship with their brothers and sisters in need.[47] Greed isn't neutral, or solely personal. Greed can destroy the lives of weak and poor.[48]

BUSINESS LAWS FOR THE POOR

Just to give you a little more background, Israel's economic system was supposed to account for the vulnerable position of the poor and protect them. People weren't just supposed to feel bad for the poor, give them a few dollars, and move on with life as usual. They were to include the needs and rights of the poor in the normal practices of their economy.[49]

Here are a few examples of Mosaic laws that took into consideration the needs of the poor:

The price of food sold to the poor couldn't be marked up. No one was allowed to profit off of the poor when selling them the basic essentials they needed to survive (see Leviticus 25:35-37).

The poor could gather food from the corners of fields, and when landowners let their fields rest every seventh year, the poor could glean the fields (see Leviticus 19:9-10, Deuteronomy 24:19-21, Exodus 23:11). This system required everyone who grew food to participate in feeding the needy in a dignifying way, by allowing the poor to gather food by their own hands.

Every third year, a tithe (ten percent) of all the nation's crops went to the priests, orphans, immigrants, and widows, "so that in every community they [had] all they need to eat" (Deuteronomy 26:12 GNT). If they looked after the poor and made sure that the needs of the priests were taken care of, God promised to abundantly bless the nation.

The poor could buy back their land. If someone fell on hard times and had to sell their land or house, they (or a relative) could buy it back within a certain time period or during the year of Jubilee (see Leviticus 25:8-34). This built redemption into their business laws. Losing a house or land meant a family had lost a source of stability, potentially sinking them even deeper into poverty. If a family fell on hard times and had to sell their land in order to survive, being able to buy their land back meant that they had the opportunity get back on their feet.

The poor benefited from the Jubilee laws. Included in the Jubilee laws in Leviticus 25 are rules that called for debts to be forgiven and slaves to go free under certain conditions. For an agrarian economy and culture, forgiving debts and giving the opportunity for land to be returned to the original owners was a huge deal. If someone had made a mistake, fallen on hard times, been forced into debt, sold into slavery, or lost their family land, they had an opportunity for redemption. Poverty didn't have to be passed on to the next generation.

GOD'S WAY TO PROSPERITY

Israel was expected to integrate the needs of the weakest and most vulnerable into the normal rules and practices of their nation. If any of the systems in their nation didn't actively include the most invisible and weak members, then it would fail. God wanted Israel's economy to have multiple mechanisms in place to incorporate the poor. Every merchant who sold food, every farmer who produced food, all the citizens who paid the tithe—everyone in every part of the system participated in meeting the needs of the poor, orphans, immigrants, and widows. If only one person or group was responsible, then it would break down. As a nation, all of their eyes were supposed to see their needs, all of their laws were supposed to reflect their value, all of their hearts were supposed to be open to compassion, and all of the cultural practices were supposed to integrate them in a dignifying way.

Israel was expected to integrate the needs of the weakest and most vulnerable into the normal rules and practices of their nation.

While many in the world act as though prosperity requires exploitation and bending the rules in your advantage, God ties blessings to respecting the needs of the poor and doing justice and righteousness (see Deut. 24:19-21, 27:19). The choice isn't to do justice and financially struggle or to exploit those weaker than yourself and become prosperous. God's blessing, which may look different from the world's, comes from stewarding your economic life in this way.

It's sad to see that people with a passion for business can feel like "social justice" movements ostracize them. Starting a business and providing job opportunities is a beautiful calling. The skills developed in the business world can be powerful tools for doing justice and righteousness. Knowing these biblical economic principles is key to making a business successful. God wants more from Christian businesses than merely making lots of money and donating it to mission projects. He wants the way business is conducted to reflect His value for people. If you make lots of money by taking advantage of people or oppressing the poor, then give that money away to a great cause, that does not honor God. Justice and righteousness should be built into the normal practices and rhythms of business.

RELIGIOUS PRIDE

Along with making it clear that God is upset about Israel's social and economic injustices, Amos tells Israel that their religious lives are out of order, too:[50]

> The Sovereign Lord says, "People of Israel, go to the holy place in Bethel and sin, if you must! Go to Gilgal and sin with all your might! Go ahead and bring animals to be sacrificed morning after morning, and bring your tithes every third day. Go on and offer your bread in thanksgiving to God, and brag about the extra offerings you bring! This is the kind of thing you love to do." (Amos 4:4-5 GNT)

You can hear the sarcasm in this writing. Amos is parodying the typical call by the priests to come in and worship. However, instead, he's telling pilgrims at religious sites to come in, sin, and give sacrifices to idols.[51] He lists the things Israel is doing, and they *look* like the right things. The Mosaic Law prescribed daily offerings (Exodus 29:38), a special tithe given to support the priests every three years (Deuteronomy 14:28), and bread offering as a show of thanks (Exodus 25:30). The sacrifices referred to here were supposed to be freewill offerings to express gratitude, either for God's goodness or in expectation of God's deliverance. The problem is that instead of giving sacrifices as an expression of gratitude, they were giving them so they could publically publish them. They were boasting before other people rather than offering thanks to God.[52]

The Israelites' religious attitudes mattered to God as much as the way they treated the poor because these things were connected in their culture. Rabbi Jonathan Sacks explains: "The message of the Hebrew Bible is that serving God and serving our fellow human beings are inseparably linked and the split between the two impoverishes both."[53] When the nation was out of order in their connection to God, it was often reflected in being out of order in their connection to their fellow Israelites. Whenever the nation was committing terrible injustices, they were also deficient in their relationship to God. Turning to idols and devaluing the poor often happened at the same time. Restoration in their relationship with God always involved restoration in their human relationships, including with the poor and vulnerable.

Isaiah 58 powerfully illustrates this connection between Israel's relationship with God and with the poor. In this chapter, Isaiah notes that Israel has been complaining to God that they have been fulfilling their religious duties—seeking God daily and fasting—and God hasn't been seeing it. Isaiah calls them on their wrong motives. They were not fasting out of a genuine desire to show submission to God, but instead, they were trying to manipulate Him to gain His favor. They were oblivious that their selfish motives were wrong.[54] Meanwhile, they also weren't paying their workers—something God took *very* seriously (see Jeremiah 22:13, Malachi 3:5). Workers were supposed to be paid a fair wage promptly each day (see Leviticus 19:13, Deuteronomy 24:14-15), and the employers in Israel weren't doing it. They were asking God for His help while ignoring His ways. God responds by telling them what He really wants:

> "The kind of fasting I want is this: Remove the chains of oppression and the yoke of injustice, and let the oppressed go free. Share your food with the hungry and open your homes to the homeless poor. Give clothes to those who have nothing to wear, and do not refuse to help your own relatives." (Isaiah 58:6-7 GNT)

God insisted that their religious practice was intertwined with how they treated the poor and victims of injustice. God considered it religious to make sure they were freed from oppression, fed, clothed, and provided with a home to live in and a family to support them—these were the religious acts He cared about.

Most Christians recognize that fasting as an important biblically-based spiritual activity. But did you know that God actually only commanded fasting twice in the Old Testament? Israel's leaders called for fasts more often than God did.[55] He commanded them to fast every year on the Day of Atonement (see Leviticus 16:29), and centuries later, He called for a fast through the prophet Joel (see Joel 1:14; 2:12, 15). It seems that God wasn't that interested in getting Israel to fast. But you know what God did command time and time again? He commanded His people to treat the poor and vulnerable with *mishpat* and to show fairness and kindness to their fellow brothers and sisters. Yes, fasting is a good spiritual discipline—one Jesus Himself modeled for us. But if fasting is that important, how much more should we see that freeing people from oppression and injustice is an important, biblically-based spiritual activity, too?

A condemnation of false religion and a call for justice is exactly what Amos delivers in Chapter 5:

> I hate, I despise your feasts,
>   and I take no delight in your solemn assemblies.
> Even though you offer me your burnt offerings and grain offerings,
>   I will not accept them;
> and the peace offerings of your fattened animals,
>   I will not look upon them.
> Take away from me the noise of your songs;
>   to the melody of your harps I will not listen.
> But let justice [*mishpat*] roll down like waters,
>   and righteousness [*sedeqah*] like an ever-flowing stream. (Amos 5:21-24 ESV)

One of the jobs of the priest was to announce when God accepted a sacrifice.[56] Here the prophet Amos announces in dramatic language that God is *rejecting* their sacrifices. The language God uses to say that He is rejecting their religious activities is emotional and dramatic: He *hates* and *despises* their sacrifices. He takes *no delight* in them. He will not *ac-*

cept them or even *look* at them. He won't *listen* to their music. What does He say that He wants instead? The Message translation puts it this way:

> "Do you know what I want?
>   I want justice—oceans of it.
> I want fairness—rivers of it.
>   That's what I want. That's *all* I want."
> (Amos 5:24 MSG)

The Hebrew words for the water analogies are significant. The phrase "roll down like waters" suggests not just a trickle of water but floodwaters moving fully and unencumbered throughout the land.[56] The fact that "waters" is plural suggests that the water would suddenly and forcefully swell. The word for stream—*nachal*—doesn't have an English equivalent. The best equivalent is the Arabic *wadi*—one of the narrow streams common throughout Israel. In the rainy season, it would gush and overflow with water, but during dry times, it would be a mere trickle if it had any water at all. So God says that He wants *sedeqah* to flow through Israel constantly, in an ever-flowing *wadi* that never runs dry.[57]

Instead of songs, sacrifices, assemblies, or offerings, God expected mishpat *and* sedeq *to flow unencumbered continually from that generation onward, never growing dry no matter the season.*

Instead of songs, sacrifices, assemblies, or offerings, God expected *mishpat* and *sedeq* to flow unencumbered continually from that generation onward, never growing dry no matter the season. According to God, the only real outward sign of religious devotion is for *mishpat* and *sedeq* to be reflected in His people's political, religious, and social order. Most of us can get that God desires religious activities like prayer and fasting. But God also says that: "To do righteousness [*sedeqah*] and justice [*mishpat*] is desired by the Lord more than sacrifice" (Proverbs 21:3 NASB).

What does this tell us about how God views worship and religious practices? Worship is not just songs and lyrics. The way we behave in our economic lives and the level of justice we give the poor are considered part of our worship. Sacrifices and religiosity can't make up for a lack of justice and righteousness.

HOPEFUL FUTURE

Israel may have had stability and prosperity on the surface, but they were not living in *shalom*. Remember, justice in their culture was focused on *what life should be like*. Life should *not* be like the rich oppressing the poor, wives nagging their husbands to pamper them by taking advantage of the vulnerable, or businessmen living with an all-consuming drive for profit. This shows a perfect picture of a nation full of pain, suffering, and misery.

Like the other prophetic books, however, Amos does not leave his audience without hope that God will bring healing and restoration to their nation. His prophetic message ends with the promise that God would rebuild Israel again: "A day is coming when I will restore the kingdom of David, which is like a house fallen into ruins. I will repair its walls and restore it. I will rebuild it and make it as it was long ago" (Amos 9:11 GNT). Despite the fact that the nation fell short of their call to be a faithful, righteous, and just nation, God was going to bring a redeemer who would save them. Israel's leaders couldn't bring God's justice and righteousness to earth, so God was going to do it personally.

This is the perfect place to end our study of justice and righteousness in the Old Testament: the promise that in the middle of the terrible mess Israel made, God Himself would restore them and set the world right again. This is how the first part of the biblical story ends. In the next section, we will pick up with the New Testament, Act II of the biblical story where we see the next part of God's redemptive plan to bring His justice and righteousness to victory. God's powerful revelation of His justice and righteousness in the Old Testament sets the stage for an even greater revelation of His justice and righteousness in Jesus.

STUDY QUESTIONS

Do you ever see Christians trying to make up for injustice and sin by becoming more religious? Think of a few historical events where this may have happened.

Do you see any places where sin and injustice are becoming normal in your nation?

What prophetic voices do you see acting as a "destabilizing presence" calling out sin and injustice?

If you feel a call to business, what would it look like to integrate justice and righteousness as part of it?

JUSTICE IN THE NEW TESTAMENT

CHAPTER TEN

WHEN I FIRST STARTED studying what the Bible said about justice topics, I thought I knew exactly how to find them: search for the word "justice." But there's a problem with looking for justice in the New Testament. If you type "justice" into a Bible word search engine, it doesn't appear much. "Justice" appears only 11 times in the ESV translation,[1] 9 times in the NASB,[2] and 8 times in the NKJV.[3] For those translations, "justice" shows up more in the book of Isaiah—around three times more, in fact—than in the *entire* New Testament.[4] In the few instances where the word "justice" appears, the word primarily refers to legal justice, which feels distant from the Hebrew *shalom*-centered ideas of justice in the Old Testament. Verses like "Mercy triumphs over judgment [*krisis*]" (James 2:13b), or "Judge [*krino*] not, that you be not judged" (Matthew 7:1) make it seem like justice and judgment are opposite of mercy and, therefore, don't belong in the New Testament.

It's hard to see that the New Testament values justice when it seems almost silent on the subject. Given this near-silence, I used to wonder if justice, especially "social justice" topics, simply didn't belong in a New Testament paradigm. Maybe God meant us to leave behind anything that looked like humanity's old ways of relationship, including the Old Testament's model of justice.

Thankfully, I kept reading and discovered just how much justice is part of the New Testament—I just had to learn to see it. My simple Bible word search couldn't show it. As we saw at the beginning of the Old Testament section, the differences in the language and culture of our modern, English-speaking world and the ancient Hebrew world make it challenging to understand justice and righteousness in the Old Testament. The same problem applies to the New Testament, which was written in first-century Greek to a mixed audience of Jews and Gentiles.

TRANSLATION PROBLEMS

Translating *mishpat* into English can make it challenging to see God's justice in the Old Testament. Translating the Greek words for justice into English gives us yet another set of challenges. The Greek word most often translated "justice" in our English New Testament is *krisis* and is related to "judgment," *krima*. The root is *krino*, meaning to sift and separate, like when a person evaluates something and makes a decision.[5] That's a good picture of God as Judge—the compassionate, all-knowing one who sifts and makes judgments. That's His job, not ours, because He sees things we can't see like people's hearts. The definitions of *krisis* line up with our English definitions: legal decision, condemnation, the authority to judge, punishment, or judgment.[6] *Krima* has similar legal definitions.

But these meanings miss the more holistic dimensions of justice we saw in the Old Testament. Those dimensions *do* show up in the New Testament, however, through the Greek word *dikaiosune*. *Dik*-stem words are common in the New Testament, showing up around 300 times. The concept of *dikaiosune* is captured by *two* English words—righteousness and justice—yet is almost always translated as *one* of the two: "righteousness."[7] Likewise, other *dik*-stem words, like *dikaios* and *dikaioo*, are translated as *"right-"* words—righteous, righteousness, right, etc.—instead of *"just-"* words.[8]

JUSTICE IN THE NEW TESTAMENT

The concept of dikaiosune is captured by two English words—righteousness and justice—yet is almost always translated as one of the two: "righteousness."

At the time the New Testament was written, however, *dikaiosune* was not just used to mean "righteousness."[9] In fact, translators of classical Greek literature usually did the opposite when translating *dikaiosune* into English, opting for "justice" instead of "righteousness."[10] In classical Greek, *dikaiosune* meant "well-ordering," and it was an important word for understanding justice and government at the time. Plato's *Republic*, written almost four hundred years before Jesus' birth, was among the most influential books on the ideal structure of government of the day and was much concerned with "justice"—*dikaiosune*.[11] To Plato, justice was important for understanding the human soul as well as the state.[12] It was more than a personal quality; it was particularly demonstrated in relationships.[13] A "just" or "righteous" person fulfilled their proper role in civilized society.[14]

Not every language has the same challenge that we English-speakers have. Romance languages like Spanish and French don't have a word for "righteousness," so *dikaiosune* is translated almost always as "justice." But if you look for the English word "justice" in the New Testament, it isn't in there much. If you look for "righteousness," you'll see it all over. This translation problem helps explain why the New Testament seems almost silent on justice. When English-speakers like me read the Bible, it seems like righteousness is what we are supposed to pursue, not justice. And because righteousness in our world is connected to private, personal morality, it can seem like the highest goal of Christian life is to be clustered inside of church buildings, never doing wrong, instead of doing right in the wider world.

When I went back and looked at *dikaiosune* in the New Testament with this new understanding of its significance, I saw a different picture:

- "But seek first His kingdom and His righteousness/justice [*dikaiosune*]." (Matthew 6:33a NASB)

- "Blessed are those who hunger and thirst for righteousness/

justice *[dikaiosune].*" (Matthew 6:33a NASB)

- "…those who receive the abundance of grace and of the gift of righteousness/justice *[dikaiosune]* will reign in life through the One, Jesus Christ." (Romans 5:17b NASB)
- "But even if you should suffer for righteousness/justice' *[dikaiosune]* sake, you are blessed." (1 Peter 3:14a NASB)
- "For the kingdom of God is not eating and drinking but righteousness/justice *[dikaiosune]* and peace and joy in the Holy Spirit." (Romans 14:17 NASB)

So *krisis* and *krima* are translated as "justice" and "judgment," making it easy for us to see how the legal dimensions of justice carry over and conveniently fit into our Western understandings of justice. But God's transformative, dynamic, eternal justice remains the same, even when the words we use to describe His justice make it challenging for us to see it.

As we will explore in the coming chapters, God's love for justice and righteousness is as real in the New Testament as it is in the Old. In fact, the work of redemption that transitions us into a new paradigm brings justice and righteousness to the earth in a deeper, more permanent way. The gospel of Jesus is the good news of the justice and righteousness of God.

IDEAL BLUEPRINT

As we start the New Testament, we have to be clear about what the New Testament instructions were *not*. They weren't a blueprint for a perfect society. Neither did they tell the Roman government how it should rule. When I first started looking for justice in the New Testament, I wanted to find something like I saw in the Old Testament. Because God's plan in the Old Testament is revealed through an organized nation, you can see justice and righteousness through things like laws and rulers. The Old Testament picture of justice and righteousness felt practical and tangible because there were rules about the exact obligations of a whole society.

Instead, the New Testament shows how justice and righteousness were fulfilled and demonstrated by God Himself. This solution was not administered through external laws and government but through the saving work of Christ, which makes a way for all of humanity to come into the "kingdom of God." Thus, while we will see justice and righteousness, it will be in a new way, through lives fully reconciled to God in Christ and transformed by that relationship made whole.

The New Testament's instructions on how to live are all directed toward those who have entered into this reconciled relationship with God through faith. This is a diverse community united by their loyalty to Christ and His redemptive work in their lives. From the beginning, the boundaries that this community crossed were massive—gender, socioeconomic class, race, and religious upbringing. Making peace with God spilled over into making peace between people who had been historically divided. They freely lived out justice and righteousness in a way that no one had ever seen—building off of the justice and righteousness of Jesus and finding themselves able to go to lengths people never could before Christ came. In imitation of Jesus, this community humanized those the world dehumanized, empowered those the world disempowered, and offered freedom from sin, hatred, and shame.

The way Christians are expected to live out righteousness in loving community with each other is impossible without faith in Christ and the transformation He brings. Neither the Roman government nor any other was ever expected to do this. There is no law book or blueprint for a perfect society in the New Testament. God is constantly trying to get at what a law code and government can never transform: our hearts. His community of redeemed Christ-followers operate within the world's systems, through the unity of God's Spirit, bringing salt and light anywhere they happen to be. God's people bring hope where there is despair, healing where there are wounds, and restoration where there is destruction.

STUDY QUESTIONS

Before starting the New Testament section, ask yourself if you see justice and righteousness in the New Testament that is consistent with what you just learned about in the Old Testament?

From what you learned about justice and righteousness in the Old Testament, where can you see Jesus doing justice and righteousness?

THE LIBERATING KING

CHAPTER ELEVEN

TO START OUR STUDY in the New Testament, we are going to look at how Jesus' life and work of redemption fit into the full biblical story. Christians too often get the message that it's only important to read the New Testament. Thanks to the way the Bible is taught (or not taught) in some churches, many come away with the impression that everything "Old" is really not that relevant to them. Unfortunately, what people with this approach miss is that both Testaments provide the essential pieces of God's redemptive plan throughout history. Leaving out any of those pieces prevents us from seeing the full plan.

Bible scholar John Goldingay uses the illustration of a two-act play to describe the unity of the Old and New Testaments. If you think of the Bible as a play, with the Old Testament as Act I and the New Testament as Act II, then you know it's essential to read the whole story to know what's going on in either Act. Limiting yourself to the New Testament is like coming to a play at intermission and trying to get a full grasp of what is happening. You may know how the story ends, but you won't understand the journeys of the characters or the problem that's being resolved.[1]

THE FULL STORY

Act I begins with Creation, a scene that gives us a beautiful picture of *shalom*. Every part of this newly created world is pronounced "good" by the Creator (see Genesis 1). The relationships between God and humans, man and woman, and humans and nature are all flourishing, intimate, and whole.

You know what happens next. The people God appointed to steward His good creation rebel, eat from the tree of the knowledge of good and evil, and are banished from the garden. The wholeness is shattered, and the effects are devastating. Murder, violence, oppression, slavery, misogyny, and every other form of injustice spread throughout the human race. Through Adam and Eve's sin, brokenness and pain touch every relationship in the world (see Genesis 2-3, Romans 5:12, 1 Corinthians 15:21).

Yet, Act I also shows us the first stages of God's plan of restoration. God calls a childless man, Abraham, into a covenant relationship and promises that an entire nation will grow from his family and bless the world. This promise comes to pass because Abraham teaches his family line to keep "the way of the Lord by doing righteousness [*sedeqah*] and justice [*mishpat*]" (Genesis 18:19 ESV). In every step of God's plan, justice and righteousness are essential. They are foundational to His throne and central to how He reigns, so it makes sense that they characterize everything He does, and that He requires His people to follow His ways.

The rest of Act I shows how this promise plays out. Through miracle after miracle, God increases, blesses, delivers, and guides Abraham's descendants and brings them as a nation—Israel—into a covenant relationship with Him. Essential to this covenant is the Law of Moses, which reflects God's justice and righteousness. In the Law, God expresses His passion for His people to walk in right relationships with Him and one another and gives a clear picture of what right relationships look like. Relationships are central to God's design for life, and they are meant to be full of *shalom* with Him, His creation, and one another.

Tragically, Act I shows us that while God is always faithful to uphold His side of covenant relationship with Israel, they are not so successful on their end. Again and again, God responds to this failure by raising up leaders who call His people back to their covenant with Him.

The standout among these leaders is King David. Not only is he "the man after God's own heart" (1 Samuel 13:14), but his rule demonstrates his connection to God's heart: "David administered justice [*mishpat*] and righteousness [*sedeqah*] for all his people" (2 Samuel 8:15b NASB). At the end of David's life, God makes him a promise: "Your throne shall be established forever" (2 Samuel 7:16b ESV). The promise of God's eternal kingdom is given to a king, who was connected to God's heart and ruled with *mishpat* and *sedeq*.

Unfortunately, most of Israel's history after David isn't good. Leaders and everyday people alike turn away from God and everyone in the nation, especially the most vulnerable, suffers as a result. In response, God sends prophets to confront the kings and the people, but ultimately, the nation never turns back to God. Instead, they degenerate until everything falls apart—they are conquered by foreign empires and taken into exile.

At this point in Act I, things look pretty bad. God's people have hit rock-bottom. He's sent judges, kings, and prophets, but none of them have been able to create lasting reform in the nation beyond a generation or two. In the face of this seemingly hopeless situation, God makes a stunning announcement through the prophet Isaiah:

> The Lord has seen this, and he is displeased that there is no justice [*mishpat*]. He is astonished to see that there is no one to help the oppressed. So he will use his own power to rescue them and to win the victory. He will wear justice [*sedeqah*] like a coat of armor and saving power like a helmet. He will clothe himself with the strong desire to set things right and to punish and avenge the wrongs that people suffer. (Isaiah 59:15b-18a GNT)

This is the promise that sets the stage for Act II: God isn't going to send another judge or prophet to save His people. He is going to do justice Himself. As we pick up the story of God in Act II (the New Testament) we see this God, so passionate about rescuing the oppressed and bringing justice, coming Himself to rescue us.

As Act I wraps up, the promise of a coming Messiah has begun to take hold of God's people. The Old Testament prophets give us a picture of what He will be like, and their descriptions of what He will do make something quite clear: He will succeed where other kings had failed to do justice and righteousness. Isaiah prophesied that the Messiah will be "one who judges [*shaphat*] and seeks justice [*mishpat*] and is swift to do righteousness [*sedeqah*]" (Isaiah 16:5b ESV). Psalm 72, which we looked at to see a picture of Israel's ideal ruler, is also a prophecy about Israel's coming Messiah. It says, "May he judge your people with righteousness [*sedeq*], and your poor with justice [*mishpat*]!" (Psalm 72:2 ESV). Similarly, in Jeremiah, there are two prophecies that the Messiah will "execute justice [*mishpat*] and righteousness [*sedeqah*] in the land," and that He would become righteousness for us (Jeremiah 23:5-6, 33:15 ESV).

Isaiah 9, the famous passage many of us read every year at Christmas, tells us the form in which the Messiah will come: "Unto us a child is born, unto us a son is given" (Isaiah 9:6 ESV). God Himself will be coming as a child, and the passage goes on to say what He will do:

> Of the increase of his government and of peace
>   [*shalom*] there will be no end,
> on the throne of David and over his kingdom,
>   to establish it and to uphold it
> with justice [*mishpat*] and with righteousness
>   [*sedeqah*] from this time forth and forevermore.
> The zeal of the Lord of hosts will do this.
> (Isaiah 9:7 ESV)

The Messiah would come to bring an endless kingdom, one whose *shalom* and government would never end. What this new kingdom would be built with should sound familiar: *mishpat* and *sedeqah*. As the curtain falls on the first half of God's story, we see a remnant of Jews returned from exile and starting to resettle and rebuild their homeland with hopeful expectation of this coming Messiah.

THE SAVIOR

When the curtain rises on Act II, about four hundred years have passed since the deaths last Old Testament prophets. In those four hundred years, the Jewish people have never returned to being an independent nation. Instead, they have remained a religious minority ruled by a chain of superpowers.[2] As a result, many in Israel expect the Messiah to be a liberator who will set them free from the government that is oppressing them with cruel taxes and military force. They are praying for and expecting a mighty warrior who will drive out their enemies and re-establish Israel as an independent kingdom.

Act II opens with the announcement of the coming of this expected Messiah. Two angelic visitations to His parents provide the critical pieces of information about who He will be. First, Gabriel says to Mary:

> "You will become pregnant and give birth to a son, and you will name him Jesus. He will be great and will be called the Son of the Most High God. The Lord God will make him a king, as his ancestor David was, and he will be the king of the descendants of Jacob forever; his kingdom will never end!" (Luke 1:31-33 GNT)

This Son of God would be a great king from the line of David, bringing a never-ending kingdom. Then, after Joseph finds out that Mary is pregnant and wants to break off their engagement, an angel appears to him, saying, "Joseph, descendant of David, do not be afraid to take Mary to be your wife. For it is by the Holy Spirit that she has conceived. She will have a son, and you will name him Jesus—because he will save his people from their sins" (Matthew 1:20b-21 GNT). The Messiah would come in the form of a child and son, and He would be given the name Jesus, meaning "Jehovah is Salvation."

The message to Mary and Joseph *was not* that they would raise a mighty political leader. There was no promise that Jesus would save His people from Rome. People needed to be freed from sin rather than an earthly oppressor.

THE KING AND LIBERATOR

Fast-forward thirty years or so to the beginning of Jesus' public ministry. The Gospels record two different announcements Jesus makes at the start of His ministry, both of which are significant. First, in Matthew, Jesus preaches, "Repent, for the kingdom of heaven is at hand'" (Matthew 4:17b ESV). Then in Luke, we find the account of Jesus getting up in the synagogue to read from Isaiah:

> "The Spirit of the Lord is upon me,
> because he has chosen me to bring good news to the poor.
> He has sent me to proclaim liberty to the captives
> and recovery of sight to the blind,
> to set free the oppressed
> and announce that the time has come
> when the Lord will save his people."
>
> "This passage of scripture has come true today, as you heard it being read."
> (Luke 4:18-19, 21b GNT, quoted from Isaiah 61:1-2)

Jesus announces both a kingdom and a liberation mission. Many in His audience would have instantly understood what He was saying: "Your long-awaited Messiah is standing in front of you."

There is a challenge for us modern audiences when it comes to understanding what Jesus meant by the "kingdom." The Jews had prophecies of a coming kingdom—one that God Himself would bring from heaven (see Daniel 2:44, 7:13-14). God had been communicating with Israel in these terms for generations. This is why Jesus never defines "kingdom"—His audience already knew what that meant.

The Hebrew word for "kingdom," *malkuth*, has the primary meaning of a domain, reign, or rule.[3] A secondary meaning is the place where that reign happens—the territory or realm.[4] Our modern English language puts the emphasis on that secondary meaning—the physical place where a kingdom exists—while the Old Testament puts the emphasis on the first. For example, when it says that Solomon's "kingdom [*malkuth*] was firmly established" (1 Kings 2:12 ESV), it didn't mean his nation had strong borders and good laws. It meant that Solomon's authority to rule was totally settled. From then on, what he said was *the* authority in the land.

The Greek word for "kingdom," *basilea*, is similar. It means dominion, reign, rule, or the act of ruling.[5] In both the Old and New Testaments, the words for "kingdom of God" refer to the sovereign, active rule of God on the earth.[6] When the *basilea* of God is present on earth, God is *the* authority. What He says, goes. His will and intention for human life is happening.

When Jesus announces that the kingdom of God is at hand, He is telling His audience that the redemptive reign of God is in front of them, bringing the world back to what God originally intended for creation.

When Jesus announces that the kingdom of God is at hand, He is telling His audience that the redemptive reign of God is in front of them, bringing the world back to what God originally intended for creation. However, Jesus seems to surprise everyone with the way He teaches about and brings this kingdom—and fulfills His mission of liberation. As Jesus' ministry progresses, He never organizes a rebellion against Rome to reclaim the kingdom for Israel. He never once takes up a sword or gives dramatic speeches to gather armies to go to war against a physical enemy. Nor does He allow the people to carry out a plan to make Him king (see John 6:15). He doesn't even seem to care about announcing Himself to those in power. Rather, He chooses a group of blue-collar, average joes to be His disciples, and spends His time befriending the disenfranchised, healing the sick, feeding the hungry, liberating the spiritually tormented, teaching the spiritually hungry, forgiving sin, and raising the dead.

THE DEATH OF THE MESSIAH

Jesus' death brings the events of Act II to their climax. The action begins during Passover week, when Jesus makes a triumphal entry into Jerusalem. Crowds surround Him; shouting "Hosanna," which means "salvation now," and quoting from Psalms: "Blessed is he who comes in the name of the Lord!" (Psalm 118:26a ESV, Mark 11:9). These people recognize that their promised king has come to bring them the salvation they desperately need. However, unlike any other conquering king, who would have ridden into the capital city on a horse or chariot accompanied by lots of instruments and fanfare, Jesus rides into Jerusalem on an unbroken colt, an event prophesied in Zechariah 9:9.[7] By riding in on a donkey instead of a war horse, Jesus makes a powerful statement about the kind of king He is and how He will bring His kingdom into being—through humility, not military might.

However, none of the witnesses to Jesus' triumphal entry on Palm Sunday anticipate what their hoped-for king will endure less than a week after they welcome Him into Jerusalem. He is soon betrayed by one of His closest friends, arrested, tried, and executed as a criminal. Almost all of His disciples abandon Him, believing all is lost.

Then comes the greatest plot twist. Three days after being buried in a tomb, Jesus resurrects. Of all the unexpected surprises this Messiah pulled off, none can compare to this—coming back from death itself.

Jesus' followers have about six weeks to try to wrap their minds around the significance of the resurrection, when Jesus drops another surprise on them. As they're all together one day, hanging out on the Mount of Olives, Jesus starts instructing them to wait in Jerusalem until they are baptized in the Holy Spirit. Their hearts full of anticipation, the disciples ask Him, "Lord, will you at this time restore the kingdom to Israel?" (Acts 1:6b GNT). Even after spending years with Jesus, they *still* expect that His announcement of a kingdom means the restoration of Israel as its own nation. Yet once again, Jesus reverses their script:

> Jesus said to them, "The times and occasions are set by my Father's own authority, and it is not for you to know when they will be. But when the Holy Spirit comes upon you, you will be filled with power, and you will be witnesses for me in Jerusalem, in all of Judea and Samaria, and to the ends of the earth." After saying this, he was taken up to heaven as they watched him, and a cloud hid him from their sight. (Acts 1:7-9 GNT)

Jesus returns to heaven—promising He'll be back. His mission as the Messiah has been fully accomplished. Through the power and revelation of the Holy Spirit, who comes as promised on the Day of Pentecost, Jesus' disciples finally begin to understand who this King, this Redeemer, this Messiah truly was, and what He had come to do.

He had come to save, liberate, and redeem His people—not from a physical enemy, but from sin, death, and the spiritual forces of evil.

He had come to bring justice and righteousness—not through military force or political laws, but through love, humility, service, and self-sacrifice.

He had come to sit on a throne—not in Israel, but in every human heart.

And He had come to establish a kingdom—not with geo-political boundaries and not even just among God's covenant people, but in the lives of every person who would accept the rule and reign of God and God's Spirit in their lives.

Justice and righteousness are first foundational to how God reigns on His heavenly throne. They mark His chosen people on the planet. The Messiah permanently completes them. And finally, they are fundamental to the reign of God that Jesus announces. In Act I of the story, justice and righteousness are revealed through a chosen people and their nation. In Act II, it is through the work of Christ and a never-ending, heaven-anchored kingdom.

God invites us into that story. And it is as we enter into it—when this King becomes *our* King—that we discover just how He has been establishing justice and righteousness in the world, and will do the same in and through our lives.

STUDY QUESTIONS

If you read the Old Testament prophecies about Jesus, what kind of king would you have expected?

You serve a liberating King, and He reigns over your life—what do you think that means for you?

You are a part of this story. How do you see your life fitting in?

Read Isaiah 61:1-2, quoted in Luke 4:18-19. How do you see Jesus doing the things He announces He will do with His life?

VICTORIOUS JUSTICE

CHAPTER TWELVE

IT IS EASY TO turn Jesus into the mascot for our justice work instead of the foundation and the center of it. When Christ is the center, all people—especially the poorest and most invisible in the world—are best served. He does more than teach good ideas that we can include in our projects. He makes our justice victorious before we ever start any work. In this chapter, we're going to explore just how He does this.

Isaiah 42 declares that the Messiah will "bring forth justice to the nations." When this passage is quoted in Matthew, it uses the phrase "brings justice to victory." Here are the passages side by side:

ISAIAH 42:1-4 ESV	MATTHEW 12:18-21 ESV
Behold my servant, whom I uphold, my chosen, in whom my soul delights; I have put my Spirit upon him; he will bring forth justice *[mishpat]* to the nations. He will not cry aloud or lift up his voice,	Behold, my servant whom I have chosen, my beloved with whom my soul is well pleased. I will put my Spirit upon him, and he will proclaim justice to the Gentiles.

or make it heard in the street;
    a bruised reed he will not break,
        and a faintly burning wick he will not quench;
    he will faithfully bring forth justice [*mishpat*].
He will not grow faint or be discouraged
    till he has established justice [*mishpat*] in the earth;
        and the coastlands wait for his law.
	He will not quarrel or cry aloud,
	    nor will anyone hear his voice in the streets;
	a bruised reed he will not break,
	    and a smoldering wick he will not quench,
	until he brings justice to victory;
	    and in his name the Gentiles will hope.

These are profound promises about the victorious justice Jesus brings. First, Isaiah says that He brings *mishpat* "to the nations." Before Jesus, God's *mishpat* had just been for Israel—His covenant people.[1] When it says that the Messiah will "bring forth *mishpat* for the nations," it means God will extend that relationship and covenant to everyone with all its benefits.[2]

Second, Isaiah says *how* Jesus brings *mishpat*. He doesn't go around crying out in frustration or screaming for someone to pay attention to Him. He brings justice to the nations through gentleness and meekness, not violence and force.[3]

Third, Isaiah uses two images—bruised reeds and smoldering wicks—to describe the way the Messiah would treat people. At the time Isaiah was writing, reeds were a common material used in a lot of everyday objects. They were so common that if the fibers were bruised, they were just discarded. Their use was gone and there were plenty more to replace them. Similarly, wicks in oil lamps would smolder when the oil had been consumed, so instead of producing light, they would produce smoke. Their purpose of creating light had ended. "Bruised reeds" and "smoldering wicks" represent people who are viewed as useless and cast off. Jesus' purpose is to save, not destroy—including saving those that the world casts off as without value or use.[4]

Jesus' purpose is to save, not destroy—including saving those that the world casts off as without value or use.

Finally, the passage in Matthew says that the Messiah will "[bring] justice to victory." What does this mean? It sounds like the prophet is claiming that the Messiah will successfully conquer and eliminate all injustice. But if Jesus is the one who *has brought* justice to victory, what does that mean for us living in a world that is clearly still filled with brokenness and injustice?

THE REAL PROBLEM

There can be no victory without a clearly defined enemy. Jesus demonstrated through His life, death, and resurrection that the true enemy of Israel and of all humanity was not a physical enemy, but a spiritual enemy. Dealing with this enemy first makes it possible to fix any man-made problems.

The only way for Jesus to accomplish true and ultimate victorious justice is to unravel the effects of the fall, when humans betrayed their relationship with God through sin and unleashed sin's impact on everything God made. In both the Old and the New Testament, there are a lot of words to describe sin: iniquity, lawlessness, rebellion, trespassing. Sinning means taking the wrong path, overstepping a boundary, rebelling, and missing the mark. Because God made us with free will, we can cross the boundaries He sets in life.[5] And crossing those boundaries comes with catastrophic consequences.

The first consequence of sin is that it separates us from God, leading us into spiritual bondage and death (see Romans 6:23, 1 Corinthians 15:56, 2 Timothy 2:26, Hebrews 2:15, James 1:15, 2 Peter 2:19). Jesus says that "everyone who sins is a slave of sin" (John 8:24 NLT). We aren't only hurt by sin; we are *slaves* to it—totally under its influence and authority with no hope to get out, in a relationship that leads to death. Even worse, sin enslaves the most fundamental, core, intimate parts of a person—your private thoughts, emotions, drives, and habits. And it is not limited by anything man-made, like walls or borders. It enslaves *anyone* who sins.

By violating our relationship with God, sin also ends up violating all our relationships— with ourselves, with others, and with creation. This is why sin was social in the Old Testament. The book of Amos gave a terrible picture of what happens when sin takes over the order of a nation—oppressing the poor, twisting the law, and perpetuating other injustices. And it wasn't just people who were hurt; the physical land was cursed because of Adam's sin (see Genesis 3:17). Where there is sin, there is also darkness, disease, isolation, and death. Every level of life, from individuals to families to countries to the world, is wrecked by the impact of sin.

When you look at injustice in the world, it's easy to make the person committing the injustice the enemy—a foreign nation, a criminal, or whoever else. But Jesus addressed the real enemy: sin, the impact it has on humanity, and spiritual forces that drive it. This is why Jesus didn't ride into Jerusalem on a warhorse to conquer Israel's earthly oppressors. No weapon of war can change the impact of sin. What if the Messiah had showed up, categorized people into "good guys" and "bad guys," and then killed all the bad guys, leaving the world free for the good guys to enjoy? That would mean that only *some* people are defective. Instead, the Bible insists that "all have sinned and fall short of the glory of God" (Romans 3:23 ESV). Sin impacts *all* of us—we all have the same problem and need the same solution: Jesus.

JESUS' JUSTICE

The only thing that can undo the *shalom*-shattering effects of sin and bring restoration to all our violated relationships is God's justice—His *mishpat*. This was the purpose of Jesus' sacrificial death—to fully bring about God's justice.[6] Go back to what the Jewish philosopher Eliezer Berkovits said about *mishpat*:

> *Mishpat* is done not that justice prevail, but that life prevail...Thus, while *mishpat* may be grim, it will always be an act of saving and deliverance...It is a principle of preservation; the restoration of a disturbed balance which is needed because life has become unbalanced.[7]

The balanced and ordered life God first created for us in the garden of Eden became unbalanced because of sin. Remember the Hebrew definitions of *mishpat*—it is a heavenly norm on earth, the custom of God, the

VICTORIOUS JUSTICE

balance and order that life rests upon, and it is transformative and dynamic. To bring back that original, intended order for the world, God in His love sent His Son to make His justice victorious. That victory came in an unexpected way: the Son of God executed on a cross.

The crucifiction was grim and tangled in human injustice. Jesus didn't just keel over and die at an old age. He was falsely accused and condemned to die by Israel's religious leaders and the Roman authorities (see Luke 22:66-71, 23:1-24). This took place during Passover, when the custom allowed the Roman governor to release one prisoner. This gave the people an opportunity to *free* Jesus. In response to this opportunity, however, the religious leaders convinced the crowd to demand that the notorious murderer Barabbas be freed instead (see Luke 23:18-24). Jesus was then brutally whipped and forced to carry a cross through the streets in public humiliation (see Matthew 27:27-34). Finally, He was crucified between two common criminals, while almost everyone He loved abandoned Him (see Matthew 27:38, John 19:25-27). The injustice and betrayal that brought Jesus to the cross were cruel and intense—yet even more grim was the unfathomable suffering Jesus experienced on the cross as He took on the weight of our sin. The cross was the one-time, once-and-for-all act of divine justice for all human sin. Jesus' sacrifice didn't make the burden He bore any less heavy. Rather He took the full impact of sin on Himself.

Now, on other side of the cross, God frees us from sin instead of punishing us for it. He no longer has any need to punish sin. Yet our human response to sin and injustice is often that we passionately desire punishment instead of restoration. If we mistakenly believe that God's justice wants to punish people, then we will live in fear of His justice, and live out a punishing version of justice with the people around us. Instead, we must show the world that since punishment for sin has already been carried out, God's justice is not focused on punishing what's wrong, but on restoring what's right.[8] Naturally, depending on the act of injustice, punishment might be part of that process because we live in nations governed by human laws.

God's justice is not focused on punishing what's wrong,
but on restoring what's right.

God's ultimate goal in sending His beloved Son to the cross was to restore His design for life, originally seen in the *shalom*-filled garden of Eden. Jesus' definitive sacrifice for sin allows God to extend forgiveness to us and ultimately reconcile our relationship with Him. In the Old Testament when God forgives sin, the Hebrew word used is *nasa*, which means "to carry."[9] When God forgives, He literally carries the burden and responsibility for sin, so that the forgiven person can be lifted up again from under its weight. He carries the responsibility for our sins, forgives us, and no longer remembers our offenses against Him (see Hebrews 8:12, Jeremiah 31:34).

RE-THINKING NEW TESTAMENT JUSTICE

Learning more about God's justice made me realize how much I needed to re-think New Testament justice is by reframing its connection to punishment. First I saw I had only thought about New Testament justice in legal terms. Many in the Western world are likely to interpret Jesus' justice through a legal lens, because our ideas of justice are so often legally flavored. The "legal" account of the Atonement is that we stand before God as judge, and He is able to pronounce a "not guilty" verdict for us because of what Jesus has done on our behalf (see Romans 2-3). This is only *one* dimension of the Atonement but it was the *only* way I had thought about it. I had to learn that there is more to God's justice than an abstract legal pronouncement and more to *us* than accused lawbreakers. Paul uses a lot of metaphors to explain what Jesus' death does for us.[10] Another metaphor, which shows a different dimension of how God sees us, is that we are also adopted sons of God (see Romans 8:15). Becoming a son or daughter is a beautiful picture of what Jesus did—He made God a Father to us. He put us under a new authority that gives us intimate fellowship with God, a new identity, and a new way of life in His Spirit.[11]

Another important image is that Jesus is also our Redeemer:

> In him we have redemption through his blood, the forgiveness of our trespasses, according to the riches of his grace. (Ephesians 1:7 ESV)

The Greek root word for redemption means "to loose."[12] Jesus "loosed" us, or set us free, by paying our ransom with His own life (see Matthew 20:28, Mark 10:45). This is a significant image, one connected to the image we saw from Psalm 72—that the ideal king in Israel was supposed to redeem the poor and needy from oppression (see Psalm 72:14). Likewise, Isaiah describes God's intimate relationship with Israel as "our Father, our Redeemer" (63:16) and "your Maker, your Husband, and your Redeemer (54:5)."[13] Jesus is our ultimate *go'el*, kinsman redeemer, releasing us from our bondage by paying the price with His own blood.

RESTORATION

The second way I've had to re-think New Testament justice is by reframing its connection to punishment. Because I had connected justice primarily to punishment, I thought that justice in the New Testament must be a display of God's anger. No wonder God's justice seemed scary to me—it felt angry and malicious. But Christ took the full penalty of sin on Himself, carrying out that aspect of God's justice once and for all *so that* His saving, restorative justice can be demonstrated toward us. True to His character, God saves, heals, and restores; and His justice is an uncompromising display of that.

This justice leads to restoration for us, not punishment. Jesus' act of *mishpat* restores our direct relationship with God and gives us a totally new nature. Our old self, which was bound by the power of sin and death, has died with Christ:

> And we know that our old being has been put to death with Christ on his cross, in order that the power of the sinful self might be destroyed, so that we should no longer be the slaves of sin. For when we die, we are set free from the power of sin. (Romans 6:6-7 GNT)

Any way that sin had power over our life is made powerless because of what Jesus did for us. His very life—His powerful, sin-free life—is now our own: "Since we have died with Christ, we believe that we will also live with him" (Romans 6:8). Being dead to sin gives us life in Christ (see Romans 6:11).

Being alive in Christ leads to radical, unparalleled transformation: "Anyone who is joined to Christ is a new being; the old is gone, the new has come" (2 Corinthians 5:17 GNT). When we are in Christ, we get to participate in life as a new creation (see Galatians 6:15).[14] Accepting this new nature is something we do through active faith. Paul tells us to "put on the new self, created after the likeness of God in true righteousness [*dikaiosune*] and holiness" (Ephesians 4:24 ESV). And this new self is constantly being renewed: "This is the new being which God, its Creator, is constantly renewing in his own image, in order to bring you to a full knowledge of himself" (Colossians 3:10b GNT).

Humans are created in the image of God but are damaged because of sin. When we receive Christ's freedom, however, we are being constantly renewed again into the original design God had for us. Because Jesus successfully dealt with sin and restored us to the Father, we now have access to His righteous and just nature. Does this mean we automatically live righteous and just lives the moment we put our faith in Jesus? No—we must learn to walk in His nature, which is a process. But we are no longer bound to repeat the same hopeless patterns of injustice that we did before we entered this restored relationship with God. And we get to enter the process of living in our new nature from a place of confidence—knowing that we don't have to work for our righteousness, but that we already are righteous in Jesus (see Jeremiah 23:6, 1 Corinthians 1:30). We get to live free of fear, shame, and condemnation. Jesus' justice leads to our renewal and transformation.

ABIDING JUSTICE AND RIGHTEOUSNESS

The third way I've had to re-think justice is by recognizing that God's active justice in the earth didn't stop with the cross. I had mistakenly thought that Jesus' sacrificial death on our behalf was the last. Yes, Jesus' death was a one-time act of justice, but that act ushered in God's kingdom of justice and righteousness. God's dynamic, restorative justice remains active in the world, constantly transforming what's wrong in the world back to what's right. Jesus' death isn't the only and final act of justice; instead it's the beginning of justice-and-righteousness-filled lives for all of us.

Jesus' death isn't the only and final act of justice; instead it's the beginning of justice-and-righteousness-filled lives for all of us.

In Amos 5, we saw that God wanted *mishpat* and *sedeq* to flow freely and continually from that generation in Israel onward, never growing dry no matter the season. Unfortunately, justice and righteousness came and went depending on Israel's actions. And contrary to God's expressed desires, they failed more often than they succeeded.

However, in a Messianic prophecy in Isaiah, we see the promise of what will happen when the Holy Spirit comes, at a time when "a king will reign righteously [*sedeq*] and princes will rule justly [*mishpat*]" (Isaiah 32:1 ESV):

> …Until the Spirit is poured upon us from on high,
> And the wilderness becomes a fruitful field,
> And the fruitful field is deemed a forest.
> Then justice [*mishpat*] will dwell in the wilderness
> And righteousness [*sedeqah*] will abide in the fertile field.
> And the work of righteousness [*sedeqah*] will be peace [*shalom*],
> And the service of righteousness [*sedeqah*], quietness and confidence forever.
> Then my people will live in a peaceful [*shalom*] habitation,
> And in secure dwellings, and in quiet resting places.
> (Isaiah 32:15-18 NASB)

When the Holy Spirit comes, *mishpat* will dwell and *sedeqah* will abide (see John 14:26, Acts 2:1-15). The Hebrew words for "dwell," *shakan*, and "abide," *yashab*, describe something that is permanently established. When the Holy Spirit comes, the justice and righteousness brought by the Messiah will be here to stay.

The result of abiding justice and righteousness through the Holy

Spirit is that there will be peace, wholeness, quietness, and confidence—*shalom*—forever. People will live in peace and safety, and the land will flourish.[15] Every part of creation, even the physical land, is transformed when the power of sin is broken and the Spirit comes. Remember that Adam's sin cursed not just humanity but the land. Other Old Testament prophecies promise that the physical land will be transformed when it experiences *sedeqah* (see Psalm 72:3, Isaiah 11:6-9, Romans 8:19-23). All of creation can prosper because of the reign of righteousness.[16] The effect is that the land won't be crushed or destroyed but will become whole, complete, and at peace.

Jesus' justice means that we get to live in a kingdom overflowing with God's justice and righteousness. It's an active, essential part of our Christian lives today.

LIVING FROM VICTORIOUS JUSTICE

As people living in the kingdom of God, we get to live *from* victorious justice. The most important act of justice—the act that makes all justice possible—has already been accomplished. There is a lot of language about "the struggle for justice" and "fighting for justice," and it's true that we must do intentional work in order to practically bring justice on the earth. But how do we go about it all? Well, victorious justice is where we start. If we are building off of Jesus—who has brought justice to victory—then justice is in us and flows through us.

Christ's victorious justice should be lived in and through our lives. Being put right again with God should not make us sit on our comfortable couches and wait for heaven. Instead, it should launch us. Jesus left us with a commission not just to camp out at the cross but also to move out to make disciples (see Mark 16:15).

Jesus defines the justice we live from by the victory of the cross. When we look at the massive injustices in the world, we can understand who we are and *run* into the middle of these problems, knowing that we are fully equipped to bring justice. To shrink back in fear is ridiculous when Jesus has already brought *mishpat* to victory.

No human injustice can stop the expanse of His kingdom. However, this doesn't mean we get to pronounce judgment on the earth and call down natural disasters on people that we deem particularly sinful. This means we get to extend the opportunity for *all* people to come back into a right, just relationship with God. The cross has brought us into victory.

WHAT HAPPENS WHEN A PERSON RECEIVES SALVATION? YOU...

Are forgiven of all your sins. *Eph. 1:7*

Are born again. *1 Peter 1:23, John 3:3*

Are set free from the power of sin. *Rom. 6:7*

Are set free in Christ. *Rom. 8:2, Gal. 5:1*

Have Christ become your life *Col. 3:3-4*

Are redeemed from the curse. *Gal. 3:13*

Are washed in regeneration and renewal by the Holy Spirit. *Titus 3:5*

Are given eternal life. *John 10:28*

Are holy and blameless before God. *Eph.1:4*

Receive the Holy Spirit through faith. *Gal. 3:14, Eph.1:13*

Become the dwelling of the Spirit of God. *1 Cor. 3:16*

Live in the Spirit. *Rom. 7:6*

Walk in newness of life. *Rom. 6:4*

Receive victory through Christ. *1 Cor. 15:57*

Enter the unity of the body of Christ, established by Christ, who is our peace. *Eph. 2:13-16*

Receive the protection of God's peace, which guards your heart and mind. *Phil. 4:7*

Overcome the world through faith. *1 John 5:4*

Live for righteousness [*dikaiosune*]. *1 Peter 2:24*

Have the mind of Christ. *1 Cor. 2:16*

Are called by God to a holy, Christ-given calling. *2 Tim. 1:9*

Have boldness and confident access to God. *Eph. 3:12*

Become the temple of the Holy Spirit. *1 Cor. 6:19*

Become a member of the body of Christ. *1 Cor. 12:27*

Have citizenship in heaven. *Phil. 3:20*

Become an heir of God and a co-heir with Christ. *Rom. 8:17*

Partake of Jesus' divine nature. *2 Peter 1:4*

Are created in Christ for good works. *Eph. 2:10*

Have access to the Father. *Eph. 2:18*	Conform into the image of Christ. *Rom. 8:29*
Become a new creation. *2 Cor. 5:17*	Get to put on a new self, created to be like God in righteousness *[dikaiosune]* and holiness. *Eph. 4:24*
Become alive in Christ. *Col. 2:13, Eph. 2:5*	
Receive a spirit of power, love, and a sound mind. *2 Tim. 1:7*	Know that everything is possible through God. *Phil. 4:13*
Are rescued from the dominion of darkness and brought into the kingdom of Christ. *Col. 1:13*	Are a light in God. *Eph. 5:8-9*
	Become the salt and light of the world. *Matt. 5:13-14*
Are seated in heavenly places in Christ. *Eph. 2:6*	Become an ambassador for Christ. *2 Cor. 5:17-20*
Make peace with God. *Rom. 5:1*	Are given a ministry of reconciliation. *2 Cor. 5:19*
	Know that everything will be worked together for your good. *Rom. 8:28*

STUDY QUESTIONS

How does victorious justice Jesus brings connect to living a life of justice and righteousness?

In what ways are the gospel, justice and righteousness linked?

How would justice and righteousness dwelling and abiding in the world practically look like?

SERMON ON THE MOUNT: RIGHTEOUSNESS IN THE HEART & IN THE WORLD

CHAPTER THIRTEEN

NOW WE ARE GOING to begin to move into what a justice-and-righteousness-filled life looks like. I need to mention a few challenges before we start. First, I don't have the space to go through all of Jesus' teachings, much less the whole New Testament. Second, defining righteousness in the New Testament is more of a debate than a simple study. Scholars have been arguing generations about what the precise definition of it is. For the purposes of this study, we will go in-depth on one of Jesus' teachings—the one that summarizes best what a life under the reign of God should look like: the Sermon on the Mount. No matter how you define righteousness in the New Testament, this teaching from Jesus is powerful and practical. It is considered one of the most influential ethics teachings in history.

It's important to understand the cultural context in which Jesus gave this sermon. As we have seen, righteousness was central to Israel's culture in the Old Testament. The Law outlined the righteous lifestyle God required of His covenant people. In the period between the Old and New Testaments, however, Jewish lawyers and scholars developed a huge body of writings interpreting the Law and defining how it should be practiced. These teachings took the laws Moses had laid out to a whole new level of detail. In Jesus' day, the scribes and Pharisees were those who prided themselves on following all of these hair-splitting rules. Their obsession with rules and religious purity led them to make all kinds of barriers between them and those they deemed "sinners."[1] To them, any association with sinners meant they were defiling themselves.

The Pharisees' interpretation of righteousness was dangerous, and it angered Jesus. Not only did it prevent sinners from going to the God they desperately needed; it also kept these so-called righteous blind to their own need for God and real spiritual principles (Luke 18:10, Matthew 9:13, 12:7, 23:13, 23:23). This is why Jesus' sternest words were directed toward the Pharisees and why He ignored their legalistic rules of righteousness. Their rules actually violated the character of God. Jesus revealed God's heart to seek out sinners and bring them into intimate fellowship. Instead of distancing Himself, Jesus pursued sinners and addressed their needs so He could minister to them.[2] This is the heart of the gospel—God is the One who takes the initiative to look for and save the lost.

A LIFE DISPLAYING RIGHTEOUSNESS

Jesus directly exposes the flaws in the Pharisees' teachings about righteousness in the Sermon on the Mount. The Sermon appears in both Matthew and Luke, but we are going to focus primarily on Matthew's account.

Matthew, written to a Jewish audience, regularly quotes the Old Testament prophets throughout his Gospel in order to show how Jesus fulfilled the prophecies about their long-awaited king.[3] The kingdom of God is also central in Matthew's Gospel. The Sermon on the Mount presents a vivid picture of what it looks like to live out the kingdom's principles, both as an individual Christ follower and as a Christian community.

It's important to understand that Jesus wasn't presenting new laws or new requirements for salvation in this sermon. Rather, He showed how those with a restored relationship with God live. Jesus painted a mind-boggling picture of those who have been so dramatically changed by the kingdom of God that their lives display its righteousness.[4]

The Sermon starts out with the famous "Beatitudes" (*beatitude* comes from the Latin word for blessing).[5] Each of the Beatitudes starts with a promise: "Blessed…" The Greek word here was often used in the religious texts of the day to translate a Hebrew word that means "Oh, the happiness of…" It is sometimes translated as "happy," "fortunate," or "God blesses."[6] Yet when we read Jesus' descriptions of who is "blessed," they sound like those the world would label as the *least* happy or fortunate. The kingdom way is often opposite to the world's way.

If you want a life and community full of blessing, this is a great instruction manual. Remember that God puts up boundaries in your life to keep happiness and blessing in, not to keep it out. Let's look at each of these "blessed" promises more closely.

POOR IN SPIRIT

Jesus' first Beatitude—"Blessed are the poor in spirit, for theirs is the kingdom of heaven" (Matthew 5:3 ESV)—resonates with Isaiah 61:1, which promises that the Messiah will "bring good news to the poor" (ESV).

"Poor in spirit" means you realize that you are totally bankrupt apart from God.[7] Jesus gave this promise first because it marks the starting point of the kingdom lifestyle. We can't receive the kingdom of God without recognizing that on our own, we have nothing.[8] We have to be emptied of ourselves—our selfishness and our efforts to be perfect on our own—before God can fill us with Himself.

Jesus wasn't saying that being materially poor makes you closer to God. True, those who have fewer possessions have less stuff to get in the way of fully trusting and surrendering to God.[9] But the materially poor can be just as proud and unwilling to recognize their need for God as the materially rich, and the rich can also be humble and poor in spirit. Most would say that poverty and dependency are the *least valuable* qualities in the world. But God takes these qualities and makes them spiritually the *most valuable* ones that everyone should pursue.

Jesus' promise is for anyone who embraces this posture of humility and need, and the reward for doing so is enormous: "Theirs is the kingdom of heaven." Another way to put this is that the poor in spirit get "the good things God gives to those who are a part of His reign."[10] To gain these good things, you have to recognize that on your own, you have nothing.

THE MOURNERS

The next Beatitude is, "Blessed are those who mourn, for they shall be comforted" (Matthew 5:4 ESV). This verse connects to the promise in Isaiah 61:3, that the Messiah will comfort "those who mourn."

Jesus doesn't give a reason these mourners are mourning. It could be from recognizing their own personal sin or from experiencing evil in the world.[11] Whatever the cause might be, the promise is that God Himself will come close and comfort them.

When we allow God to come close to us in our grief and bring His comfort, it brings an incredible blessing into our lives—not the least of which is that it enables us to pass through mourning and come out on the other side. This allows us to lean into grief rather than avoiding it.

It's easy to think that in order to stay happy and avoid depression, we have to ignore all the pain and injustice going on in the world. But God promises that happiness comes *through* mourning. In the kingdom, we don't have to live with emotional detachment from our own experiences or from what we see going on in the world. Being present in pain is hard, but it positions us for God's comfort. The Beatitudes recorded in Luke say it this way: "Blessed are you who weep now, for you shall laugh" (Luke 6:21b ESV).[12] Laughter comes by allowing yourself to weep. Conversely, cutting yourself off from pain cuts you off from joy. If you want happiness and comfort, it won't come through ignorance and emotional detachment but through being emotionally present and engaged.

This has a huge application for living God's justice and righteousness. How can we be moved to action if we stay detached from the emotional impact of injustice? God is not detached. He hears the cry of the poor and is moved by compassion to help them. To be led by God's genuine love for people, we have to have real, whole, connected hearts.

Many of the greatest social reformers in history started because they saw and were moved by the agonizing impact of sin on people's lives, both socially and personally.[13] Seeing the impact of terrible injustices on God's children will cause you to weep and mourn, but this is where doing justice begins. Being fully connected to the pain of sin and injustice moves you to act until full restoration comes.

THE MEEK

The next Beatitude is, "Blessed are the meek, for they shall inherit the earth" (Matthew 5:5 ESV). This verse connects to a promise in Psalms: "But the meek shall inherit the land and delight themselves in abundant peace" (Psalm 37:11 ESV).[14] Being meek doesn't mean that you become weak or a doormat. The Greek word translated "meek" is *praus,* and it means "strength under control."[15] It can also be translated "gentle" or "humble," and it describes those "who don't trust in their own power."[16]

Meekness is an attitude toward God before it is an attitude toward others.[17] In fact, this humble position before God is what *makes* a person kind and gentle toward others.[18] Jesus Himself is our perfect model of meekness. He even describes Himself as *praus* and humble in heart (see Matthew 11:29).[19] When He calls for a community to be marked by meekness, gentleness, and humility, He is calling it to display His own character and leadership to the world (See Galatians 5:22-23, 6:1; Ephesians 4:2; Colossians 3:12; James 1:21, 3:13, 3:17; 1 Peter 3:15). Some of the greatest leaders in the Bible are described as meek or humble: Moses, David, Saul, Solomon, Paul, and Jesus. Being humble is a mark of a great leader—even military and political leaders.

Jesus promises that the meek will be given the entire earth as their inheritance. Think about how many people spend their lives pursuing wealth, believing it will lead to power and happiness. Many are taught to get what they want through methods like force, selfish ambition, and sacrificing relationships and integrity. But God promises that the whole earth will belong to a very different sort of group—those who live out Christ's meekness.

HUNGRY AND THIRSTY FOR RIGHTEOUSNESS

Next, Jesus blesses "those who hunger and thirst for righteousness, for they shall be satisfied" (Matthew 5:6 ESV). In the Old Testament, the metaphors of hunger and thirst are used to show longing for God,[20] describing a desire so intense that you feel pain.[21] The desire for righteousness here means a desire "to see God's will be done"[22]—for His will and standards to happen in all areas of your life.[23] This righteousness is a gift from God, not something you can achieve on your own.[24] The type of righteousness we should long for is the righteousness we can't have apart from Jesus.

Many people want *some degree* of righteousness. This verse is saying that you have to desire *full* righteousness—the kind equal to the righteousness found in God.[25] Few actually seek that. On our own, we can do some righteousness; but to live God's full righteousness, you need God. And to get it, you have to desire it like you desire food and water. When you experience that level of longing, God will satisfy it. Theologian James Boice paraphrases this Beatitude like this: "O how happy is the man who knows enough not to be satisfied with any human goodness. He alone is happy who seeks for the divine righteousness, because God certainly will provide it."[26]

THE MERCIFUL

"Blessed are the merciful," Jesus continues, "for they shall receive mercy" (Matthew 5:7 ESV). A common rabbinic saying in first-century Jewish culture was, "As God is merciful, so you must be merciful."[27] This also echoes the Micah Mandate to "do justly, love mercy, and walk humbly."[28]

Jews understood mercy to be an essential quality of God (see Exodus 34:6). Reflecting God's mercy is a privilege, because it's a way to show the world what He is like. We have experienced so much mercy and forgivingness from God, so we should treat others in the same way we have been treated. Being merciful includes being kind, generous, compassionate, and forgiving toward others, as well as ministering healing.[29]

Showing mercy is essential, because when we don't forgive, it keeps us imprisoned. In another passage in Matthew, Jesus tells a parable

SERMON ON THE MOUNT: RIGHTEOUSNESS IN THE HEART

about an unforgiving servant. This servant owes his master millions of dollars. The servant begs for mercy, knowing that he can never repay the debt. Moved with compassion, the master forgives the *entire* debt. In response, the newly freed servant turns and demands that his fellow servant repay him a debt of around a few thousand dollars—almost nothing compared to what he has just been forgiven.[30] Right after he has been shown mercy, he turns around and shows no mercy to his fellow servant. When the master hears what his servant has done, he is furious. He calls the servant before him and rebukes him: "You should have had mercy on your fellow servant, just as I had mercy on you" (Matthew 18:33 GNT). He then throws the unmerciful man in prison until he can pay back his debt. Jesus concludes: "That is how my Father in heaven will treat every one of you unless you forgive your brother from your heart" (Matthew 18:35 GNT).

God forgives you, but He can't forgive *for* you. When you don't show mercy, it puts *you*, not the person you aren't forgiving, in prison. All Christians have received extreme mercy from God. Showing mercy and forgiving others is a way to show the world what our God is like—and we are blessed as a result. This is also the model of how we should all respond to every act of injustice against us personally. In a sin-distorted world, all of us will experience injustice in life. We are all given the same remedy for it: to show mercy and forgive. That doesn't necessarily mean forgetting about the injustice, or not pursuing legal action if necessary. However, forgiveness is our first response to it—one that will keep us out of spiritual prison.

PURE IN HEART

Jesus' next Beatitude is, "Blessed are the pure in heart, for they shall see God" (Matthew 5:8 ESV). This verse connects to Psalm 24:3-4, which says that those who are welcome before the presence of God in the temple are those with "clean hands and a pure heart."

"Pure in heart" emphasizes inner purity over outward religious purity.[31] The heart is more than the emotions; it's the very core of a person's being.[32] When righteousness reigns in a person's core, it changes everything about his or her motivations.[33] Trying to keep a pure and holy lifestyle when your heart isn't pure is exhausting and unsustainable. But when God gives a pure heart, He not only makes a heart washed clean by forgiving sin; He also gives you pure motives that transform how you live.

Purity of heart enables you to "see" God. In Romans, Paul describes the "foolish hearts" of the unrighteous as "darkened" (Romans 1:21). When your heart is darkened, it makes it hard to see God.[34] But when your heart is pure, you get to experience intimate fellowship with God, which allows Him to impart His heart and character to you and enables you to see Him and know Him.[35]

THE PEACEMAKERS

Next, Jesus says, "Blessed are the peacemakers, for they shall be called sons of God" (Matthew 5:9 ESV). Again, peace—that spectacular word, *shalom*—means "wholeness" or "the state of something being complete as it was designed to be." In particular, *shalom* is focused on people and relationships being whole and complete. When you love people, you love peace.[36]

Working for peace expresses God's character in the world. When the world sees *shalom*-loving people, it points them to what God is like—they are acting like sons and daughters who accurately represent their Father.[37] In Jesus' day, this would have been a radical statement about what His kingdom is like. Revolutionaries were hoping for a violent overthrow of the Roman oppressors to bring the kingdom of God.[38] Instead, Jesus says that God's blessing will be on those who work for peace. Violence brings chaos and pain, and it destroys life. Peace creates an atmosphere for people to grow and prosper.

Paul describes our peacemaking call in 2 Corinthians as a "ministry of reconciliation":

> All this is from God, who through Christ reconciled us to himself and gave us the ministry of reconciliation; that is, in Christ God was reconciling the world to himself, not counting their trespasses against them, and entrusting to us the message of reconciliation. (2 Corinthians 5:18-19 ESV)

SERMON ON THE MOUNT: RIGHTEOUSNESS IN THE HEART

Our message to the world is reconciliation, not judgment. God wants to bring people separated by sin back to Him again. When we act as peacemakers and reconcilers—those who are restoring wholeness in the world—we show what our Father is like.

THE PERSECUTED

The first Beatitude concludes, "for theirs is the kingdom of heaven," and the final Beatitude concludes with the same promise: "Blessed are those who are persecuted for righteousness' sake, for theirs is the kingdom of heaven" (Matthew 5:10 ESV).

"Persecuted for righteousness' sake" can also be translated, "Persecuted because they live as God wants people to."[39] Living a righteous lifestyle is strange. Though you actively work for *shalom*, your lifestyle will be abrasive to the world's. But even when suffering and persecuted, the righteous are blessed by God.

The key part of this Beatitude is that people are persecuted "for righteousness' sake." Plenty of Christians act like a nuisance, then call people's response to their insulting methods "persecution." If you act like a judgmental jerk and people call you out on it, that's not persecution. The only kind of persecution you are blessed for comes from being like Jesus—showing His meekness, mercy, and power, and actively living the gospel. When you do this, the kingdom of heaven is yours.

THE PARADOX OF THE KINGDOM

Jesus' teachings in the Sermon on the Mount are about keeping happiness inside your life, not out of it. Following God's ways may seem like a strange route to a happy life. Yet when your life is transformed by God's reign, a pure heart, mourning, peacemaking, and all the other things Jesus lists actually lead to happiness and fulfillment.

The Beatitudes all seem personal—mourning, recognizing your need for God, and keeping a pure heart. Yes, first God profoundly changes a person's heart, and the Christian life should be marked by personal purity and morality. But *immediately* after declaring the Beatitudes, Jesus calls His followers to a place of influence in the world. He could have easily told them to go make a utopian community where they could live out this righteousness far away from the evil and corruption of the surrounding culture. In fact, at the time, there were Jewish groups that separated themselves into remote communities for this reason. But instead, Jesus tells His followers that they are the "light of the world" (Matthew 5:14)—a beacon to show the way to eternal life in the midst of spiritual darkness—and the "salt of the earth" (Matthew 5:13)—people whose lives add heavenly flavor and act as a preservative to those around them. Salt was used to preserve food, so if salt lost its saltiness, food would spoil. Jesus' followers are sprinkled in the world to keep it from decaying.[40] These are metaphors for influence. The righteous in the kingdom are not to make their own separate community. Rather Christ's followers will stand out by showing a heavenly character.[41]

Righteousness has always marked God's influence in the world. Rabbi Abraham Heschel puts it this way: "Life is clay, and righteousness the mold in which God wants history to be shaped."[42] God's "rightness" or His standard for life now comes into the world through His followers. Living kingdom righteousness will impact society in a way that brings light and preserves from decay.

Throughout history, Christians have been tempted to leave the evils of the world and make their own separate utopias. I thought it was just my generation that was tempted to do this, but I learned that disengaging from the world entirely has been a temptation for centuries—a temptation that would destroy the mission Jesus gave us. John Wesley wrote that the belief that people should "wholly withdraw from the world"[43] is "the simplest of all devices with which Satan has perverted the gospel of Jesus."[44] Ouch. He said that times of spiritual retreat were good for the soul, but too much time away would "destroy, not advance, true Christianity."[45] The reason is, "Christianity is essentially a social religion. To turn it into a solitary religion is to destroy it."[46]

Being in the world shouldn't change our heavenly character. Our righteousness comes from being connected to God, and living that out in the world doesn't decrease its potency. So when we see darkness and deterioration in the world, our response shouldn't be to ask God why He's allowing it to happen. We should recognize that a part of the world is in desperate need of some salt and light. We should step in to show the way and bring out the flavors of heaven.

When we join our lives with a community of salty light-bearers, we can transform the world. Our Christian communities will always be diverse with different talents, passions, skills, and callings. But this sermon shows what look and flavor we should all have. Wherever we all are—as government officials, church leaders, teachers, or parents—we should all bring light and salt into that part of the world. The blessed life of being meek, merciful, righteous, poor in spirit, pure in heart, and totally dependent on God should be a defining characteristic of our Christ-following communities.

HIS RIGHTEOUSNESS

The Beatitudes challenge what most of us think of as the "blessed" life. And Jesus doesn't stop there. As the Sermon on the Mount continues, He takes "righteousness" to a whole new level. He begins by saying that "unless your righteousness [*dikaiosune*] exceeds that of the scribes and Pharisees, you will never enter the kingdom of heaven" (Matthew 5:20 ESV). He goes on to declare that hating a brother is the same as murder, and looking lustfully at someone is the same as adultery. He says that every single thing out of our mouths should be truthful. He says we are to love our enemies, turn the other cheek when someone hits us, and give someone more than what they demand of us. He commands us not to worry about anything but to fully trust God to meet our physical needs. With every command He goes for the heart, which makes fulfilling the command even more impossible. Anyone can control their behavior for a little while, but who can make their innermost being feel, think, and react in this way constantly?

The key to understanding Jesus' words is to recognize that He was indeed calling His followers to a standard that is totally impossible *on our own*. The Pharisees proved that. They were giving righteousness the best of human effort, yet they couldn't hope to fulfill Jesus' guidelines. The only way this righteousness can become ours is if God gives it to us. And as it just so happens, that is exactly what Jesus came to do.

The righteousness Jesus was describing is, in fact, His own. We receive it not by human effort, but by entering into a relationship with Him and by putting our full trust in Him. When we put our faith in

Him, the first thing He goes after is our heart. The righteousness of the Pharisees was concerned with outward behavior. But God's righteousness is focused first on who we *are*, not what we *do*.[47] A transformed heart motivated by love and free of selfishness is capable of extraordinary, unimaginable behavior, such as forgiving your enemies and blessing those that curse you. That's where the real power for righteous living comes from.[48]

The Sermon on the Mount is the description of a new life, not a new legal system.[49] The righteousness of the kingdom is given to us when God reigns in our life. Reading Jesus' description of kingdom living should make you realize that you are totally, utterly, and completely unable to live it out on your own. Thankfully, living righteousness is not dependent on you. As the theologian George Eldon Ladd said, "The righteousness which God's Kingdom demands, God's Kingdom must give." [50] Your only hope of being able to live it isn't to study a law that tells you the exact limits of your behavior; it's to fall at Jesus' feet and admit that apart from Him, you can't hope to live out His righteousness.

The Sermon on the Mount is the description of a new life, not a new legal system.

Putting Jesus' teaching into action sets you up for a strong, long-lasting life (see Matthew 7:24-27). The Sermon goes on to give instruction about prayer, fasting, giving to the poor, money, and more—practical topics that we will continue to explore.

ACTIVE, KIND, EMPOWERED JUSTICE

Growing up, I had this idea that justice isn't possible in the New Testament because Jesus taught things that were the opposite of justice, like goodness and kindness. But Jesus' teachings are actually the opposite of things like hatred and retribution, not justice. I've seen Christians twist the Sermon on the Mount to justify keeping people oppressed, telling them that they need to turn the other cheek and wait for heaven. But Jesus telling people to love and be kind to their oppressors doesn't mean being passive when faced with unjust people and systems. He

SERMON ON THE MOUNT: RIGHTEOUSNESS IN THE HEART

gives active responses. In response to hatred, love (see Matthew 5:44). In response to oppression, be kind (see Matthew 5:41-42). In response to injustice, forgive (see Matthew 6:14). In response to abuse, stand firm and give more than demanded of us rather than retaliating (see Matthew 5:39-41). In response to unjust demands, give extra (see Matthew 5:41). In response to persecution, pray for the persecutors (see Matthew 5:44, which He demonstrates in the Lord's prayer a few verses later). We should take their unjust action and respond, turning the evil they brought into the world into good.

Jesus' teaching harmonizes perfectly with God's active way of bringing justice and righteousness into the world. Remember the Micah Mandate, which links justice, mercy, and humility (Micah 6:8, see also Hosea 12:6, Zechariah 7:9, and Jeremiah 9:24)? Mercy and kindness have always been a way that God has done justice in the world. The Sermon on the Mount shows that justice and righteousness don't come by using the world's methods of hatred, violence, and retribution. Instead, they come by being empowered through kindness, forgiveness, truth, and the love of your enemies.

RIGHTLY-ORDERED TRANSFORMATION

I've seen two problems Christians face when they want to "change the world," and the Sermon on the Mount gives us a great solution to both of them. The first problem appears when people pursue transformation out of a wrongly-ordered life. The second problem is reacting to how some have pursued transformation out of order by never doing anything.

Often, "social justice" is talked about in terms of the "big forces" in the world—economics, politics, social order, etc. When those "forces" are unjust, they hurt people, so naturally we want to change them. Yes, those "big forces" impact all of our lives, and there is biblical wisdom for how to improve them (the Old Testament in particular shows God's intense response to His people committing injustice through those "big forces"). But the first step for Christians to take when they want to "change the world" is to let God transform their own heart. As the Russian writer Leo Tolstoy wrote during a time of great social turmoil in Europe: "There can only be one permanent revolution—a moral one;

the regeneration of the inner man... Everybody thinks of changing humanity, and nobody thinks of changing himself."[51] We have to remember that humanity first fell in Eden, a perfect environment. Therefore, bringing a perfect environment back into the world won't solve the source of man's problem in his own heart.[52]

It's easy to react to how some have worked *only to* "change the world" by then focusing *only* on internal transformation. But if our Christ-transformed lives never influence the world, it cuts off salt and light from a world that desperately needs them. Righteousness is right, does right, and makes right. To focus on the "is right" part means you are living the *first* instead of the *full* expression of righteousness. We get to be active participants in molding history with God's righteous influence. The Sermon on the Mount is where Jesus teaches His people to pray, "Your kingdom come, your will be done, on earth as it is in heaven" (Matthew 6:10 ESV). Some approach this as a passive prayer, as though all we need to do is sit around and look at the sky waiting for God to do His thing. If it's His reign and He's all-powerful, then it should be on Him to change things, right? But that's not how it works. Even the Jews at Jesus' time understood that God ruled sovereignly over everything, and yet they still prayed every day for His reign to be established over everyone now. They recognized that God's kingdom comes into the physical world when people submit themselves to His rule.[53] The reign of God begins in human hearts, making it timeless and limitless. To see that reign come practically, for God's will to come on earth, we submit to His rule and let His kingdom happen through our lives.

We get to be active participants in molding history with God's righteous influence.

To do this, we must embrace the not-yet-but-already-here tension of the kingdom in which we live. Jesus also describes the kingdom as something that is immediately in front of people (see Luke 17:20-21), something we are to pray for (see Matthew 6:10), and something that has not yet come (see Luke 19:11-12).[54]

The question then becomes, how do we pursue bringing God's just and righteous kingdom practically in the world from an internally-transformed life? Civil rights icon Dr. Martin Luther King, Jr. has wisdom about how to do this. He talked about the need for people who were "maladjusted" or "transformed nonconformists"—those who wouldn't adjust and conform to the evil and unjust order of the world, and thus would bring a different way of life. He listed the "maladjusted" people of their time we should use as models: the prophet Amos, Jesus of Nazareth, Thomas Jefferson, and Abraham Lincoln.[55] He said, "The world is in desperate need of such maladjustment. Through such maladjustment, I believe that we will be able to emerge from the bleak and desolate midnight of man's inhumanity to man into the bright and glittering daybreak of freedom and justice."[56] The kingdom of God, His righteous and just reign, is fully inside our hearts but not quite visible in the world. The Sermon on the Mount shows how maladjusted and non-conformed people can use God's ways to bring His transformation into the world.

RIGHTEOUSNESS AND OPPRESSION: HOWARD THURMAN'S LIFE

Let's look at one example of how a modern "maladjusted" person's righteousness-filled life transformed an unjust society: Howard Thurman. His life demonstrates just how powerful God can make someone within the limits of the most oppressive man-made structures. You may not know Thurman's name, but everyone in the United States has felt the impact of his life. Many leaders and participants in the Civil Rights Movement used Thurman's teachings to spiritually ground their work. He was one of Martin Luther King, Jr's, seminary chaplains. In fact, during the Montgomery bus boycott, King kept Thurman's most famous book, *Jesus and the Disinherited,* with him to read continually. Thanks to Thurman's influence, the Civil Rights Movement adopted a revolutionary non-violent stance.[57] Instead of a violent overthrow of the political order, Thurman showed that the oppressed in a society must fight first for internal transformation.

Jesus' teaching on how to live a righteous lifestyle doesn't include things like "make an army and rebel against your oppressors"—things I would probably want to do if I were living under oppression. On the surface, it can seem like God wants His people to be passive and powerless. So how *does* Jesus want us to live in the face of injustice?

To answer these questions, let's look at Thurman's message in *Jesus and the Disinherited*. The book lays out the theological foundation for the oppressed to work for social change. Thurman wrote the book in 1949, a time when African Americans in our nation faced an intense amount of oppression. Thurman spoke from the perspective of those with "their backs against the wall"—the poor, the oppressed, and the dispossessed of the world.[58] His perspective and voice are essential to the body of Christ, because in Christ, the free and oppressed are integrated. It's important for us to tune our ears to listen to those whose experiences are different than our own.

It's one thing for me—rich, free, and powerful compared to much of the world—to tell people who are oppressed that "Jesus is enough for you." As Thurman says, though, it's not good for "the man who is not forced to live in a ghetto to tell those who must how to transcend its limitations."[59] Instead, we must listen to the perspective of someone who has experienced what it's like to be crushed and oppressed, and who has found freedom in God.

To Thurman, it was significant that Jesus was born into a time and place where He too was among the oppressed of His day. Jesus could have risen up as a revolutionary political reformer, overthrowing the government like others in His day tried to do. But Jesus carried out another revolution. Jesus' revolution allowed the oppressed to find freedom from what Thurman identified as three natural human responses to living under injustice: fear, deception, and hatred. Thurman emphasized the importance of *first* finding transformation on the inside, since that was the focus of Jesus' own message. A person with a victorious spirit inside them, with life flowing from their hearts, cannot be destroyed by any external force in the world.

Thurman taught that Jesus shows the way to become free from the spiritually-imprisoning forces of fear, deception, and hatred. He said the answer to fear is first to recognize that you are a child of God. Born in 1899 in the segregated South, Thurman was raised by his grandmother, who was born a slave. He told the story of how she had the idea drilled into her by a fellow slave and preacher that, "You—you are

SERMON ON THE MOUNT: RIGHTEOUSNESS IN THE HEART

not niggers. You—you are not slaves. You are God's children."[60] When the world disempowered and dehumanized her and her fellow slaves, she chose to remember that she was actually a child of God, and that she had dignity and worth. God is the one who gives identity first. It's easy to accept a man-made label like "slave" and let that identity disempower you. But grounding your identity as God's own child should make you fearless.

Thurman understood that as God's child, fear of other humans is ridiculous, especially as this puts a person in God's place: "Do not fear those who kill the body but are unable to kill the soul; but rather fear Him who is able to destroy both soul and body in hell" (Matthew 10:28 ESV). Recognizing that you are a child of God also lets you own your development process, changing fear into "the power to strive, to achieve, and not to yield."[61] To Thurman, that meant the lack of opportunity for the oppressed shouldn't be allowed to define your potential as God's child.

Once free from fear, Thurman explained, you can become free from deception. When you are fearless, you can speak truth and reject hypocrisy. In an unjust environment, many people learn to lie as a survival mechanism. If you are weak and disempowered, using deception to appease the powerful and manipulation to get your needs met can become normal. But if you lie enough, you *become* the lie. Jesus taught that we are to speak the truth and keep our word, no matter what (see Matthew 5:37). Sincerity replaces deception. Though the culture says your relationships are between categories like the weak and strong, God only sees a relationship between two human beings, both of whom deserve sincerity.[62] This means that both the poor and oppressed are free to speak the truth, even the hard-to-hear stuff to powerful people, because everyone deserves honesty.

To become free from hatred, Thurman taught it's essential to follow Jesus' own example. Jesus had many opportunities to become bitter toward Roman oppressors. But instead, Thurman observed, "Jesus rejected hatred because he saw that hatred meant death to the mind, death to the spirit, death to communion with his Father. He affirmed life; and hatred was the great denial."[63] When Jesus taught His disciples to love their enemies, Israel's main enemy was their Roman rulers. Loving an enemy requires the relationship to be reconciled with barriers taken down. When you love an enemy who has done terrible things to you, that means you have to recognize that they too are a child of God.[64] You can't see them in the broad category of your "enemy"; you have to shift so you can see them as a human again. For someone to do this after experiencing so much injustice, they have to keep bitterness from rooting in their hearts. That's a hard challenge, but Jesus had to do it, too.

The survival strategies of fear, hatred, and deception only lead to spiritual imprisonment. Thurman taught that Jesus shows the way out of that imprisonment. Every person has power, agency, and ownership over their life and needs never be defined by the oppression and injustice of another. This means everyone has the opportunity to have a free life—free from hatred, unforgiveness, bitterness, and shame. Instead, life is full of love, power, and freedom.

Thurman emphasized that change must first happen *inside* the person who is experiencing oppression. Yet significantly, Thurman's influence shaped a political movement that led to the external and political changes needed to free his people from oppression. Thousands in the Civil Rights Movement took his teachings and used them to fuel their actions. Freedom in the heart led to greater freedom in society. A redeemed man—freed from hatred, fear, and deception and filled with love—is what led to the very changes needed for the external freedom. In this example, inner transformation led to outer transformation.

SALT AND LIGHT RISING UP

The Sermon-on-the-Mount way of living isn't violent, but it is resistant to power structures in the world. To not accept the political, economic, and social orders that define and limit your life will probably get you into trouble. Jesus' life and the early church demonstrate this truth well. It's a way of life that requires living in tension—a tension that brings transformation first *to* you, and then *through* you. German theologian Karl H. Rengstorf explains, "…redemption, like sin, takes place within existing social structures, so that the first priority is not to change the structures but to achieve a life which is conformable to that of Jesus. Such a life will in due time break down the structures…"[65] The fact that Jesus never preached about how to fix or perfectly order a society doesn't mean that He didn't care about it.[66] Rather, He showed where it starts: from an individual's transformed heart and character. Instead of passively accepting evil in the world, we use God's forces (humility, love, pure hearts, forgiveness, mercy, emotional connection, truth) to establish His justice and righteousness. We are to be justice-and-righteousness-filled *people,* living justice-and-righteousness-filled *lives,* molding a justice-and-righteousness-filled *world.*

Our salvation, freedom, and empowerment are not dependent on "social justice." Yet when we live our Christ-centered lives, justice and righteousness will happen. Bringing salt and light into the sin-distorted world—seeking justice where there is injustice, peace where there is chaos, connection where there is disconnection, and restoration where there is destruction—demonstrates to the world what our God is like and reveals His design for human life to thrive. But the difference is where it all starts—a redeemed heart set free from sin and death. Time and time again, we see God's people taking His heart to see people thrive and using their own lives to make Jesus' "on earth as it is in heaven" prayer a practical reality. The gospel is not dependent on human systems, but human systems can be transformed when the people of God rise up as the salt and light of God.

STUDY QUESTIONS

Do you feel like you've received the radical righteousness of Jesus? What would it look like for you to live from the righteousness of Jesus?

For each of the Beatitudes, think of Christians that you know who are doing them well. What are they like? How are they displaying God to the world?

What would it look like for you to pursue transformation in the world from a place of transformation in your heart?

LAWLESS LOVE

CHAPTER FOURTEEN

ONE OF THE MOST challenging things about understanding the New Testament paradigm for living out righteousness and justice is that it is no longer focused on adhering to a rulebook. As we have seen in the Old Testament, justice and righteousness included keeping the Law. The Law of Moses clearly laid out a community's exact obligation for the poor, business laws, and all that other practical stuff, which made it easy to see how God expected His people to live out justice and righteousness. Our own Western views of justice are similarly focused on keeping laws and punishing those who break them. However, when Jesus showed up with the new paradigm, He didn't bring a new rulebook to go with it or a new code of behavior to better express justice and righteousness. Instead, Jesus brought us a fully restored relationship to God, a new nature, complete freedom, and access to the Holy Spirit. He brought us into a totally new kind of life—a life that flows from within and is guided by a transformed heart. So how do we live out justice and righteousness without a rulebook?

ISRAEL'S *PAIDAGOGOS*

To answer this question, we must first understand the original purpose for the Law. Paul uses a helpful illustration to show why God chose the Law as His first paradigm for guiding His people into justice and righteousness: the *paidagogos* (Galatians 3:24-25). This Greek word is usually translated "tutor" or "guardian," but the *paidagogos* was very different from the helpful teacher-type of person that I picture when I hear "tutor." A *paidagogos* was a trusted slave charged by a child's father to watch over the child twenty-four hours a day and to manage his moral development and education.[1] Greek and Roman families used them, and even some wealthy Jewish families adopted the practice. The *paidagogos* had a lot of authority over a boy in his youth, limiting his freedom and keeping him within strict boundaries for a season of his development. In addition to escorting the boy to and from school and making sure he studied, the *paidagogos* was in charge of teaching him manners and putting him on a path toward virtue.[2] He also protected the child from harm in public. Though the *paidagogos* served a good purpose, the popular image was that he was harsh, discipline-focused, and willing to use strong physical punishment to get his charges to obey.[3] One person described the *paidagogos* as a "lover of fault-finding."[4] Whether respected or despised, the *paidagogos* served an important, but always temporary, role in a child's life.[5]

FREEDOM

The *paidagogos* had a goal for his charge: freedom.[6] When the child came of age as a teen, he was freed from the round-the-clock surveillance of his strict *paidagogos* and trusted to control himself. It was a scary time in a father's life, watching to see what his child would do with his freedom for the first time. Fathers hoped that the moral training they had invested in their child made a difference, and that the decisions the child made on his own would be good. If you have ever watched a child with a strict upbringing go to college and experience freedom for the first time, you know that adolescents don't always make the best choices without someone else telling them what to do.

In Galatians 5, Paul recognizes that freedom is the goal, but also a challenge. First, he says that freedom is what Jesus came to bring us: "It was for freedom that Christ set us free" (Galatians 5:1 ESV). Freedom is Christ's goal for us, so we shouldn't go back to living under the Law. But how will we use our newfound freedom? Freedom can easily turn into self-service, so Paul warns the Galatians, "As for you, my friends, you were called to be free. But do not let this freedom become an excuse for letting your physical desires control you. Instead, let love make you serve one another. For the whole Law is summed up in one commandment: 'Love your neighbor as you love yourself'" (Galatians 5:13-14 GNT).

Paul goes on to describe what people are like when they are led by their "physical desires"—what he also calls the "flesh"—versus when they are led by the Spirit. Being led by our flesh produces a lot of things that the Law prohibited, like orgies and worshiping idols (see Galatians 5:19-21). In contrast, the things that the Spirit naturally produces aren't things that you can control through laws: "But the Spirit produces love, joy, peace, patience, kindness, goodness, faithfulness, humility, and self-control. There is no law against such things as these" (Galatians 5:22-23 GNT). Our Christian freedom should be marked with this "fruit" of the Spirit.

The Law, with the central command to love, gave specific rules to control Israel's behavior that could limit some of the damage caused by sin. But its role was temporary. As Paul says, it was "our guardian [*paidagogos*] until Christ came" (Galatians 3:24 ESV). Sin is destructive, and therefore God's people needed something to limit its impact. But it couldn't actually save people from sin or give life (see Galatians 3:19-21).

Now, those in Christ are filled and led by the Spirit of God, living under the "law of liberty" (James 1:25, 2:12), and empowered to manage themselves and produce good behavior from within through their unity with God. In particular, our freedom needs to be managed in community with people. The purpose of our freedom is not to serve ourselves, but to love and serve others. The New Testament writers are constantly working for unity and mutual love in a diverse community where everyone is called to freedom.

The purpose of our freedom is not to serve ourselves, but to love and serve others.

Freedom in Christ calls us to live from our hearts, which forces us to confront our true desires. When offered absolute freedom, what we really want has the chance to come to the surface. With the news that we are no longer ruled by the Law, we can say, "Sweet! No more rules! No one can tell *me* what to do." Some believers respond to freedom like kids going, "Mom and Dad aren't home tonight! I'll have candy for dinner!" This immature response totally misses what freedom from the Law was supposed to bring. There's a reason you shouldn't eat candy for dinner, and there are reasons you shouldn't use your freedom to be a jerk. Both of those lead to an unhealthy, unhappy life.

The Law exposes how hopeless we are without Christ. This sets us up to see the incredible solution Jesus offers us—to trust that Christ has put us right with God by perfectly fulfilling the Law and by liberating us from sin and death on the cross. By putting our faith in Him, we enter into a relationship in which His law becomes written on our hearts (see Hebrews 10:16). His Spirit transforms us, teaching and empowering us to live out the heart of the Law through grace.

THE HEART OF THE LAW

When a group of Pharisees got together to grill Jesus about the Law, they asked Him what He thought the greatest commandment was. He answered:

> "You shall love the Lord your God with all your heart and with all your soul and with all your mind. This is the great and first commandment. And a second is like it: You shall love your neighbor as yourself. On these two commandments depend all the Law and the Prophets." (Matthew 22:37-40 ESV)

Jesus was saying that everything in the Mosaic Law—from the Ten Commandments to the rules for worship and sacrifices (and yes, even the weird stuff we can't relate to)—was all centered around living out love for God, other people, and ourselves. Likewise, the admonitions of all the prophets to call a sinful nation back to the Law were essentially calling them back to love. Remember that message Amos delivered to

Israel? The rich and powerful in the nation were ridiculously corrupted because of sin. They were hurting the poor and vulnerable. God had to specifically tell them to stop sexually abusing their servant girls and selling human lives for something material and cheap. All of that line-by-line instruction could be summed up in this this simple command: "Love your neighbor."

Paul reiterates the same point in Romans, and says that "If you love others, you will never do them wrong; to love, then, is to obey the whole Law" (Romans 13:10 GNT). Paul is emphasizing that there is a Big Law governing all the small laws and *this* is the real Law to which we are obligated. Love is why we are commanded "do not lie," for example. The reason we shouldn't lie isn't that God will be mad at us if we do; it is that lying violates and harms our relationships. Instead of asking, "Can I get away with hiding this little part of the truth and still not break the law?" we say, "I want to always tell the truth in love because it protects my relationships with God and others." When we are governed by the law of love, we aren't trying to see how close we can get to the "line"; we are seeking to love God, and to love people the way God does.

Jesus said this about what He did to the Law: "'Do not think that I have come to do away with the Law of Moses and the teachings of the prophets. I have not come to do away with them, but to make their teachings come true'" (Matthew 5:17 GNT). Jesus fulfilled every rule in God's rulebook perfectly. He not only performed the outward actions of righteousness; He did them with completely pure motives—to simply and totally love God and others unconditionally. Now, He gives us His heart and the grace to live like He does.

If Jesus completed the Law, then when we express the love of Christ, we should be even more effective and sincere in our care of the poor and vulnerable than if we were just trying to keep Old Testament laws. While we don't have books of rules to obey now, we are still obligated to adhere to the same core principle behind the old rules. Love holds you to a higher standard than any laws.

In addition to love, Jesus gave one additional guide for how we treat people without a law: "'Do for others what you want them to do for you: this is the meaning of the Law of Moses and of the teachings of the prophets'" (Matthew 7:12 GNT). As you wrestle through how to treat people, put yourself in someone else's position and consider how your actions affect them. Your decisions have to be guided by searching your heart and asking what you would want done for you. This keeps your heart and mind engaged, relating your actions directly to people instead of an often impersonal law.

NOT A NEEDY PERSON AMONG THEM

A community of believers who learn to walk in freedom and love is a community that will demonstrate a level of justice and righteousness that far exceeds the actions of a community governed by the Mosaic Law. In Deuteronomy, God set the ideal standard in Israel that "there will be no poor among you" (15:4), yet never in the Old Testament did that happen. In the New Testament, however, we do see a community with no needy—the early church:

> There was not a needy person among them, for as many as were owners of lands or houses sold them and brought the proceeds of what was sold and laid it at the apostles' feet, and it was distributed to each as any had need. (Acts 4:34-35 ESV)

Did Jesus set up a law where people had to sell their land so they could help each other? No. All He said was, "'This is my commandment, that you love one another as I have loved you. Greater love has no one than this, that someone lay down his life for his friends'" (John 15:12-13 ESV). By living out the law of love, the early church fulfilled the ideal of the Mosaic Law. Israel could not accomplish this, because the Law alone couldn't make Israel treat each other with compassion and justice. But in the first generation of the church, the first collective group of people to experience the power of salvation, the ideal of "no poor among you" happened. When Jesus deals with sin and transforms us, our natural selfish ambition is replaced with humble service as modeled by Christ. Radical acts of justice and righteousness happen without rules.

Without exact rules telling us to demonstrate compassion, care, and justice, it might seem like we are taking a step back from doing those things that God previously required under the Law. In fact, the New Testament shows how these qualities go to new levels. With Jesus as our justice and righteousness, now it is possible for more justice and righteousness to happen than ever before. This is possible because Christ took care of the effects of sin and made us just and righteous before God. That is our starting place. We can imagine what is possible with God instead of what we are obligated to do under the Law. This love is lawless, and this love is limitless.

With Jesus as our justice and righteousness, now it is possible for more justice and righteousness to happen than ever before.

LOVE COMPLETES JUSTICE

From the Old Testament to the New, the rule of law changes to the rule of love. Justice continues to be expressed through our love and freedom. God's love fully repairs our relationship with Him. And when love is ruling our communities, justice will be done. Remember the definitions of *mishpat*. It's the way life should be—right, life-giving order. Now, the order of our lives and communities are guided by love.

Justice and love are linked. Scholar Nicholas Wolterstorff says it like this: "God desires the flourishing of each and every one of God's human creatures; justice is indispensable to that. Love and justice are not pitted against each other but are intertwined."[7] Both love and justice are needed in order for people to live in the world as God originally designed it. Think of the description of love in 1 Corinthians 13—it is patient, kind, not envious, keeping no records of wrong, rejoicing in the truth, never giving up. What would it look like to live justice in this world *from* that place of love? It doesn't tell you *not* to do justice, but *how* to do it.

WHO IS MY NEIGHBOR?

God is not passive toward injustice, nor should we be. The attitude of love is active against injustice. How do we know this? Let's look at the well-known story of the Good Samaritan.

Jesus tells this parable after an expert in Jewish law asks for more specific instruction about the "love your neighbor as yourself" command. "'Who is my neighbor?'" he asks Jesus (see Luke 10:29). Like a good lawyer, he wants to know the fine print on this simple command to discover the loopholes. If your neighbor is only someone who lives in your town, then you can legally get away with ignoring the rest of the world.

Jesus answers the lawyer's question by telling a story (see Luke 10:25-37). The story goes that a man is attacked by robbers while traveling along the road from Jerusalem to Jericho—a famously dangerous path with lots of places for ambushers to hide. The robbers leave the man beaten, naked, and half-dead along the road. His only hope is for a stranger to find him and help him.

The first person who comes along seems like a lucky break: a priest. But instead of helping, the priest sees the injured man, crosses to the opposite side of the road, and continues on his way. Next, a Levite, whose job was to assist the priest at the temple, comes along. Again, this seems like it would be fortunate. But the Levite does the same thing the priest did.

Finally, a Samaritan comes along. When he sees the beaten man, he immediately feels compassion. His compassion moves him to stop and clean the beaten man's wounds. Then he puts the man on his own donkey and brings him to an inn, where he pays the innkeeper to take care of him and promises to return and pay more. The Samaritan puts himself at risk of being robbed, and gives his time and money to help someone he doesn't know.

In this story, Jesus uses two people who were distinguished members of religious community—a priest and a Levite—as the example of what *not* to do. It's shocking. These two religious men probably both had a good reason for passing the man by. If they had touched the man and he turned out to be dead, for example, they would have been considered unclean. Priests weren't supposed to touch a dead body at all unless it was a close relative (see Leviticus 21:1-3). Or maybe they were afraid that if they stopped, they too would be robbed. Fear and rule-keeping seem legitimate until you consider that a man's life was at risk and withholding help, even if for a good reason, could mean his death.

If it was shocking to make a bad example out of a priest and a Levite, it was even more scandalous for Jesus to choose a Samaritan as the hero of the story. Samaritans lived north of Judea, making them close neighbors. However, they were ethnically and religiously different. In the 8th century BC (after Assyria conquered Israel), the king repopulated the region of Samaria with conquered people from other nations, who then intermarried with some remaining Jews in the land. Jews considered Samaritans a mixed race, second-class, religiously incorrect, quasi-terrorists, and generally detestable. The two groups had a long history of animosity toward each other, and it was still alive and well in Jesus' day.

After the end of the parable, Jesus asks the lawyer which of the men in the story proved to be a neighbor to the man beaten by robbers. The expert says, "'The one who showed him mercy.'" And Jesus says to him, "'You go, and do likewise'" (Luke 10:36-37 ESV). Through His parable, Jesus doesn't give an answer about the limits of who a neighbor could be, but instead puts the focus on our hearts and actions. What will our response be when we see someone in desperate need of a neighbor?

What I love about this example is that you see the continuation of God's active attitude toward injustice. Too often when we ask about why there is so much heartbreaking suffering, the "Christian answer" we get is a complex one that involves philosophical arguments about people using their "free will" to do destructive things. And how God has to allow free will in order to allow people to love Him. I feel frustrated with how this point is used in the face of injustice because it doesn't paint an accurate picture of the loving God I know. He's not distant, crossing His arms on His throne and making intellectual arguments about why injustice is given a pass by Him. Yes, free will causes sin in the world and that sin brings pain. But merely pointing that out isn't helpful.

It's like a parent hearing their child screaming, running out to find the child lying on the ground with blood gushing out of a gash on their forehead, and then sitting down next to their precious child to explain why such a thing was allowed to happen. "Well sweetie, there is this thing called gravity…" Is that what a parent does in response to their child's suffering? No, they don't explain the mechanics of why they are in pain. A child would never be satisfied by an explanation like that, even if it were logically correct, because the pain would still be real. There's a time and place to explain the mechanics of physics—usually in a classroom with a textbook and not at the side of a traumatized child. Why, then, is that how we Christians respond to a hurting world asking why so much pain and injustice is possible? Giving them a logically correct answer can never show the full picture of our heavenly Father, who is deeply grieved at the pain His children experience, and who wants to see healing and restoration.

I think many of us Christians have been trained to be passive toward injustice, because we have been trained to respond to suffering with intellectual reasoning. And when we find that reason, that is enough for us to explain away our own role in bringing change. It's like we say that because we aren't actively causing injustice, therefore injustice is not *our* problem. And that's what we show to the world—a bunch of people washing their hands clean of doing justice because "injustice is not *our* fault." Instead, the Christian answer to suffering should be partnered with actions that demonstrate God's passion for restoration and healing.

The Christian answer to suffering should be partnered with actions that demonstrate God's passion for restoration and healing.

This story of the Good Samaritan shows a very different response to seeing a hurt and dying person on the side of the road. The response of love is based on actions, not the right arguments. The priest and Levite had legitimate reasons not to help, and it wasn't *their fault* he was hurting. This means neither guilt nor obligation moved the Samaritan to respond to the injustice. He was motivated by something else entirely: compassion. Because of compassion, the Samaritan spent himself on behalf of someone he didn't know to fix a problem that wasn't his fault.

Compassion is an essential part of Jesus' and God's relationship with us. In the Old Testament God is described as compassionate, while in the Gospels, Jesus is continually moved by compassion for people to perform some of His most dramatic miracles (see Matthew 14:14, 20:34; Mark 1:41, 6:34, 8:2; Luke 7:13). Compassion towards others is essential in reflecting God's love to the world.

If we are asking what our exact duty toward justice is, we are acting like that expert in the Law: "God, give us a list of dos and don'ts. We want to maximize our comfort and minimize our guilty emotions, and we need laws in order to do that. Give us rules instead of love."

This way of thinking leads us to limit our love rather than to explore what a limitless, lawless love could possibly do. Is that the way we really want to live? God, in His extravagant mercy and justice, stopped at nothing to make our relationship right again—a relationship that was broken by our fault, not His. We who have received His love and compassion for ourselves should get excited when we have an opportunity to show mercy to someone beat up by an injustice in the world. For us, seeing injustice is a practical opportunity to demonstrate love.

By the way, we are not only called to be neighbors to the poor. We should be able to line up everybody, from the most famous celebrity, to the most average and mundane, to the poorest and most vulnerable, and love them all. We all reflect the image of God, and how we treat each other should reflect that.

LOVE INTENSIFIES THE CALL OF JUSTICE

Now that we are governed by love instead of laws, some Christians seem confused about why we should do justice. Is it because we have to do it to go to heaven? Of course not. Salvation is dependent on Jesus. A much better question to ask is, now that Jesus is our justice and righteousness, and we have a whole lifetime to build off of that, where will we go from here?

Our actions matter because they can display God's love to the world. While works of the Law don't save us (see Romans 3:28, Galatians 2:16), action-less faith is dead (James 2:17). When we truly trust in Jesus, that trust will manifest in our actions. Good works don't save us; good works are the fruit of faith. When we put our faith in Jesus, good works must flow from our lives. Good works breathe life into our faith, giving it a shape and form for the world to see.

Love only intensifies our passion for justice. When God's love sets us free from guilt, shame, and selfishness and restores our value, we naturally want the same for everyone else. How in the world could we ever hurt or take advantage of someone else? People aren't just a resource to exploit to make more money. That would be ridiculous in light of their true, infinite value. In fact, we care about those who can do nothing for us *because* of their value. We rush to help others when they are hurt, no matter whose fault the pain is. Our love becomes justice in action. Having a lawless love frees us up to live out justice in ways outside of a courthouse. A lawless love has the potential for limitless justice.

If we use the fact that we are now governed by love as an excuse to disengage from other people, then we should probably question whether or not we have God's love. Love doesn't disengage. Love doesn't look for excuses. Love doesn't think about itself before others. Love doesn't keep a record of what you can possibly do to not give love anymore. Instead of spending energy memorizing rules, we can let compassion rule our hearts and let our minds engage with the reality of others' lives.

A lawless love is not a selfish love. It's not unconcerned about justice because it's moved on to fluffy sentimentalism. It may seem severe to insist that now we actually *have* to have compassion and to consider the unique circumstances of others who we are not legally obliged to help. But since when is the path of following Christ easy? It's a call to come and die so that you can find true life. I heard a pastor once say, "If you've given your whole life to God, and He's asking you to give your jacket away to someone who needs it, then what's the big deal?" We shouldn't need laws to tell us what our exact obligation is if our hearts and minds are connected to God's immense love for every individual. A reconciled relationship between people and God is the key to all reconciled relationships in the world.

Now that Jesus is our justice and righteousness, we can focus on expressing a love that is only possible with God. A lawless love may not give us what most Westerners think we need in order to do justice—a rulebook and guidelines for punishment when the rules are broken. But by the grace of God, we are given redemption in Christ and a new life full of freedom. Our best form of justice as Christians isn't pointing out and condemning everything the world is doing wrong. Instead, it's actively doing right, restoring what's broken, and living a love not limited by laws.

LAWLESS LOVE

STUDY QUESTIONS

Now that Jesus is your justice and righteousness, what would you want your life to display?

What would it look like for you to live a life filled with freedom, and marked with service and righteousness?

What do you think living a lawless love in relationship to the poor and vulnerable in the world looks like now? How do you think it should look responding to injustice?

JUSTICE & RIGHTEOUSNESS IN EVERYDAY KINGDOM LIFE

CHAPTER FIFTEEN

I THINK PART OF why the church has been held back from living out justice and righteousness is because we try to apply them to the limits of our religious lives. Where does justice fit into a place like a church building? Are we just supposed to bring the poor to Sunday services? Or give sermons about justice every once in a while? Most of life doesn't happen inside a temple or church. If righteousness is going to mold history, then it has to be let out of church buildings. God's justice and righteousness will happen the most outside of the church's walls.

While most of us in America talk a lot about church or religion, Jesus constantly talked about the kingdom of God. In fact, Jesus only says the word "church" three times (see Matthew 16:18, 18:17). He also says that His kingdom and His righteousness [*dikaiosune*] should be our first pursuit, not church (see Matthew 6:33). Entering the kingdom is different than joining a religion or a church. A religion may define how you spend your Sundays or the types of music you listen to. You will probably spend something like 5% of your life inside a church building, but 100% of your life should be shaped by the reign of Jesus.

This should feel empowering. For one, it means that even if your church isn't on-board with justice stuff, then you still have your whole life in which to live it out. It also means that justice is something we should be living out in every aspect of our lives, not just in church.

We don't have time to explore all the basic principles for practically displaying the kingdom of God in our lives, but I want to give you a brief overview of how the New Testament teaches the concept of living out justice and righteousness within our social and economic lives. Today's culture often divides the practical from the spiritual—yet the Bible always gives *both* practical life teachings and spiritual principles all at the same time. And the Bible holistically approaches issues, such as justice in marriage, families, and relationships as well as justice in money, work, or business within the same conversation. Let's take a look at what it means to view these aspects of our life from a kingdom perspective.

PROBLEM OF THE SOCIAL TRANSLATION

Some of the revolutionary social parts of Jesus' life and teachings are missed because we are so far removed from the His cultural context. The more you study Jesus' life in the context of His time, the more it becomes clear what a revolutionary He was, particularly when it came to the people with whom He chose to socialize. Remember that metaphor of the bruised reeds and smoldering wicks (see Isaiah 42:3, Matthew 12:20)? Jesus' justice saves those who have lost their value and use in the world's eyes, so it makes sense that we constantly see Him with these people during His ministry.

Jesus had nothing to do with the sexist and racist attitudes normal for His culture. We see Jesus touching lepers, staying with Samaritans, welcoming children into His arms, eating at the house of tax collectors, and inviting women to sit at His feet and learn. To us, this may not seem that exciting, but in His time, these acts were revolutionary. Lepers weren't allowed to be touched because it made you unclean according to the law, yet Jesus touches them to heal them (see Matthew 8:3, Mark 1:41). He broke a man-made religious tradition to heal on the Sabbath, demonstrating the value of human life (see Luke 14:1-6). He commanded that hospitality be shown to the outcasts and the destitute by throwing them dinner parties (see Luke 14:12-14). These are just a

JUSTICE & RIGHTEOUSNESS IN EVERYDAY KINGDOM LIFE

few examples, and as you read the Gospels for yourself, you should look for how often He crosses man-made labels and barriers.

His attitude toward women is particularly revolutionary for His time. They are named as His followers (see Luke 8:1-3), affirmed as part of His family (see Mark 3:35, Luke 8:19-21), and offered as models for faith that men and women should follow (see Matthew 12:42, 13:33, 25:1-13; Mark 12:41-44; Luke 13:20-21, 15:8-10, 18:1-8). Jesus told Martha to set aside her feelings of obligation to take care of domestic duties, and instead sit and learn at His feet along with her sister Mary (Luke 10:38-42). At the time, women weren't allowed to be taught, yet Jesus makes the statement that women should be taught—and taught *religious* subjects, too. He talked to an adulterous Samaritan woman alone at a well on one of His travels (see John 4:4-26). This was scandalous—a Jewish man of His day wouldn't talk to a woman at all in public. Jesus listened to her questions and responded, which was also scandalous, since men wouldn't talk about theological subjects with women, let alone a Jew talk with a Samaritan.[1] Jewish literature of the day said that if a man talked too much to a woman, even his own wife might go to hell: "A man who talks too much with a woman brings trouble on himself, neglects the study of Torah and in his end will inherit Gehinnom (hell)" (m.Pirkei Avot 1:5).[2] Knowing this, consider the significance of this fact: Jesus' *longest* recorded conversation with anyone in the Gospels is with this Samaritan woman. With this one single encounter, Jesus broke all the normal religious, ethnic, gender, and social boundaries. From the beginning, with the uncompromising faith of His mother Mary, to the end, with women serving as the first witnesses and proclaimers of His resurrection (Matthew 28:1-9, John 20:1-2), women have an important, public place in Jesus' story.

Our Savior was a revolutionary. Jesus attracted everyone across races, nationality, gender, age, social, and religious backgrounds. Even those participating in injustice receive an opportunity for healing and redemption from Jesus. We who claim to follow Him must seek to imitate His example. These radical kingdom values—often opposite of how the normal social world teaches us to think—should be an integral expression of how we live the kingdom of God in our everyday life. We should be touching the untouchable, inviting the outcasts to dinner, valuing and including the poor, and eating at the houses of the tax collectors in our world—not in the name of "social justice," but because we hold God's perspective on all people.

MARRIAGE AND FAMILY

When God first created humans, they weren't organized into a nation complete with a government and economic system; they were organized into a family. The founders of the human race were a father and a mother, Adam and Eve. Since that first marriage, that family has grown much bigger and now needs things like governments to organize it. But we should remember that every institution and system has come from a family.

When God first created humans, they weren't organized into a nation complete with a government and economic system; they were organized into a family.

Jesus' teachings on marriage, family, and divorce were also as radical in His day as they are in ours. Let's look at the answer Jesus gives to the religious leaders' questions about divorce:

> And Pharisees came up and in order to test him asked, "Is it lawful for a man to divorce his wife?" He answered them, "What did Moses command you?" They said, "Moses allowed a man to write a certificate of divorce and to send her away." And Jesus said to them, "Because of your hardness of heart he wrote you this commandment." (Mark 10:2-5 ESV)

A little context here would be helpful. The fact that the religious leaders even ask Jesus about divorce suggests that it was a big issue at the time. Different rabbinical schools argued over how to interpret the Mosaic Law about divorce (see Deuteronomy 24:1). One side said that the Law allowed for divorce only in the case of adultery, while the other said that a man could divorce his wife if she did anything that displeased him,

JUSTICE & RIGHTEOUSNESS IN EVERYDAY KINGDOM LIFE

such as cooking a meal that he didn't like.[3]

When Jesus addressed this, He began by stating the reason Moses had to write a divorce law in the first place: hardened human hearts. People rebelled against God, and the Law was set up to limit the impact of human sinfulness. The Law wasn't encouraging divorce; it was a concession to protect someone who could potentially be put in a vulnerable position because of sin. If a man divorced his wife and didn't give her a certificate, she wouldn't be allowed to remarry. That could put a woman at that time in a destitute position. A divorce certificate gave her a way to rebuild her life.

Then Jesus drew the attention back to the bigger picture: God's original design for marriage:

> "But from the beginning of creation, 'God made them male and female.' 'Therefore a man shall leave his father and mother and hold fast to his wife and the two shall become one flesh.' So they are no longer two but one flesh. What therefore God has joined together, let not man separate." (Mark 10:6-9 ESV)

Jesus draws our vision back to God's intent for human partnerships. God made man, then woman from the man's rib, each carrying God's divine image. In the same way you can't separate God, you can't separate a marital union. From that first union, all of human society came.

Of course, the Bible shows us that humans have always had a lousy success rate at living out the "biblical definition of marriage." The Old Testament starts out with a good marriage—even Noah and his sons each had one wife. However, there are plenty of examples of terrible forms of marriages or laws that allowed for weird rules about marriage. Women could be treated as property. Polygamy, a highly problematic and unjust form of marriage, is common in the Old Testament. That one-flesh-covenant marriage ideal was rarely followed in Old Testament history—and the negative consequences of this are plainly seen in the Bible.

What's powerful about Jesus' teaching here is that He goes back to the very beginning, before human sin—even the kind committed by God's chosen people—got in the way. He didn't affirm King David's multiple marriages or even the different forms that the Mosaic Law allowed. He affirms the first, the one that was in line with God's original intent and design. And the rest of the New Testament teachings are in line with marriage as a monogamous, life-long covenant (see Matthew 19:1-12, 1 Corinthians 7, 1 Timothy 3:2, Ephesians 5:22-33, 1 Peter 3:1-7, Colossians 3:18-19). The Old Testament issue of marriage is messy to wrestle through, but what we do know is that in the kingdom of God, monogamy is the one and only form of marriage allowed, because it reflects God's *shalom*-loving design.

Sometimes the family gets lost in justice work. Unfortunately, many great social reformers and Christian leaders were terrible spouses and parents. But when you really think about how central the family is to God's original design for society, it makes sense that we connect family with doing justice and righteousness—fulfilling the demands of personal relationships within God's intention for relationships. Think of how many big, terrible justice issues are tied to broken families. Families are taken for granted when they are functional, but huge brokenness is created when they fail. Family responsibilities are some of the easiest to overlook, but they are essential to the level of order, health, and justice in the world.

Family responsibilities are some of the easiest to overlook, but they are essential to the level of order, health, and justice in the world.

If you are in the stage of life where you are giving a majority of your energy to raising a family, then you are a powerful, active example of living justice and righteousness every day (not to mention gaining important leadership skills). If the government or a non-profit had to pay to provide all of the services that you freely give, they would need tens of thousands of dollars. Parents usually get sleepless nights and blog articles about how they are doing everything wrong. Parenting is not a career that gets a lot of praise for being "social justice-y." But really, if you are married with children, the most "social justice-y" role you can have is to be an actively engaged parent and/or spouse. A healthy marriage has a social impact—it contributes to the stability and well being of an entire community. Do you want to bring peace and justice into the world? Love your spouse and children and let them experience family the way God intended. Likewise, singles, love and engage in your natural and spiritual family relationships because that has the same peace and stability-bringing impact.

YOUR TREASURES

If you look for economic justice between the Old and New Testament, it can be confusing. You don't see Jesus advocate for worker's rights or speak out against the crushing Roman taxes. This silence might make it seem like God doesn't care as much about that part of our lives in the New Testament. But remember that the contexts in the Old and New Testament are different. In the Old, God addresses government leaders and business people and sets up an economic system that values the poor. In the New, He doesn't tell a government how to rule.

What is consistent between the Old and New Testament is the way the Bible talks about money. Jesus, in particular, talks about money *a lot*. In fact, fifteen percent of His words recorded in the Gospels are about money. He talks more about money than He talks about sex, heaven, and hell.[4] This is consistent with the rest of Scripture—there are twice as many verses about money as there are about prayer and faith *combined*. Clearly, money is an important topic to God, whether it's how the nation of Israel uses their money or how followers of Jesus steward their resources.

If we are going to live lives that impact eternity and bring heaven to earth, we have to hold our temporary resources in a way that honors our heavenly calling, rather than takes our eyes off of it.

Why would Jesus talk about money so much if He came to bring a new kingdom and eternal life? I think it's pretty simple. If we are going to live lives that impact eternity and bring heaven to earth, we have to hold our temporary resources in a way that honors our heavenly calling, rather than takes our eyes off of it. The gospel is practically reflected in how we steward our own resources.

The best summary of Jesus' teachings on money, in my opinion, is found in the Sermon on the Mount. He says:

> "Do not store up riches for yourselves here on earth, where moths and rust destroy, and robbers break in and steal. Instead, store up riches for yourselves in heaven, where moths and rust cannot destroy, and robbers cannot break in and steal. For your heart will always be where your riches are." (Matthew 6:19-21 GNT)

Again, we see that Jesus is primarily concerned about our hearts. It's not that riches are bad. If our hearts are centered on heaven, we will be concerned about storing up eternal riches there. If they are centered on earth, the riches we accumulate are temporary and easily lost.

Jesus goes on to say: "You cannot be a slave of two masters; you will hate one and love the other; you will be loyal to one and despise the other. You cannot serve both God and money" (Matthew 6:24 GNT). Money is easy to worship and make your master. However, God wants to be the only object of your desire. When you make Him so, your whole life will be ordered around Him. If you put something material in that place or try to put both God and money in that place, you will live a divided life.[5] Also, when you make money your master, you are ordering your life around something that's going to rot away someday versus that which is going to last forever. It should be obvious which is more valuable. Money by itself isn't bad, but its value cannot compare to God and the eternal blessings He brings into our lives when we make Him our only Master and desire. God always works for our benefit, so if He's asking us to follow Him and not money, it's in order to lead us to an abundant life full of peace, joy, and righteousness. He always promises to take care of our material needs (see Matthew 6:31-34).

The Bible doesn't only teach right from wrong, but also how to order the good and right things in your life. Many may read this and think they aren't serving money because they don't want a huge house or a

JUSTICE & RIGHTEOUSNESS IN EVERYDAY KINGDOM LIFE

BMW. But just because you don't want extravagant luxury doesn't mean money isn't your master. Are you anxious about your needs? If your life is guided by the fear of going broke, it will stop you from following God. That's a huge sign that money is your master. Your 401k, bank account, or salary shouldn't guide your life. They are part of your life. While they're not bad things, they should not be what primarily guides you. You don't need lots of money in order to make it your master. You can be poor and serve money or be wealthy and serve God.

Jesus concludes His teaching on money in the Sermon on the Mount with the famous verse: "But seek first the kingdom of God and his righteousness [*dikaiosune*], and all these things will be added to you" (Matthew 6:33 ESV). He is not saying that our material needs aren't important; He is saying that we are not to put them first in our lives. It's all about the right order. When we make the kingdom of God our aim, we can be confident that our material needs will be met by our loving Father.

Stewarding money and resources to impact eternity is powerful—whatever the volume of resources that flow through your life. For some, stewardship may look like developing a successful business that provides jobs and uses its profits to improve the standard of life in a community. For others, it may look like opening your home to abandoned children or forgoing a job opportunity with a large salary in order to pursue the call of God to serve in another area. Whenever you take what is temporary and point its impact toward eternity, you will gain treasure that will never rust or rot. The simple, biblically-centered calling for each of us isn't to be rich or poor but to be generous managers of all the resources God has given us, allowing God to be our one true desire.[6] No matter our income level, whether we are like the widow with two mites (see Mark 12:42) or are wealthy and influential (see Matthew 19:16-22, Acts 10:1-6), we must be generous with what we have. It's only temporary and doesn't belong to us anyway.

Moving from the Old Testament laws about money for the nation of Israel to the New Testament view of money in the kingdom of God makes economic justice personal and applicable for everyone. The place where economic justice starts is your own heart, over which you have full ownership. Though you may not be stealing a widow's cloak or withholding pay from a worker harvesting your field, the question is still: how do you hold material objects in your heart? You were made for eternity. Making money your aim in life or hurting any of God's precious children in order to get it is contrary to your design.

Between the Old and the New Testament, God is consistent with how He talks about money. Hard work is emphasized, greed is condemned, practical help is always given to the vulnerable, living a generous lifestyle is praised, trusting God to meet your needs is always necessary, and using your financial power to oppress the weak is never okay. Whether it's an Old Testament king enslaving his own people to build a fancy palace (see Jeremiah 22:13-14) or the rich in a church not paying their workers (see James 5:1-5), God condemns it. The Bible equally condemns the New Testament false prophet who manipulated people for money (see 2 Peter 2:3) and used the appearance of being godly to gain wealth (see 1 Timothy 6:5) and the religious leaders in Amos' day that manipulated the vulnerable and used their position for their selfish benefit.

When the world looks at Christians, they may not see us all having the exact same opinions about politics or economics, but what they should see are generous people who take care of our communities and have nothing to do with greed. Money is a powerful tool to serve people, yet we have a bad habit of using people to serve money. What a powerful display we could give the world if all Christians everywhere only used their money to serve God and people. This is where we as the church can find our unity. Choosing to work hard, managing all our resources toward growth, and being generous with what we have can change lives—including our own. We all have to use money in order to function in the modern world, so it is such a practical way to express justice and righteousness every day. If we want heaven to come to earth, then we need to express heavenly values in what we do with our possessions and resources.

In order to live with eternity in mind, we have to have the right mindset about what's temporary, especially money. Wealth seems to be the compass so many people use to guide their lives. The gospel should transform our attitude toward work and money, especially as it draws our focus to eternity and the eternal value of all people. Instead of being our compass, money becomes just one more tool by which we bring *shalom* in the world and enable people to thrive.

JUSTICE & RIGHTEOUSNESS IN EVERYDAY KINGDOM LIFE

ONE BODY, ONE FAMILY

There is so much in the Old Testament about relationships between the rich and poor. In the kingdom of God, God gives us a new metaphor for understanding our relationships: a human body. As Paul says to the Ephesians, Jesus has made "one new man" out of Jews and Gentiles (see Ephesians 2:15). In 1 Corinthians 12, he dives further into what it means that everyone who calls Jesus their Savior is fully connected and integrated as one:

> Christ is like a single body, which has many parts; it is still one body, even though it is made up of different parts. In the same way, all of us, whether Jews or Gentiles, whether slaves or free, have been baptized into the one body by the same Spirit, and we have all been given the one Spirit to drink. (1 Corinthians 12:12-13 GNT)

Those things that typically separate people—national or ethnic backgrounds, gender, economic status, etc.—should no longer separate us now that we are joined as one entity. In most societies, people naturally gravitate toward people who are like them. Having real, authentic relationships across boundaries is hard when there's barely a chance to interact in daily life. But Christ gives the opportunity for the most diverse people on the planet to unite in a powerful and intimate way. I love the moments in church when I look around and see people from such different experiences and backgrounds than mine, and I know that we get to experience a unity that goes beyond any earthly labels.

The passage in 1 Corinthians goes on to say:

> And so there is no division in the body, but all its different parts have the same concern for one another. If one part of the body suffers, all the other parts suffer with it; if one part is praised, all the other parts share its happiness. (1 Corinthians 12:25-26 GNT)

This is a great place to start thinking about how we should be living out our love and concern for the poor. Those who are materially poor are powerful and essential members of Christ's body, *just as much as* the materially rich. They are not merely consumers in the body; they are contributors. Their talents and unique callings are a part of making the body of Christ on earth what it is.

The richest and poorest Christians in the world are connected through Christ. When the poor in our own neighborhoods or across the planet are hurting or suffering, all of us should feel it. We often act like helping the poor is doing *them* a favor, that it is a one-way relationship and *they* get all the benefit. But I think if we really understood everything the world is missing out on because poverty and injustice have stolen the contributions of so many people then we would do everything possible to help, because it's for our own and our family's benefit. There isn't an *us* and *them*. We are one body, and we want all parts fed and healthy. Meeting material needs is essential because it feeds the body that's expanding the kingdom. Poverty is against God's design for the world, and it takes away strength from the world. The most prosperous, peaceful, stable world is one where everyone has the ability to have the strength and power inside of them expressed.

The New Testament talks about the material needs of the poor. Acts 6:1-4, 1 Timothy 5, and James 1:29 all describe different parts of the early church offering practical help to widows, who were one of the poorest and most vulnerable groups in their day. This gives us a great peek into how the early church coordinated help for the poor. Guess what? It wasn't always an easy process. The two times the New Testament talks in detail about projects to help feed widows, it addresses the challenges the programs were facing. The early church, known for dramatic miracles and rapid conversions, also had logistical troubles.

Paul gave specific instructions to Timothy about how to manage the care that Timothy's church was giving to widows, implying that there were some who were abusing the church's charity (1 Timothy 5:2-16).[7] He came up with a better list of criteria for which widows should receive help from the church, and which ones should get help from their families. Even though their system had problems, that didn't mean they should stop trying. Instead of telling Timothy to stop the program or condemn the widows, Paul came up with a solution for

JUSTICE & RIGHTEOUSNESS IN EVERYDAY KINGDOM LIFE

how to handle the challenges.

In the earliest days of the church, a dispute came up when the Greek-speaking Jews felt that the Hebrew-speaking Jews were overlooking their (Greek) widows when distributing food to those in need (see Acts 6:1-7). The apostles came up with a solution: they had everyone choose seven men who were known to be full of the Holy Spirit and wisdom and put them in charge (Acts 6:2-4). Stephen, the first martyr, was among this group. Instead of the apostles dropping what God had called them to do in order to manage the food distribution, they set up a better system, and everyone was happy with the solution.

Anyone who has worked in a program with the vulnerable has probably experienced similar challenges—people abusing the charity and arguments about how to run a project. However, even though there are problems, this doesn't mean that the practical help should stop. Logistics are fixable. It's tempting to blame failures on those you are trying to serve, but the Bible shows us that we should recognize *any* failures as part of the learning process and keep moving forward.

If you are having a hard time tailoring your projects to best help those in need, know that you are in good company. Even the early church, while seeing dramatic miracles and salvations, had their own set of practical challenges in coordinating aid for the needy. Get some advice and continue to fine-tune your project.

MATERIAL NEEDS MATTER

In the Sermon on the Mount, Jesus gives guidance about giving to the poor as an expression of "practicing your righteousness [*dikaiosune*], (Matthew 6:1 ESV). He teaches that you should give in secret so that you don't draw attention to yourself (see Matthew 6:1-4). The teaching isn't *if* you should give to the poor, but *how* to when you do. Meeting the material needs of the poor is a vital part of a righteous lifestyle.

Jesus met people's material needs all the time. He fed them and healed their physical bodies. While it may not seem like the most glamorous subject, think about the effects when material needs are not met. When people don't have shelter, clothes, or food, they can't survive. God hears the cries of the poor and oppressed, even in the New Testament. When James rebukes some wealthy members in the early church who refused to pay their employees, he says that the cries of their workers reached God's ear (see James 5:4). That same image of God's ear hearing the cries of victims is in the Mosaic Law (see Deuteronomy 24:15). Imagine hearing every cry of a mother pleading for the food her children need to live or the cry of every person experiencing the injustice from another.

In the New Testament, caring about the needs of fellow brothers and sisters was an essential part of expressing love. 1 John 3:16-17 says, "This is how we know what love is: Christ gave his life for us. We too, then, ought to give our lives for others! If we are rich and see others in need, yet close our hearts against them, how can we claim that we love God?" (GNT; see also James 2:15-16 and Romans 12:13). Say what you want, but shallow words of comfort do nothing to meet a very real need for food and clothes. Practical demonstrations of love look like giving resources when needed. Hebrews 13:16 calls this kind of sacrificial giving to meet needs "the sacrifices that please God" (GNT), which should sound familiar after seeing how God tied religious practices to doing justice and righteousness in Israel. All the material stuff—money, food, clothes—will eventually pass away, but love is eternal (see 1 Corinthians 13:13). Taking something that is temporary and using it to express love will make an impact into eternity.

It matters to God that people are hurting for lack of basic material needs. He created us as physical beings in a physical world, and we have real physical needs—ones our heavenly Father recognizes. It's a spiritual activity to meet these needs, to build businesses to employ people, to "break the fangs of the unrighteous" (Job 29:17), and to strengthen the weak and needy in our own body of Christ. We should stop asking God why He's not doing something about all the people suffering because their basic needs aren't getting met, and start asking ourselves why *we* are not taking action, especially when He's already said and proven His care in His Word.

We should all continually ask ourselves: "Am I responding toward my brother's and sister's practical needs?" Are we honoring those in need in our own church families—the single-parent families, military veterans with lingering injuries from war, the elderly, victims of trauma and abuse, foster children, and more? Do they receive practical support, healing, and strength from their connection to the body of Christ? This will look different for each of us, but we should all to be united in being alert to the needs of our brothers and sisters. People of every income level can participate; it's not just a one-way relationship from the powerful to the vulnerable. Everyone has strength and resources to bring to the body.

FIGHTING THE REAL ENEMY

We Christians aren't just put into families and told to have comfortable lives. We are given fighting instructions. In Ephesians 6, Christians are commanded to put on the "full armor of God," a military symbol—not for the purpose of fighting other people or nations, but to *stand firm* against the "schemes of the devil." Ephesians 6:12 reminds us that we aren't battling flesh and blood, but "spiritual forces of wickedness in heavenly places." Yes, we are commanded to fight. But the fight is so much different than gathering warhorses and chariots to attack a physical enemy.

In Ephesians 6:14-17, we are given a list of the armor and weapons of this kingdom:

- Truth (belt)
- Righteousness (breastplate)
- Faith (shield)
- Salvation (helmet)
- The Word of God (sword)

Instead of having the biggest guns or the most sophisticated body armor, the military garb to put on in this kingdom is truth, salvation, righteousness, and the word of God. Jesus has already won, and the time to bring about God's purposes through military war has ended. No amount of violence can fix the effect of sin on a human soul. With a physical war, you can't win what is most important to God—human hearts.

When Paul describes all the obstacles he was facing to spread the gospel, he mentions one weapon he used: "We have righteousness [*di-*

kaiosune] as our weapon, both to attack and to defend ourselves" (2 Corinthians 6:7b GNT). If you want to be aggressive in expanding the kingdom of God and resisting the enemy, use your righteousness.

Recognizing the true source of injustice—spiritual slavery to sin and the enemy—should change the way we see those who are doing all the terrible injustices in the world. Too often, when we witness injustice, we want to destroy the person or people committing it. But now we know Jesus' death means that the perpetrators of injustice have the opportunity for redemption, too. This also changes how we fight injustice. Our job isn't to judge another person or to discern their hearts and decide their fate.[8] Since we are not sitting in the judge's seat, it frees us up to pursue healing reconciliation with all people, even the ones who do sinful stuff in the world. What if we saw that gang members, corrupt politicians, pimps, cheaters, and tyrants aren't really the ones we are fighting? Those people were hand-knitted by God in their mother's womb just as much as we were, and they are just as valuable to Him. They are in bondage to sin, and God's desire is for them to have the same spiritual freedom He has given to us. We can address the forces of darkness in their life while believing that God created them for a better purpose.

We can see examples of this in Jesus' and Paul's lives. Jesus sparked controversy by befriending tax collectors, who were far from popular in His day. Instead of collecting taxes from their conquered nations themselves, Romans hired locals who were familiar with the people to do the job for them. Tax collectors notoriously raised the taxes so that they could skim off a cut for themselves. That being the case, there was a lot of greed and corruption in the system. Not only were they helping the oppressive Roman government; they were also taking advantage of their own people. To the Jews, this was especially terrible because they thought the Roman oppression already made them victims—the fact that their own brothers were participating in the oppression seemed like the worst treachery.[9]

But Jesus didn't distance Himself from those who were active in this terribly unjust system. He saw them as real people and even invited one of them, Matthew, to be a disciple. Jesus didn't stand far away, yelling at them or talking about what terrible things they were doing.

JUSTICE & RIGHTEOUSNESS IN EVERYDAY KINGDOM LIFE

Participating in injustice is contrary to our design, so Jesus called those doing injustice to come close to Him and discover they were made for more than the way they were living. Those who did so, of course, naturally changed. When Jesus invited Himself to the house of the chief tax collector, Zacchaeus, the man's response was to tell Jesus that he was going to give half of his belongings to the poor and pay back four times what he had stolen to everyone he had cheated (see Luke 19:8). Jesus didn't tell him to do any of that; He simply invited Himself to dinner. But when Jesus comes into your house, conviction about what doesn't belong there will make you want to make it right.

In Ephesians, Paul powerfully addresses a way to respond to criminals when they come into Christian community:

> Those who used to rob must stop robbing and start working, in order to earn an honest living for themselves and to be able to help the poor. (Ephesians 4:28 GNT)

Paul sees that the thief doesn't need to banished from a community. He needs to stop stealing and become what God intended him to be—a hardworking, contributing member of a community. Rather than demonizing the thief, we are to call him to his true purpose. Our prayers shouldn't be for destruction but for transformation. We are to see the person involved in injustice as God's precious child, and the spiritual forces of darkness as the enemy needing to be taken out. Paul himself was a terrorist and a murderer, and restoration to God meant restoration to the community he had at one point victimized. Nations do need to worry about things like laws and punishment. But as Christians, we have more options. The justice we get to live in the world looks like restoration and redemption. Making sure people are properly punished for their sins isn't what our justice looks like. Even when punishment is needed because we submit to the authority of national government, restoration and relationship is our goal.

The justice we get to live in the world looks like restoration and redemption.

The freedom Jesus brought and the way He brought it should open up new opportunities to bring solutions to injustices in the world around us. In America today, we like to try to solve most problems with money or laws. Unfortunately, this can make us feel disempowered or apathetic. If the problem is with the government, and we don't think we can directly change it, then we can feel like it's not our job to do anything. Limiting our solutions to the law and politics can make us judgmental, too. Instead of connecting with people caught up in an injustice and participating in a solution, we sit back and think that having the "right" political opinion is the answer.

LIVING LIVES FULL OF JUSTICE & RIGHTEOUSNESS

Living with a Christ-centered mentality in everything we do means that all parts of our lives reflect justice and righteousness. We can't compartmentalize our public work from our private lives. What matters is how we love our own families, steward our money, connect to the vulnerable, and respond to those committing injustice. Justice and righteousness belong in all parts of the world, which means they belong in all parts of your world.

JUSTICE & RIGHTEOUSNESS IN EVERYDAY KINGDOM LIFE

STUDY QUESTIONS

How can you keep your family a priority in the midst of doing justice and righteousness in the world?

How do you hold money in your heart? Does it have a greater say on the direction of your life or your emotional state than God?

What do you think it would be like for Christians to pursue transformation for people who are currently the "bad guys" of the world—the tax collectors, criminals, gang members, etc.?

CONCLUSION: GOD OF HOPE

CHAPTER SIXTEEN

HAVE YOU EVER BEEN completely overwhelmed when looking at an issue of injustice—especially one that feels huge and totally out of your control? You want to just let your heart break over it, but there's so much going on and it feels enormous and unsolvable. That doesn't seem like the ideal circumstance in which to feel hope.

But our God is a God of justice, love, and compassion—and all of that is joined with the most hopeful perspective on injustice. It's so important that we as Christians reflect the hope our God has, especially when we look in the face of seemingly hopeless situations.

To understand the hope God calls us to carry, we are going to look at a situation in the Old Testament, in which the prophet Ezekiel confronted the nation of Israel over their massive, huge complicated layers of injustice:

> Again a message came to me from the Lord: "Son of man, give the people of Israel this message: In the day of my indignation, you will be like a polluted land, a land without rain. Your princes plot conspiracies

just as lions stalk their prey. They devour innocent people, seizing treasures and extorting wealth. They make many widows in the land. Your priests have violated my instructions and defiled my holy things. They make no distinction between what is holy and what is not. And they do not teach my people the difference between what is ceremonially clean and unclean. They disregard my Sabbath days so that I am dishonored among them. Your leaders are like wolves who tear apart their victims. They actually destroy people's lives for money! And your prophets cover up for them by announcing false visions and making lying predictions. They say, 'My message is from the Sovereign Lord', when the Lord hasn't spoken a single word to them. Even common people oppress the poor, rob the needy, and deprive foreigners of justice. (Ezekiel 22:23-29 NLT)

This is an ugly picture of injustice influencing every part of a nation. Let's break this down. Who are all of the people listed in the passage and what are they doing wrong?

1. **Political leaders:** The princes are devouring innocent people, seizing treasures, extorting wealth, and making widows by killing men.
2. **Religious leaders:** The priests aren't following God's laws or honoring Him.
3. **Government officials:** The leaders are tearing apart innocent victims and destroying precious people's lives for money.
4. **Prophets, the mouthpieces for God:** The prophets are covering up for everyone by giving false messages.
5. **Normal citizens:** Everyday people are going along with everything—oppressing the poor, robbing the needy, and not giving justice to immigrants.

When you look at justice issues in the world, it's all too common to see

CONCLUSION: GOD OF HOPE

a picture like this—an intertwining of political, cultural, and religious leaders who are all doing horribly wrong things, while the average person just goes along with it. There is layer after layer of complicated, systemic injustices. Unfortunately, all the people who *should* be standing up and doing what's right are actually perpetuating it. It's overwhelming to look at. No one person could change a picture like that, right?

Well, take a look at what Ezekiel goes on to say God is looking for:

> "I looked for **someone** who might rebuild the wall of righteousness that guards the land. I searched for **someone** to stand in the gap in the wall so I wouldn't have to destroy the land, but I found **no one**. So now I will pour out my fury on them, consuming them with the fire of my anger. I will heap on their heads the full penalty for all their sins. I, the Sovereign Lord, have spoken!" (Ezekiel 22:30-31 GNT emphasis mine)

Whoa. Hold on. Though almost an entire nation is doing wrong, God isn't looking for an entire nation to change first. Instead, He is looking for one person willing to stand in the gap.

Over and over again in the Bible, we see that when there is a huge, seemingly overwhelming crisis, God solves the problem by raising up one person. When Israel was oppressed by Egypt, He raised up a liberator, Moses. When the world was going to be destroyed by a flood, He raised up Noah to save humanity. When Nineveh was facing judgment, He raised up Jonah to be His mouthpiece in order to give the city a second chance. When Haman plotted to destroy all the Jews, He raised up Esther to stand before the king and to convince him to save God's beloved people.[1] When the Gentiles needed the gospel, God raised up a former Jewish murderer, Paul.

God sees the complexity of injustice, but He is not looking for all that huge, complicated, heartbreaking stuff to change first. He is looking for some*one*. Really? That wouldn't be my way of solving anything. I would command all those people doing bad stuff to stop it. With so much going on, what good will one person do?

But what feels giant and overwhelming to us looks different from God's perspective. We don't think our lives contain the power to do anything, but one person who submits to God can shift history. When our emotions tell us that the problems in the world are too big, we need to look again with God's perspective. God can see an oppressed nation, *and* see the liberator for it. God can see a coming worldwide flood, *and* see the person who will join with His plan to save humanity. God sees a nation in dire need of righteous and just leadership, *and* He sees the perfect king for the job. Get excited that God can change problems entangling millions by raising up one person.

For us humans, it's often hard to see both. We feel like we either have to see the problem or see what God can do. It takes some time to train our brains to think differently about injustice. When we see intense issues of injustice—the kind that is so complicated and tangled that it seems like there is no solution—we should have an extreme amount of hope. We mustn't let ourselves give into hopelessness and fear. But how can we be filled with hope when we are constantly faced with seemingly hopeless situations?

GOD OF HOPE

When I first started getting involved in justice projects, I only wanted to learn about issues that I could possibly solve. I preferred to stay ignorant about the issues I couldn't fix because they were way too depressing. While I cared about people, I had a really difficult time opening up my heart to what felt like the overwhelming reality of what was going on in the world.

At some point, I started to sense God knocking on my heart and challenging me not to look away from the reality of what He saw every day. Initially, this felt like too much, so I still chose to avert my eyes. Everything felt so intractable—kids dying of AIDS, rainforests being destroyed, huge wars. Why should I let my heart feel for kids dying of famine when I was powerless to change it? *It would all continue, whether I knew about it or not.* My logic was that if I knew about what was going on, it would just make me sad and powerless, and what good would it be to have one more sad person in the world? Instead, I decided I would

CONCLUSION: GOD OF HOPE

concentrate on problems I could potentially help with, because then I would at least *feel* productive.

One day, God showed me just how wrong my logic was. I was driving home from work, and I could feel the familiar tug from God to stop shutting my mind and heart off to all the injustices in the world. Frustrated, I said out loud, "What's the point? The more I know, the more depressed I will feel. Wouldn't you prefer that I have hope?"

I sensed God gently say back, "I have more information than you do—and more hope."

I drove the rest of the way home in stunned silence. What I had been calling hope, God was calling ignorance. It hit me: Hope is a perspective, not the amount of information you have. My feeling of hopelessness was on me, not Him, and ignoring what's going on in the world for the sake of what I called emotional stability was not healthy. Thinking I needed a warped view of the world to keep my hope alive was wrong and sad. Hope is a decision that God invites us to make.[2]

Hope is a perspective, not the amount of information you have.

God knows *way* more than I do, and He has *way* more hope. And for Him, it's personal. He sees and hears the agony that every single one of His precious children experiences. God hand-knits every human on this planet (see Psalm 139:13, Jeremiah 1:5). He knows the number of hairs on their heads (see Luke 12:7, Matthew 10:30). He hears their cries when they are hurting. Yet, in the midst of knowing the personal, intimate impact of every act of injustice against His precious children, God is a God of hope:

> May the God of hope fill you with all joy and peace in believing, so that by the power of the Holy Spirit you may abound in hope. (Romans 15:13 ESV)

In a world full of injustice and suffering, knowing that we are deeply anchored in a God full of hope is essential. Keeping hope isn't easy. Living a life abounding in hope requires the power of the Holy Spirit. In God,

GOD LOVES JUSTICE

hope thrives. And in God, we can get a real, clear picture of the massive number of injustices that are tearing people apart. When we as the body of Christ only allow ourselves to be exposed to issues of injustice that we *think* we can fix, we shrink to the limits of our abilities. But in God, all things are possible.

When you know the real enemy and that Jesus has already defeated it, you should never be intimidated by a problem, no matter how big it may seem. When you fight the world's problems with the world's solutions, you only get results the world can give. They aren't bad or wrong, but their impact is limited. When you fight the world's problems with God's solutions, you get results only God can achieve. This is a major reason why I think we as Christians should have a ridiculous amount of hope even while looking at injustice and the challenges facing the world. If the problems seem so big that only God can fix them, then good. It's totally possible. Jesus' victory over sin brings us into a lifestyle of hope, courage, strength, and resiliency—even when we face seemingly impossible problems.

NOT ALONE

I know how hard it is when you look around the world and see so much injustice. In the face of millions of orphans, widows, and slaves, as well as massive, tangled issues of injustice in business and governments, how can any single person feel empowered?

There's something important to remember: We aren't called to everything. The great part about being in the body of Christ is that because we are joined together, *we* can actually make big changes.

Here's an example. There are an estimated 8 million orphaned children living in orphanages and institutions—very destructive environments for children to be raised in.[3] God's heart is for each of them to experience the love and stability of a family. When you hear that number, it sounds overwhelming. I want a house with 8 million beds to take them all in. But that's just not realistic. I have a single income, two arms, and twenty-four hours in my day. My limited resources are not enough to take care of 8 million kids.

But think about this: There are over 2.1 billion Christians world-

CONCLUSION: GOD OF HOPE

wide.[4] If only .0038% of Christians adopted a child, the need would be solved. I think *at least* .0038% of Christians have the desire and ability to take in one child.

Put any injustice into the perspective of the size and reach of our God—and the global body of Christ—and there's no reason to be overwhelmed. No single person has 8 million arms. But *we* are integrated into a body that has billions of arms, and it is more than capable of reaching out to all the orphaned and hurting people in the world. Any single body doesn't contain enough resources. But the body of Christ is immensely bigger than any one of us, and the resources available through all of us joined together in relationship to a limitless God are more than enough.

When the heart of the body of Christ reflects God's own love for justice and righteousness, we will watch the world change. We aren't alone in living out justice and righteousness. This isn't an excuse to disengage because someone else will take care of injustice. But instead, this should free us all up to fully engage with the people and tasks to whom and which He's called us, knowing that everyone else in the body of Christ is engaging in their unique positions, too.

BRINGING HOPE

Gaining God's hope for the world will ultimately motivate us to carry that hope into the world, to become active as salt and light in our neighborhoods, cities, and nations. Hope gives us a new perspective on both world issues and our own actions. No issue is too big for God, and none of our own actions are too small or hopeless. Church history is filled with amazing stories of believers who have stepped into hopeless situations with the hope of God, and who have seen everything change. Just as beautifully, they've all done it in different, creative, and powerful ways. The potential for what it can look like to live out God's justice and righteousness in the world is limitless.

Remember that Jesus wasn't concerned with having the right political opinion. We have so many tools in our kingdom tool belt to solve issues, and politics is just one of *many* tools. If we follow the Holy Spirit, He may lead us to address injustice with things like prayer, using art to tell stories and change a society's perceptions, discipleship, or a million other non-political activities. Spiritual freedom is the source of all true freedom, and the more we learn to live in it, the more we can offer it to others.

One person may say that the church should take care of the poor and develop ways for the church to meet their needs. Another sees how government resources can be used to care for the vulnerable in a way that benefits a whole nation. A CEO, teacher, pastor, non-profit leader, government employee, community activist, and stay-at-home parent will all have different perspectives on how to live God's justice and righteousness. The diversity we have as the body of Christ should make us feel *more* empowered and free to live out the exact call and passions we have in our life. Honoring passions and positions that are different than our own should give us more freedom to fully pursue our own unique calls.

There are a lot of ways Christians can bring hope and be salt and light in the world. Here are a few models Christians have used, as well as some examples from more recent history:[5]

1. Working inside the world's systems: Some will be called to influential places in the world. Being in a place where important decisions are made that influence the rest of a nation is an opportunity to bring salt and light to the systems of the world. You could be like Daniel or Joseph, serving an important government leader and using wisdom and strategy from God to work for a nation's success. Or you might be the pro-athlete, business leader, or media professional working in a field that you love, while bringing salt and light into the world through your passion.

An example of this is William Wilberforce, a significant influencer in the abolitionist movement in England. After converting to Christianity in his twenties, he used his position as a member of the British parliament to promote justice in the nation. For decades, he worked within the British political system to bring the changes in the law needed to end slavery. He felt called to use his position of public power to serve God. It took a lifetime of work, but his perseverance paid off. Three days before he died, the Slavery Abolition Act of 1833 passed.

Another example from England is Florence Nightingale. Nightingale was born in 1820 to a wealthy family, and at seventeen, she felt a call from God to give her life to service. She later wrote in her diary, "God

CONCLUSION: GOD OF HOPE

called me in the morning and asked me, 'Would I do good for Him, for Him alone, without reputation.'"[6] Instead of following the societal expectations for a young woman from a wealthy family, Nightingale chose to become a nurse. At the time, nursing was a tough profession. Most nurses survived the smell and conditions by staying drunk—not the most reputable profession for a good Christian woman. After training at a German Lutheran hospital, her first major assignment put her in charge of a battlefield hospital during the Crimean War. Reports of the poor medical care the soldiers received had shocked the British public, so she was charged with improving the care of the wounded. When taking over the hospital, Nightingale and her team of nurses worked tirelessly to make sure all the wounded soldiers got proper care. Thanks to her work, the death rates of soldiers dramatically declined. When she returned home to England after the war, the nation gave her a hero's welcome. The Nightingale Fund was set up in her honor and thanks to generous donors, she started the first modern nursing school. Her accomplishments were vast. During her lifetime, she wrote over 200 books and reports, and she used statistical data to improve health care. Through her work, the culture of care in hospitals changed, with patients being cared for in clean, hygienic, attentive environments. Her model of nursing spread around the world. Because of her response to a call from God at seventeen, Nightingale forever changed the quality and delivery of healthcare.

2. Making alternative institutions: When there is a need in society and a government can't meet it, Christians have frequently developed their own ways to meet the need. This has given Christians more freedom to directly express their faith. Hospitals, addiction rehab centers, orphanages, hospice, and more recently, crisis pregnancy centers, have all come from Christians stepping in to meet a need. Reflecting God's value for the poor, the sick, the elderly, and the orphan by developing institutions when a government or other institution can't or won't is a tangible way to live out justice and righteousness.

3. Disaster relief work: When disaster hits, Christians have a long history of stepping in to bring aid. The founder of the Red Cross, Henry Dunant, was a devout Christian. Raised by parents devoted to helping orphans and the poor, he founded a chapter of YMCA as a young man in Geneva. The idea for the Red Cross came when he witnessed a battle in Italy in 1859 that left tens of thousands of soldiers wounded on the battlefield with no help. Dunant organized people from neighboring towns to give aid to the soldiers so that they could save as many lives as possible. A few years later, Dunant and a group of other men from Geneva officially founded the International Committee of the Red Cross. Soon after, it led to the history-making Geneva Convention, an agreement that twelve governments signed that allowed care for the wounded on the battlefield. Medical care is now considered "neutral," so the wounded in battle, no matter the side, can be cared for. That shift in international law started with a Christian man who saw suffering and destruction and moved in to help.

4. Prayer: Prayer should stay central to all of our lives and especially to our justice work. Doing justice can feel action-oriented, while prayer can feel passive, but they should work together. One modern example of how powerful prayer is to justice work is the story of the prayer movement that ended the bloody, decades-long civil war in Liberia. The situation in Liberia was a lot like the scenario we saw in Ezekiel 22—a massive, complicated tangled injustice that seemed to have no solution. And in that very messy situation, God empowered a single mother of five, Leymah Gbowee to spark a peace movement in Liberia. She had a dream that God told her to gather women and pray for peace. She started out gathering Muslim and Christian women to pray for peace, and moved into more public activism and work. Her bravery was extraordinary. She personally confronted the brutal dictator Charles Taylor when he was in power and later organized a group of women to barricade the warring groups inside of the room for peace talks until the groups reached a deal. With a foundation in prayer, this movement was essential in solving a problem that was so complicated that the smartest, best-trained professionals in the world couldn't fix it. Gbowee went on to win the Nobel Peace Prize, and she is the subject of the documentary *Pray the Devil Back to Hell.*

So many Christian social reformers and activists have built their lives and work on a foundation of prayer—Sojourner Truth, Martin Luther King Jr, William Wilberforce, and Dietrich Bonhoeffer, to name a few. It's essential to anchor your life and work in that intimate place with

CONCLUSION: GOD OF HOPE

God where you can be completely vulnerable and honest, letting Him give you strength when it gets hard. In that place, you will get lined up with His values, and get a strategy for what you do. We may never fully know the impact of prayer outside of our own personal lives on this side of eternity, but I have a feeling when we go to heaven, we will be in awe of how much history was shaped by faithful, everyday people who devoted themselves to prayer.

5. Evangelism: The place where God's reign begins is the human heart. Evangelism (and discipleship) will always change the world for the better because it transforms the deepest core of a person's life. A life redeemed from sin will have an impact on a society.

Not only that, the perspective of an evangelist gives a powerful lens for doing justice and righteousness. In fact, many evangelists have been major supporters of justice. William and Catherine Booth, the founders of the Salvation Army, preached the gospel in the darkest, most ignored places of London. At the same time, they started practical projects to help the poor.

The first advocate for universal human rights was an evangelist—Bartolome de las Casas. He was born in 1484, before Christopher Columbus made his first journey to the Americas. He became a Dominican friar on the island of Hispañola (where modern-day Dominican Republic and Haiti are currently located), and he owned farmland with indigenous slaves. Later, after meditating on a section of Catholic Scriptures about justice, he realized that the system in which he was participating was unjust. Immediately, he gave up his land and slaves, and he became an advocate for the indigenous people. Las Casas believed that the native people in the Americas should not be murdered or enslaved but instead treated as full humans and God's children—all so that they could have the opportunity to hear the gospel. Because of this belief, he became an influential thinker, writing about law, history, politics, and anthropology. Along with his advocacy, he set up missions in modern-day Guatemala to evangelize the native Mayans. His work helped to change the Spanish laws that made enslaving the indigenous people illegal.

In the United States, John Perkins, the founder of Christian Community Development Association, started his community development work in rural Mississippi out of a heart for evangelism. Perkins wrote, "As we responded to all these felt needs, God had given us an abundant spiritual harvest. For hand in hand with our social action, our economic development, and our work of justice has gone the work of evangelism....Everything else we have done has grown out of this gospel we preach."[7] Evangelism and justice work can be done in a way that amplifies the impact of both.

6. Prophetic tradition: Since the time of Israel, God has raised up prophetic voices. Christians can all act as a "destabilizing presence" when sin and injustice have become the accepted norm. Throughout history, bold, righteous men and women have stood up and been willing to "speak truth to power."

One example is William Cooper, an Australian Aboriginal rights leader born in 1860. A man of deep Christian faith, he fought for the rights of his Aboriginal people, believing that the God of the Bible wanted the native Aborigines to live as equals in their native land. He co-founded the Australian Aboriginal League and worked to start a nationwide Day of Mourning to recognize the unjust treatment of the Aborigines. During his life, he petitioned political leaders for Aboriginal representation in government and rights to their land. In his writings, he used biblical images and language—for example, that their land was "by right and gift from God."[8] He's also known for being the only person in the world to organize a private protest of the Nazi's treatment of the Jews following *Kristallnacht*. In fact, there are now 70 Australian trees planted in Israel in his honor. Most of his goals were not achieved in his lifetime. But thanks to his legacy, he influenced new generations of activists and his ideas gained recognition.

7. Church body: From the first generation of the church, people have used the church body to pool resources and meet needs. In the New Testament, we see programs to feed widows, individuals showing hospitality, and churches from one area supporting churches in another. They weren't focused on changing the government but on modeling a loving community using their own resources.

There is an uncomfortable side to all of this history. Plenty of people have used the label "Christian" to do terrible, selfish, unjust things in the world. When Bartolome de las Casas was advocating for rights of the murdered and enslaved indigenous people in the Americas, he didn't end up fighting atheists or people of other religions. Sadly, he had to fight other Christians who were justifying the murders and slavery. Again and again, he called out his fellow Christians for what they were doing and held them to a higher standard, saying things like: "The reason the Christians have murdered on such a vast scale and killed anyone and everyone in their way is purely and simply greed."[9] Those are harsh words. Las Casas used his voice to bring truth to topics that many did not want to discuss. He wrote a book, *History of the Indies*, to show the reality of the atrocities to those living in Spain, who were ignorant about what was being committed in the name of their nation. Lies are instruments of enslavement, and the Spanish needed the truth so that the slaughter of the native people would stop. This will always be a challenge to wrestle through. The label "Christian" isn't enough. We need to be lined up with biblical values, and willing to work in community with each other to confront greed, selfishness, or injustice when they try to take over.

CONCLUSION

My prayer is that this book would be a foundation for movement in your life. If you want to see a justice movement on the earth today, you won't see it in the news or on social media. If you want to see a justice movement, look in the mirror. It looks like you, with your exact talents, callings, gifts, and passions. The world will miss out on so much if you feel like you have to fit into a cookie-cutter idea of what a "social justice" person is supposed to look like. The world needs you to be fully *you*. The invitation is not for you to join a cause or a project, but to use your full life to reflect God's own heart.

*If you want to see a justice movement,
look in the mirror.*

Justice and righteousness start in God, flow into us, transform us, and then flow through our lives. All of us can live justice and righteousness exactly where we are. If we are grounded in God's word, we can all learn what life is supposed to be like. All of us can have compassion-filled hearts, set the standard for integrity, be engaged in our natural and spiritual families, and act as salt and light to a world that needs it. Instead of making justice and righteousness a cause or a project, let's make it an integrated, normal part of everything that we do, so that we reflect the heart and character of God.

God gives justice His best, and so should we. For some, we will be called to do justice through more traditional ways, like politics and non-profit work. But there are so many other ways to work toward creating a world where everyone is able to enjoy life as God created it to be—to do justice through families, science, missions, sports, education, business, evangelism, the arts, technology and more. Think about *what life should be like*, where your calling fits in, and then invest your own life into building that. No matter what your authority and influence look like, you can use them to restore what's broken, reconcile relationships, and contribute to the *shalom* and wholeness of the world God created. Your resources—your job, talents, words, time, voice, spiritual gifts, art, church community, and so much more—are immense. Point those toward filling the world with justice and righteousness.

God loves justice and righteousness. Living a life full of justice and righteousness will never take away from "more important" spiritual priorities, because they *are* God's priority. So I am going to leave you with a simple challenge: *Love justice and righteousness.* That's the message. There are three simple steps to walking this out:

> 1. Ask God to show you how to love justice and righteousness like He does.
>
> 2. Ask Him to show you what the justice and righteousness He loves look like.
>
> 3. Ask Him to lead you into a life that displays the justice and righteousness He loves.

That's it. Love justice and righteousness like God does. Grow in what that looks like in your life. Get big ideas to solve massive issues of injustice. You will probably have to wrestle through what it looks like for you to live it out. There isn't one way to do it.

CONCLUSION: GOD OF HOPE

His kingdom coming on earth should look practical and tangible, bringing that heavenly norm on earth. Heaven on earth—the reality of God's reign made tangible here—looks like a reign of *mishpat* and *sedeq*.

APPENDIX: APPLICATION GUIDE

Take a deep breath. Saving the world isn't on you. But you get to partner with the Savior of humanity in finding the ways you are uniquely positioned and called to live out and establish God's justice and righteousness in the world. God's justice is focused on what life should be like, creating a world full of *shalom*. To bring *shalom*, you get to be creative. Doing justice and righteousness isn't supposed to make you feel like you need to fix everything or that you should add 15 things to your already-too-maxed-out schedule. The following are a few ideas and exercises you can use to find out what it looks like for you to integrate justice and righteousness into your normal lifestyle—the everyday habits and rhythms, cyclical practices, and impact that you are building toward.

Invite God into your process: Spend time in prayer, asking God to give you creative ideas and strategies for doing your life calling from a place of righteousness and justice. Do some journaling and look in the Bible for inspiration.

Meditate on Scripture: The Bible has so many verses about justice, righteousness, and the poor. Our culture so often shapes what we think about issues in the world, and it can be hard to separate which ways of thinking are based on the culture and which are based on the Bible. If there is an area, such as a specific social issue, in which you want God to shape your thinking, then spend time reading about it in the Bible. Take one Scripture or passage on a subject and meditate on it.

Today's widows and orphans: Who are the "poor, widows, orphans, and immigrants"—the people the Old Testament includes as the most vulnerable—in your nation today? Who do you think would be categorized as vulnerable? Who are those likely to be victimized or forgotten about—the ones with the least amount of power and position? How do those people find support? Who is listening to them? Who is working to make sure that they get the justice they need to thrive? What are some ways Christians could meet their needs and see that they get justice?

Your life calling: Because justice is often expressed in limited parts of the world, through limited career choices, it can be a process to wrestle through what it would look like in your personal life calling. Remember that God's justice is creative, dynamic, and transformative—focused on creating what life should be like in the world. Every calling in the world can contribute to fostering what life should be like, including yours. So how could you express justice in new and creative ways within your unique calling? How could you connect your talents, passions, skills, calling, ministry, career, etc. to justice? What part does your career choice play in contributing to the wholeness and restoration of the world?

Look for inspiration: Do a little research and find some people who are integrating justice and righteousness in effective ways through their life calling. How are they are integrating the needs of the poor and vulnerable in their work? How are they contributing to the *shalom* of the world? What are they doing to set a standard of integrity, honesty, and kindness in their career?

Your own wholeness: The wholeness of your own life is part of the wholeness of the world. What are ways that you can build healthy body, soul, and spirit habits to keep your own *shalom*? If there are areas of brokenness in which you are still walking out healing, are there resources that you are connected to? What are ways that you can stay connected to enriching community?

Think outside of money: Sometimes when we think of giving or using our resources for justice, we only think about money. What other resources do you have available—time, an extra seat at your dinner table, your words, networks, a blog, influence, talents, skills, etc.? How could you use those non-monetary resources for justice?

One-degree changes: There are all sort of statistics out there about how destructive small, unconscious habits can be when lots of people are doing them. It can be daunting to look at all the parts of your life and sort through them all, so take one portion of your life at a time and consider whether there are any habits you could adjust. Are your everyday eating, drinking, transportation, and shopping habits reflecting justice and righteousness? If not, what do you think is a better option? What are habits you can change so that justice and righteousness are integrated as normal habits in your life? Analyzing and changing everything at once is overwhelming and probably wouldn't last long-term anyway. But small, one-degree changes taken a little at a time add up to big changes.

Steward the earth: What are habits you can develop to steward the earth in a way that keeps it healthy and thriving for the next generation to enjoy?

Social media: Social media and being online are a huge part of modern lives. When you are interacting with people online, are you still doing justice and righteousness? If you use social media often, what would it look like for you to use it with justice and righteousness?

Golden Rule: When you are confronted with big issues in the world, take a moment and apply the Golden Rule to them. Put yourself in the shoes of someone impacted by the issue and think about what you would want done for you. You can't fix everything in the world, but if you are putting yourself in someone else's situation, it will help you to stay connected to the human side of the issue.

Reconciliation: Are there any groups that have historically been divided in your community—by race, age, gender, economic status, geographic area, etc.? How could you be a minister of reconciliation to those areas?

Supporting your spiritual family: If a problem arises in your city and you hear your vulnerable brothers and sisters asking for help, do you listen and respond? What are ways you can support your fellow brothers and sisters when they ask for help, even if the problem they want help with isn't one that impacts you directly?

Learn about available resources: If you meet someone who needs more help than you can provide, do you know of existing resources that you could connect them to? You may not have the training or time to help everyone you come across. Knowing resources that you can connect people to is a great way to love them. Where are the places people who need deep emotional healing or practical help can go—support groups, counseling centers, ministries, domestic violence shelters, resources for veterans, etc.? This isn't an excuse to disengage from people. We should all be involved with walking out the process of healing and transformation with some people. But the reality is, there will be more need than you have time, skill, and resources to meet. Knowing trusted resources that can help the people you can't personally help is a way of investing in their healing.

Local church community: The local church is a great place from which to do justice and righteousness. Do you see any ways in which your church could be doing justice and righteousness together? What are some ways your church is uniquely positioned to do justice and righteousness? What are some ways you can restore and build wholeness in the communities your church represents? How can you contribute to that happening? What are some ways you've seen other churches doing righteousness and justice together?

The diversity of the church: The body of Christ is so diverse, and the church is a great place for people from all sorts of backgrounds to unite and gain strength from each other. What are ways that you can connect to people from different backgrounds in your church—through ministries, volunteer opportunities, parachurch organizations, outreaches, home groups, etc.? If your church isn't very diverse, if most of the people are just like you, what are other ways you can connect to the diverse body of Christians in your city?

Get to know your own community: Sometimes the world feels really big and full of too many problems to wrap your mind around. Start by taking a look at your own community, where you are living and investing your own life. What are the poverty statistics? Are there specific groups who are typically poor? Where do the poor live, and what are those neighborhoods like? What is the quality of the school districts there? Where does most of the crime happen? Where are churches located? How many kids are in foster care? Where do the homeless populations typically live? Where do the elderly live? Are there any historic cycles of injustice and oppression? Are there Native reservations close? Are there any homeless people you see regularly in your community? If so, introduce yourself and get to know them and what they need. What do you think life should be like in your own city? Who is working in your city to build it?

Get out of isolation: Our modern Western culture is really good at isolating folks, both individually, and in social groups. People typically live in communities with people like them their entire lives. This can mean that if you are economically stable, you can live the majority of your life without ever really knowing someone who is poor, or if you are poor, you can never know other types of oppressed people. In order to really get in touch with people who are different than you, you need to get close enough to them to hear the cry of their hearts. What are the poor in your community crying out for? What are the materially wealthy yet emotionally and spiritually broken crying out for? What opportunities, habits, practices, and rhythms will help connect you to the poor and suffering in your community regularly so that you stay aware of their reality?

Get a human perspective: Think of a group you know who has been historically victimized or oppressed, yet from whom you haven't heard a personal perspective—the human side of their experience of injustice. God knows the individual people, not only the statistics. Learn the human side of the issue or statistics. What personal impact have the injustices had on them? What strength do they have to bring to the world?

APPENDIX

Find a Christian in that group and hear what they have to teach you about God.

Finding your season: You don't necessarily need to quit your day job to do justice and righteousness, even if your job isn't one that obviously connects to justice. What are the practical skills you are learning in this season? How can those practical skills be used for justice and righteousness? In your job, is there any way that you can encourage your company or co-workers to do righteousness and justice? How can you contribute to an environment of integrity, honesty, and kindness at your work? When you are given authority, how are you using that authority to promote justice and righteousness?

Family season: If you have a young family, they will probably take up a lot of time an energy. If you are in the season of raising a family, what are ways you can do justice together? It could look like inviting people over for dinner, keeping bottles of water and socks in your car to give homeless people you encounter, stopping and saying hi to someone who looks sad or lonely, volunteering together, praying for victims of injustice together, and much more. What are traditions or habits you could start to make doing justice and righteousness together normal?

Big picture: God uses everyday people all the time to do big things. What are some issues you want to make an impact on in your lifetime? This impact could be contributing to solving big problems, or intentionally investing in your own community so that it benefits the next generation. For example, maybe you want your own family to reflect a value for the poor and vulnerable. You could invest in the kids in your neighborhood or start taking in foster-care children. Or maybe you want to help heal the physical land that has been hurt by human activities. What are practical skills you can gain now to see that happen? What are some ways you can build in this season toward that bigger-picture impact?

Consistent integrity: Are you consistently living the values you want expressed in the world? It's easy to point to a corrupt government official and be mad at them, but what about your personal integrity? Are you ever willing to bend the truth a little or look the other way for any reason? If so, how can you grow in transparency and accountability with trusted people so that there is no room for corruption?

Integrity habits: What are habits you can implement now to give you accountability and transparency? Who are the people who know you well enough to call you out if they see integrity issues?

Hope Diet: Find news and information sources that introduce you to stories that give you hope. Do a little research and find some people God is raising up to solve issues—serving the poor effectively and with dignity, reaching new people with the gospel, developing technology, promoting integrity and excellence in leadership, finding ways to restore land and communities, etc. What is working? Where are solutions coming from? How are people who have been hurt by injustice finding healing? Find organizations that tell hopeful stories, sign up for their newsletters, and follow them on social media. Listen to podcasts, watch documentaries, or find news sources that expose you to who is doing right in the world. Make sure you are getting a steady diet of hopeful stories and learning about creative solutions being developed.

Growing kingdom: Find ways to get exposed to how God is growing His kingdom in the world today. That's not usually shown in the news, so you will probably have to find that elsewhere. No matter what is going on in economics and politics, God's kingdom stands through it all. Find Christian resources that tell you the stories of the kingdom coming in the world.

ENDNOTES

CHAPTER 1

1. Alden, "'ahed.", 14-15.
2. Sakenfeld. "Love (OT)", 375-381; Els "'hb.", 277-299.
3. Sakenfeld, "Love (OT)," 375-381.
4. Alden, "'ahed," 14-15.

CHAPTER 2

1. Burke, *Concept of Justice*.
2. Carroll and Shiflett, *Christianity on Trial*.
3. Burke, *Concept of Justice*.
4. Schwarzschild, "Justice," 578-579.
5. Carpenter and Comfort, "Peace", 135.
6. Gesenius and Tregelles. "שׁלום".
7. Schneider, "Judgment", 362-367; Mafico, "Just, Justice", 1127-1128.
8. Morris, *Biblical Doctrine of Judgment*.
9. Houston, *Contending for Justice*, 107, 131.
10. Ibid., 107.

CHAPTER 3

1. Leclerc, *Yahweh Is Exalted*, 425; Enns, "*Mispat.*", 1142-1144.
2. Mott, "Justice", 968-970.
3. Culver, "*Shaphat*," 947-949.
4. Ibid.

5. Duchrow and Liedke, *Shalom,* 78.
6. See Psalms 10:18, 72:4, 82:3; Proverbs 29:14; Isaiah 1:17, 1:23, 11:4; Niehr, "*Šāpaṭ*," 411-431.
7. Weinfeld, *Social Justice,* 40.
8. Not only does "social justice" have multiple meanings, but plain "justice" in English has multiple definitions. Some say it's about right order; others that it's about giving people what's due to them. I'll leave the philosophical debates to people with more education than I have, and instead introduce the range of biblical meanings.
9. For an outline of sixteen different dimensions of the meaning, see Rolf Knierim's lecture "Justice in Old Testament Theology" in *The Task of Old Testament Theology.*
10. Morris, *Biblical Doctrine of Judgment.*
11. Oswalt, "Justice and Righteousness", 606-609; Calvin and Pringle, *Commentary on the Gospel According to John.*
12. Waltke, "Creation Account", 28-41.
13. Mott, *Justice.*
14. Waltke, "Creation Account," 28-41.
15. Johnson, "*Mišpāt,*" 86-98.
16. See Proverbs 29:4; Schultz, "*Mishpat*", 837-846.
17. Schultz, "*Mishpat,*" 837-846.
18. Ibid.; Keller, *Generous Justice.*
19. Runesson, "Judgment," 457-466.
20. Sicker, *Political Culture of Judaism.*
21. Schultz, "*Mishpat,*" 837-846.
22. Culver, "*Shaphat,*" 947-949.
23. Morris, *Biblical Doctrine of Judgment.*
24. See Genesis 40:13; 2 Kings 1:7-8, 11:14; 17:26; 1 Samuel 8:9; Judges 18:7.
25. Berkovits, "Biblical Idea of Justice"; Johnson, "*Mišpāt,*" 86-98.
26. Morris, *Biblical Doctrine of Judgment.*
27. Johnson, "*Mišpāt,*" 86-98.
28. Morris, *Biblical Doctrine of Judgment.*
29. Sacks, *Fractured World,* 77.
30. Runesson, "Judgment," 457-466.

ENDNOTES

31. *ESV Study Bible.*
32. Berkovits, "Biblical Idea of Justice," 135.
33. Ibid., 147.
34. De Fraine and Hartman, "Justice," 1251-1252.
35. Marshall, *Beyond Retribution,* 52.
36. Berkovits, "Biblical Idea of Justice."
37. Marshall, *Beyond Retribution.*
38. Mafico, "Just, Justice," 1127-1128.
39. Strong, "Shephet"; Johnson, "*Mišpāt,*" 86-98.
40. Schultz, "*Mishpat,*" 837-846.
41. Morris, *Biblical Doctrine of Judgment.*
42. House, *1, 2 Kings.*
43. Gibbs, "Just," 1167-1168.
44. Morris, *Biblical Doctrine of Judgment,* 16.
45. Brueggemann, *To Act Justly.*
46. Gibbs, "Just," 457-466.

CHAPTER 4

1. Stigers, "*Sadaq, Sedeq, Sedeqah, Saddiq,*" 753-755.
2. Scullion, "Righteousness (OT)," 724-736.
3. Stigers, "*Sadaq, Sedeq, Sedeqah, Saddiq,*" 753-755.
4. Scullion, "Righteousness (OT)," 724-736.
5. Schtemeier, "Righteousness in the Old Testament," 80-85.
6. Von Rad, *Old Testament Theology,* 370-77.
7. Stigers, "*Sadaq, Sedeq, Sedeqah, Saddiq,*" 753-755.
8. Ibid.
9. Scullion, "Righteousness (OT)," 724-736.
10. Seebass, "Righteousness," 352-372.
11. Scullion, "Righteousness (OT)"; Reumann, "Just, Justice, Justification, Justify, Righteous, Righteousness," 262-271.
12. Stigers, "*Sadaq, Sedeq, Sedeqah, Saddiq,*" 753-755.
13. Scullion, "Righteousness (OT)"; Reumann, "Just, Justice," 262-271.
14. See Judges 5:11, 1 Samuel 12:7, Proverbs 11:4, Isaiah 41:2; Scullion, "Righteousness (OT)," 724-736.

GOD LOVES JUSTICE

15. Johnson, "Sādaq," 239-264.
16. Ibid.
17. "Righteousness (OT)," 724-736.
18. Johnson, "Sādaq," 239-264.
19. Ibid.
20. Bratcher and Reyburn, *Translator's Handbook*.
21. Johnson, "Sādaq," 239-264.
22. Stigers, "*Sadaq, Sedeq, Sedeqah, Saddiq*," 753-755.

CHAPTER 5

1. Johnson, "Sādaq," 239-264.
2. Weinfeld, *Social*; Goldingay, "Justice and Salvation," 169-176.
3. Arnold and Choi, *Guide to Biblical Hebrew Syntax*, 29-30.
4. Leclerc, *Yahweh Is Exalted in Justice*.
5. Frey, "Impact of the Biblical Idea of Justice," 91-104.
6. Weinfeld, *Social Justice*.
7. Scullion, "Righteousness (OT)," 724-736.
8. Ibid.
9. Goldingay, "Justice and Salvation," 169-187.
10. Heschel, *The Prophets*, 253.
11. Morris, *Biblical Doctrine of Judgment*.
12. Knierim, *Task of Old Testament Theology*.
13. Goldingay, "Justice and Salvation for Israel and Canaan," 169-187.
14. Mathews, *Genesis 11:27-50:26*.

CHAPTER 6

1. Gen. R. XII. 15; Cohen, *Every Man's Talmud*, 17.
2. Marshall, *Beyond Retribution*.
3. Berkovits, "Biblical Idea of Justice."
4. Kselman, "Grace (OT)," 1084-1086.
5. Coppes, "*Raham*," 841-843.
6. Millikin, "Grace," 678-680.
7. Osborn and Hatton, *Handbook on Exodus*; Stoebe, "*rhm*," 1225-1230.
8. Neusner, *Theological Dictionary*.

ENDNOTES

9. Sakenfeld, "Love (OT)," 375-381.
10. Baer and Gordon, "*Hsd*," 211-218.
11. Garrett, *Hosea, Joel*.
12. Ibid.

CHAPTER 7

1. Sacks, *To Heal a Fractured World*, 37.
2. Barclay, *We Have Seen the Lord!*, 85.
3. Pliens, "Poor, Poverty (OT)," 402-414.
4. Domeris, "*'Ebyon*," 228-232.
5. The nine words are: *'ebyon, dal, dalla, mahsor, misken, miskenut, 'ani, 'anawim,* and *ras*.
1. See Exodus 31:1-6; Ecclesiastes 9:9-10; Matthew 25:14-20; Luke 19:11-27; Romans 12:11-12; Ephesians 4:28; Colossians 3:17, 3:23-24; 1 Thessalonians 4:9-12; 2 Thessalonians 3:10-12; 1 Timothy 5:8.
6. Ellingworth and Nida, *Handbook on Paul's Letters*.
7. Martin, *1, 2 Thessalonians*.
8. Ellingworth and Nida, *Handbook on Paul's Letters*.
9. King, "Letter From a Birmingham Jail."

CHAPTER 8

1. Runesson, "Judgment," 457-466.
2. Henry, *Commentary on the Whole Bible*.
3. Whybray, *Job*
4. Reyburn, *Handbook on the Book of Job*.
5. Ibid.
6. Spence-Jones, *Job*.
7. Gesenius and Tregelles, "וָנָר".
8. Spence-Jones, *Job*.
9. Janzen, *Job*.
10. Lange, *Commentary on the Holy Scriptures*.
11. Reyburn, *Handbook on the Book of Job*.
12. Keil, and Delitzsch, *Commentary on the Old Testament*.
13. Gill, *Gill's Commentary*.

14. Reyburn, *A Handbook on the Book of Job*.
15. Spence-Jones, *Job*.
16. Keil, and Delitzsch, *Commentary on the Old Testament*.
17. Alden, *Job*.
18. Mason, *Teaching of Jesus*.
19. Reyburn, *A Handbook on the Book of Job*; Lange, *Holy Scriptures: Job*.
20. Spence-Jones, *Job*.
21. Reyburn, *A Handbook on the Book of Job*.
22. Alden, *Job*.
23. Brueggemann, *Theology of the Old Testament*.
24. Walvoord and Zuck, *Bible Knowledge Commentary*; Lange, *Holy Scriptures: Job*.
25. Spence-Jones, *Job*.
26. Reyburn, *Handbook on the Book of Job*.
27. Spence-Jones, *Job*.
28. Lange, *Holy Scriptures: Job*.
29. Spence-Jones, *Job*.
30. Lange, *Holy Scriptures: Job*
31. Spence-Jones, *Job*.
32. Reyburn, *Handbook on the Book of Job*.
33. Ibid.
34. Lange, *Holy Scriptures: Job*

CHAPTER 9
1. Goldingay, *Old Testament Theology*.
2. Scullion, "Righteousness (OT)," 724-736.
3. Goldingay, *Old Testament Theology*.
4. Jackson, "'Law' and 'Justice' in the Bible," 218-229.
5. Johnson, "*Sādaq*," 239-264.
6. See Leviticus 25:25-28, 47-49; Ruth 3:13, 4:1-6; Jeremiah 32:6-9; Young, "Redeemer, Redemption," 1827-1829.
7. Goldingay, *Old Testament Theology*.
8. Ibid.

ENDNOTES

9. Ibid.
10. Miller, *Israelite Religion and Biblical Theology*.
11. Baker, "Prophecy, Prophets," 975-986.
12. Goldingay, *Old Testament Theology*.
13. Waltke, "Kingdom of God in the Old Testament," 49-72; Miller, *Israelite Religion and Biblical Theology*; Brueggemann, *Theology of the Old Testament*.
14. Brueggemann, *Theology of the Old Testament*, 233.
15. Wood, *Amos*.
16. Smith and Page, *Amos, Obadiah, Jonah*.
17. Goldingay, *Old Testament Theology*.
18. Sacks, *To Heal a Fractured World*, 37.
19. Ibid.
20. Waard and Smalley, *Translator's Handbook on the Book of Amos*.
21. Brueggemann, *Theology of the Old Testament*.
22. Ibid.
23. Waard and Smalley, *Translator's Handbook on the Book of Amos*.
24. Ibid.
25. Smith and Page, *Amos, Obadiah, Jonah*.
26. Waard and Smalley, *Translator's Handbook on the Book of Amos*.
27. Ibid.
28. Smith and Page, *Amos, Obadiah, Jonah*.
29. Waard and Smalley, *Translator's Handbook on the Book of Amos*.
30. Wood, *Amos*.
31. Smith and Page, *Amos, Obadiah, Jonah*.
32. Waard and Smalley, *Translator's Handbook on the Book of Amos*.
33. Ibid.
34. Smith and Page, *Amos, Obadiah, Jonah*.
35. Wood, *Amos*.
36. Waard and Smalley, *Translator's Handbook on the Book of Amos*.
37. Smith and Page, *Amos, Obadiah, Jonah*.
38. Bauckman, *Bible in Politics*.
39. Goldingay, *Old Testament Theology*.
40. Smith and Page, *Amos, Obadiah, Jonah*.

41. Goldingay, *Old Testament Theology*.
42. Ibid.
43. Smith and Page, *Amos, Obadiah, Jonah*.
44. Waard and Smalley, *Translator's Handbook on the Book of Amos*.
45. Goldingay, *Old Testament Theology*.
46. Ibid.
47. Smith and Page, *Amos, Obadiah, Jonah*.
48. Ibid.
49. Brueggemann, *Theology of the Old Testament*.
50. Smith and Page, *Amos, Obadiah, Jonah*.
51. Smith and Page, *Amos, Obadiah, Jonah*.; Waard and Smalley, *Translator's Handbook on the Book of Amos*.
52. Waard and Smalley, *Translator's Handbook on the Book of Amos*.
53. Sacks, *To Heal a Fractured World*, 9.
54. Oswalt, *Isaiah*; Friesen, *Isaiah*.
55. See 2 Samuel 12:23; 1 Kings 21:9; 2 Chronicles 20:3; Ezra 8:21; Nehemiah 9:1; Esther 4:3, 9:31; Psalm 35:13, 69:10, 109:24; Jeremiah 14:12, 36:6; Daniel 9:3; Zechariah 8:3, 8:19.
56. Smith and Page, *Amos, Obadiah, Jonah*.
57. Gill, *Exposition of the Entire Bible*.
58. Smith and Page, *Amos, Obadiah, Jonah*.

CHAPTER 10

1. Matthew 12:18, 12:20, 23:23; Luke 11:42, 18:3, 18:5, 18:7, 18:8; Acts 8:33, 28:4; Hebrews 11:33.
2. Matthew 12:18, 12:20, 23:23; Luke 7:29, 11:42, 18:7, 18:8; Acts 28:4, Colossians 4:1.
3. Matthew 12:18, 12:20, 23:23; Luke 11:42, 18:3; Acts 8:33, 28:4; Romans 9:14.
4. ESV: Isaiah 1:17, 1:21, 1:23, 1:27, 5:7, 5:16, 9:7, 10:2, 16:3, 16:5, 28:6, 28:17, 30:18, 32:1, 32:16, 33:5, 40:14, 42:1, 42:3, 42:4, 51:4, 56:1, 59:8, 59:9, 59:11, 59:14, 59:15, 61:8 (28 total).
   NASB: Isaiah 1:17, 1:21, 1:27, 5:7, 9:7, 10:2, 16:5, 28:6, 28:17, 30:18, 32:16, 33:5, 40:14, 40:27 42:1, 42:3, 42:4, 49:4, 51:4, 56:1, 59:8, 59:9, 59:11, 59:14, 59:15, 61:8 (26 total).

ENDNOTES

NKJV: Isaiah 1:17, 1:21, 1:27, 5:7, 5:23, 9:7, 10:2, 16:5, 28:6, 28:17, 30:18, 32:1, 32:7, 32:16, 33:5, 40:14, 42:1, 42:3, 42:4, 51:4, 56:1, 58:2, 59:4, 59:8, 59:9, 59:11, 59:14, 59:15, 61:8 (29 total).

5. Schneider, "Judgment," 362-367.
6. Swanson, *Dictionary of Biblical Languages*.
7. Blomberg and Foutz. *Handbook of New Testament Exegesis*.
8. Wolterstorff, *Justice: Rights and Wrongs*.
9. Marshall, *Beyond Retribution*.
10. Wolterstorff, *Justice: Rights and Wrongs*.
11. Farley, *In Praise of Virtue*.
12. Schrenk, "δίκη," 174-224.
13. Wolterstorff, *Justice: Rights and Wrongs*.
14. Schrenk, "δίκη," 174-224.

CHAPTER 11

1. Goldingay, *Do We Need the New Testament?*
2. Melvin, "History of Israel, Post Monarchic Period"; Vos, "History of Israel," 1055-1066.
3. Ladd, *Jesus and the Kingdom*.
4. Ladd, *Jesus and the Kingdom*; Strong, "Malkûwth, malkûth, malkûyâh."
5. Yarbrough, "The Kingdom of God in the New Testament:" Muraoka, "βασιλεία."
6. Ladd, *Jesus and the Kingdom*.
7. Borchert, *John 12-21*.

CHAPTER 12

1. Schrenk, "δίκη," 174-224.
2. Marshall, *Beyond Retribution*.
3. Smith, *Isaiah 40-66*.
4. Weber, *Matthew*.
5. White, "Sin," 1967-1968.
6. Marshall, *Beyond Retribution*.
7. Berkovits, "Biblical Idea of Justice," 129-154.

8. Marshall, *Beyond Retribution*.
9. Goldingay, *Do We Need the New Testament?*
10. Marshall, *Beyond Retribution*.
11. Ibid.
12. Young, "Redeemer, Redemption," 1827-1829.
13. Lau, " Redemption."
14. Gaffin, "New Creation," 1827-1829, 1544-1546.
15. Leclerc, *Yahweh Is Exalted in Justice*.
16. Bratcher and Reyburn, *Translator's Handbook on the Book of Psalms*.

CHAPTER 13

1. Ladd, *Jesus and the Kingdom*.
2. Ibid.
3. Weber, *Matthew*.
4. Ladd, *Jesus and the Kingdom*.
5. Blomberg, *Matthew*.
6. Newman and Stine, *Handbook on the Gospel of Matthew*.
7. Blomberg, *Matthew*.
8. Boice, *Sermon on the Mount*.
9. Blomberg, *Matthew*.
10. Newman and Stine. *Handbook on the Gospel of Matthew*.
11. Blomberg, *Matthew*.
12. Boice, *The Sermon on the Mount*.
13. Ibid.
14. Newman and Stine, *Handbook on the Gospel of Matthew*; Blomberg, *Matthew*.
15. Barclay, *New Testament Words*.
16. Newman and Stine, *Handbook on the Gospel of Matthew*.
17. Boice, *Sermon on the Mount*.
18. Gushee, "Meekness," 518-519.
19. Ibid.
20. Newman and Stine, *Handbook on the Gospel of Matthew*.
21. Lange, *Commentary on the Holy Scriptures*.
22. Newman and Stine, *Handbook on the Gospel of Matthew*.

ENDNOTES

23. Blomberg, *Matthew*.
24. Lange and Schaff, *Commentary on the Holy Scriptures*.
25. Boice, *Sermon on the Mount*.
26. Ibid., 46.
27. Newman and Stine, *Handbook on the Gospel of Matthew*.
28. Blomberg, *Matthew*.
29. Ibid.
30. Ibid.
31. Ibid.
32. Newman and Stine, *Handbook on the Gospel of Matthew*.
33. Lange and Schaff, *Commentary on the Holy Scriptures*.
34. Boice, *Sermon on the Mount*.
35. Newman and Stine, *Handbook on the Gospel of Matthew*.
36. Ibid.
37. Ibid.
38. Hagner, *Matthew 1–13*.
39. Newman and Stine, *A Handbook on the Gospel of Matthew*.
40. Blomberg, *Matthew*.
41. Ladd, *Jesus and the Kingdom*.
42. Heschel, *Prophets*, 253.
43. Wesley, *Nature of the Kingdom*, 104.
44. Ibid., 104-105.
45. Ibid., 106.
46. Ibid., 105.
47. Ladd, *Gospel of the Kingdom*.
48. Ibid.
49. Boice, *Sermon on the Mount*.
50. Ladd, *Gospel of the Kingdom*, 93.
51. Tolstoy, *Pamphlets*, 71.
52. Lloyd-Jones, *Studies in the Sermon on the Mount*.
53. Yarbrough, *Kingdom of God*, 107.
54. Ladd, *Gospel of the Kingdom*.
55. Mieder, "Making a Way out of No Way"; Rieder, *Gospel of Freedom*.
56. Mieder, "Making a Way out of No Way," 362.

57. Smith, "Howard Thurman."
58. Thurman, *Jesus and the Disinherited*, 24.
59. Ibid., 70.
60. Ibid., 64.
61. Ibid., 71.
62. Ibid., 87.
63. Ibid., 102.
64. Ibid., 109.
65. Rengstorf, "Doulos," 182-186, 184.
66. Ladd, *Jesus and the Kingdom*.

CHAPTER 14

1. Young, "Paidagogos," 150-176.
2. Ibid.
3. George, *Galatians*.
4. Young, "Paidagogos," 150-176.
5. Ibid.
6. Ibid.
7. Wolterstorff, *Justice: Rights and Wrongs*.

CHAPTER 15

1. Borchert, *John 1-11*.
2. Sacks, trans. *Koren Siddur*, 642.
3. Brooks, *Mark*.
4. Alcorn, *Money, Possessions, and Eternity*, 3-4.
5. Schunck, "Wanting and Desiring," 866-867.
6. Alcorn, *Money, Possessions, and Eternity*.
7. Cresson, "Idle," 804.
8. See Matthew 7:1, Romans 14:4, 1 Corinthians 4:5, James 4:11; Büchsel, "κρίνω et al."
9. Miller, "Tax Collector."

CHAPTER 16

1. Cooper, *Ezekiel*.

ENDNOTES

2. Brueggemann, *Prophetic Imagination*, 68.
3. Pinheiro, *World Report on Violence against Children*.
4. Hakcett, Conrad, Grim, et al., *Global Christianity*.
5. Thanks for the inspiration for this section, "Models of Christian Influence," chapter in: Hollinger, *Choosing the Good*.
6. Nightingale, *Florence Nightingale's Spiritual Journey*, 369.
7. Perkins, *With Justice for All*, 63.
8. Attwood and Markus, *Thinking Black*, 92.
9. Casas, *Short Account of the Destruction of the Indies*, 13.

BIBLIOGRAPHY

Alcorn, Randy C. *Money, Possessions, and Eternity*. Wheaton, IL: Tyndale House, 2003.

Alden, Robert L. "*ahed.*" In vol. 1 of *Theological Wordbook of the Old Testament,* edited by R. Laird Harris. Chicago, IL: Moody Press, 1980.

Alden, Robert L. "*ahed.*" In vol. 1 of *Theological Wordbook of the Old Testament,* edited by R. Laird Harris. Chicago, IL: Moody Press, 1980.

Arnold, Bill T., and H. G. M. Williamson, eds. *Dictionary of the Old Testament: Historical Books*. Downers Grove, IL: InterVarsity Press, 2005.

Arnold, Bill T., and John H. Choi. *A Guide to Biblical Hebrew Syntax*. New York, NY: Cambridge UP, 2003.

Attwood, Bain, and Andrew Markus. *Thinking Black: William Cooper and the Australian Aborigines' League*. Canberra, ACT: Aboriginal Studies, 2004.

Baer, D. A., and R. P. Gordon. "*Hsd.*" In vol. 2 of *New International Dictionary of Old Testament Theology and Exegesis,* edited by Willem A. VanGemeren. Grand Rapids: Zondervan, 1997.

Baker, J. P. "Prophecy, Prophets." In *New Bible Dictionary*. 2nd ed. Edited by J. D. Douglas. Leicester, England: InterVarsity Press, 1982.

Barclay, William. *New Testament Words*. Philadelphia, PA: Westminster, 1974.

Barclay, William. *We Have Seen the Lord! The Passion and Resurrection of Jesus Christ*. Louisville, KY: Westminster John Knox Press, 1998.

Barry, John D., ed. *Lexham Bible Dictionary*. Bellingham, WA: Lexham Press, 2015.

Bauckman, Richard. *The Bible in Politics: How to Read the Bible Politically*. 2nd ed. London, England: SPCK, 1989.

Berkovits, Eliezer. "Biblical Idea of Justice." In *Essential Essays on Judaism*. Edited by David Hazony, 129-154. New Brunswick, NJ: Transaction Publishers, 2005.

Blomberg, Craig, and Jennifer Foutz Markley. *A Handbook of New*

BIBLIOGRAPHY

Testament Exegesis Grand Rapids, MI: Baker Academic, 2010.

Blomberg, Craig. *Matthew*. The New American Commentary Series, edited by E. Ray Clendenen et al. Nashville, TN: B&H Publishing Group, 1992.

Boice, James Montgomery. *The Sermon on the Mount: an Exposition.* Grand Rapids, MI: Zondervan, 1972.

Borchert, Gerald L. *John 1-11*. The New American Commentary Series, edited by E. Ray Clendenen et al. Nashville, TN: B&H Publishing Group, 1996.

Borchert, Gerald L. *John 12-21*. The New American Commentary Series, edited by E. Ray Clendenen et al. Nashville, TN: B&H Publishing Group, 2002.

Botterweck, G. Johannes, Helmer Ringgren, and Heinz-Josef Fabry, eds. *Theological Dictionary of the Old Testament*. Translated by David E. Green. 15 vols. Grand Rapids, MI: William B. Eerdmans Publishing Company, 1998.

Brand, Chad, Charles W. Draper, and Archie W. England, eds. *Holman Illustrated Bible Dictionary*. Nashville, TN: Holman Bible Publishers, 2003.

Bratcher, Robert G., and William David Reyburn. *A Translator's Handbook on the Book of Psalms*. UBS Handbook Series. New York, NY: United Bible Societies, 1991.

Bromley, Geoffrey W., ed. *The International Standard Bible Encyclopedia*. 4 vols. Grand Rapids, MI: William B. Eerdmans Publishing Company, 1987.

Brooks, James A. *Mark*. The New American Commentary Series, edited by E. Ray Clendenen et al. Nashville, TN: B&H Publishing Group, 1991.

Brown, Colin, ed. *The New International Dictionary of New Testament Theology*. 4 vols. Grand Rapids, MI: Zondervan, 1986.

Brueggeman, Walter. *A Social Reading of the Old Testament: Prophetic Approaches to Israel's Communal Life,* edited by Patrick D. Miller Jr. Minneapolis, MN: Fortress Press, 1994.

Brueggemann, Walter. *The Prophetic Imagination*. Minneapolis, MN: Fortress Press, 1978.

Brueggemann, Walter, Sharon Parks, and Thomas H. Groome. *To Act Justly, Love Tenderly, Walk Humbly. An Agenda for Ministers.* Eugene, OR: Wipf and Stock Publishers, 1986.

Brueggemann, Walter. *Theology of the Old Testament: Testimony, Dispute, Advocacy*. Minneapolis, MN: Fortress Press, 1997.

Büchsel, Friedrich. "κρίνω et al." In *Theological Dictionary of the New Testament*, edited by Gerhard Kittel, Geoffrey William Bromiley, and Gerhard Friedrich. Grand Rapids, MI: William B. Eerdmans Publishing Company, 1964.

Burke, T. Patrick. *The Concept of Justice: Is Social Justice Just?* London, England: Continuum, 2011.

Calvin, John, and William Pringle. *Commentary on the Gospel According to John*. Bellingham, WA: Logos Bible Software, 2010.

Carpenter, Eugene E., and Philip W. Comfort. "Peace." In *Holman Treasury of Key Bible Words: 200 Greek and 200 Hebrew Words Defined and Explained*. Nashville, TN: Broadman & Holman Publishers, 2000.

Carroll, Vincent, and Dave Shiflett. *Christianity on Trial: Arguments Against Anti-Religious Bigotry*. San Francisco, CA: Encounter Books, 2002.

Casas, Bartolomé De Las. *A Short Account of the Destruction of the Indies*. Edited by Nigel Griffin. London, England: Penguin UK, 1992.

Cohen, Abraham. *Everyman's Talmud: The Major Teachings of the Rabbinic Sages*. Revised edition. New York, NY: Schocken, 1995.

Cooper, Lamar Eugene. *Ezekiel*. The New American Commentary Series, edited by E. Ray Clendenen et al. Nashville, TN: B&H Publishing Group, 1994.

Coppes, Leonard J. "*Raham*." In vol. 1 of *Theological Wordbook of the Old Testament,* edited by R. Laird Harris. Chicago, IL: Moody Press, 1980.

Cresson, Bruce C. "Idle." In *Holman Illustrated Bible Dictionary*. Edited by Chad Brand, Charles W. Draper, and Archie W. England. Nashville, TN: Holman Bible Publishers, 2003.

Culver, Robert D. "*Shaphat*." In vol. 2 of *Theological Wordbook of the Old Testament,* edited by R. Laird Harris. Chicago, IL: Moody Press, 1980.

De Fraine, J., and Louis F. Hartman. "Justice." In *Encyclopedic Dictionary of the Bible*. Edited by A. Van den Born. New York, NY: McGraw-Hill. 1963.

Domeris, W. R. "'*Ebyon*." In vol. 1 of *New International Dictionary of Old Testament Theology and Exegesis,* edited by Willem A. VanGemeren. Grand Rapids, MI: Zondervan, 1997.

Douglas, J.D., ed. *New Bible Dictionary*. 2nd ed. Leicester, England: InterVarsity Press, 1982.

Duchrow, Ulrich, and Gerhard Liedke. *Shalom: Biblical Perspectives on Creation, Justice & Peace*. Geneva: WCC Publications, 1989.

Ellingworth, Paul, and Eugene Albert Nida. *A Handbook on Paul's Letters to the Thessalonians*. UBS Handbook Series. New York, NY: United Bible Societies, 1976.

BIBLIOGRAPHY

Els, P.J.J.S. "'hb." In vol. 1 of *New International Dictionary of Old Testament Theology and Exegesis*, edited by Willem A. VanGemeren, Grand Rapids, MI: Zondervan, 1997.

Elwell, Walter A., ed. *Baker Encyclopedia of the Bible*. 2 vols. Grand Rapids, MI: Baker Book House, 1988.

Enns, Peter. "*Mispat*." In vol. 2 of *New International Dictionary of Old Testament Theology and Exegesis*, edited by Willem A. VanGemeren, Grand Rapids, MI: Zondervan, 1997.

ESV Study Bible: English Standard Version. Wheaton, IL: Crossway Bibles, 2010.Farley, Benjamin Wirt. *In Praise of Virtue: An Exploration of the Biblical Virtues in a Christian Context*. Grand Rapids, MI: William B. Eerdmans Publishers, 1995.

Freedman, David Noel et al, eds. *Anchor Bible Dictionary*. 6 vols. New York: Doubleday, 1992.

Frey, Cristofer. "The Impact of the Biblical Idea of Justice on Present Discussions of Social Justice." In *Justice and Righteousness: Biblical Themes and Their Influence*. Edited by Yair Hoffman and Henning Reventlow, 91-104. Journal for the Study of the Old Testament. Supplement Series. Sheffield, England: JSOT, 1992.

Friesen, Ivan. *Isaiah*. Believers Church Bible Commentary Series, edited by Elmer A. Martens et al. Scottsdale, PA: Herald Press, 2009.

Gaffin, Richard, Jr. "New Creation." In vol. 2 of *Baker Encyclopedia of the Bible*, edited by Walter A. Elwell. Grand Rapids, MI: Baker Book House, 1988.

Garrett, Duane A. *Hosea, Joel*. The New American Commentary Series, edited by E. Ray Clendenen et al. Nashville, TN: B&H Publishing Group, 1997.

George, Timothy. *Galatians*. The New American Commentary Series, edited by E. Ray Clendenen et al. Nashville, TN: B&H Publishing Group, 1994.

Gesenius, Wilhelm, and Samuel Prideaux Tregelles, "שָׁלוֹם'. *Gesenius' Hebrew and Chaldee Lexicon to the Old Testament Scriptures*. Bellingham, WA: Logos Bible Software, 2003.

Gesenius, Wilhelm, and Samuel Prideaux Tregelles. "וָנָר". *Gesenius' Hebrew and Chaldee Lexicon to the Old Testament Scriptures*. Bellingham, WA: Logos Bible Software, 2003.

Gibbs, J. G., "Just." In vol. 2 of *The International Standard Bible Encyclopedia*, edited by Geoffrey W. Bromley. Grand Rapids, MI: William B. Eerdmans Publishing Company, 1987.

Gibbs, J. G. "Just." In vol. 2 of *The New Interpreter's Dictionary of the Bible: E-J*, edited by Katharine Doob Sakenfeld. Nashville, TN: Abingdon Press, 2008.

Gill, John. *Gill's Commentary.* Grand Rapids, MI: Baker Book House, 1980.

Gill, John. *An Exposition of the Entire Bible.* London, England: William Hill Collingridge, 1852.

Goldingay, John. *Old Testament Theology, Volume 3: Israel's Life.* Downers Grove, IL: InterVarsity Press, 2009.

Goldingay, John. "Justice and Salvation for Israel and Canaan." In vol. 1 of *Reading the Hebrew Bible for a New Millennium: Form, Concept, and Ecological Perspective,* edited by Wonil Kim et al., 169-187. Harrisburg, PA: Trinity International, 2000.

Goldingay, John. *Do We Need the New Testament?: Letting the Old Testament Speak for Itself.* Downers Grove, IL: InterVarsity Press, 2015.

Gowan, Donald E., ed. *The Westminster Theological Wordbook of the Bible.* Louisville, KY: Westminster John Knox, 2003.

Green, Joel B. et al., eds. *Dictionary of Scripture and Ethics.* Grand Rapids, MI: Baker Academic, 2011.

Gushee, David P. "Meekness." In *Dictionary of Scripture and Ethics.* Edited by Joel B. Green et al. Grand Rapids, MI: Baker Academic, 2011.

Hakcett, Conrad, Brian J. Grim, et al. *Global Christianity: A Report on the Size and Distribution of the World's Christian Population.* Report. Washington, DC: Pew Research Center's Forum on Religion & Public Life, 2011.

Hagner, Donald A. *Matthew 1-13.* Word Biblical Commentary Series, edited by Bruce M. Metzger. Dallas, TX: Word Books, 1993.

Harris, R. Laird, ed. *Theological Wordbook of the Old Testament.* 2 vols. Chicago, IL: Moody Press, 1980.

Henry, Matthew. *Matthew Henry's Commentary on the Whole Bible.* Peabody, MA: Hendrickson Publishers, 1991.

Heschel, Abraham Joshua. *The Prophets.* New York, NY: Harper & Row, 1962.

Hoffman, Yair, and Henning Reventlow, eds. *Justice and Righteousness: Biblical Themes and Their Influence.* Journal for the Study of the Old Testament. Supplement Series. Sheffield, England: JSOT, 1992.

Hollinger, Dennis P. *Choosing the Good: Christian Ethics in a Complex World.* Grand Rapids, MI: Baker Academic, 2002.

House, Paul R. *1, 2 Kings.* The New American Commentary Series, edited by E. Ray Clendenen et al. Nashville, TN: B&H Publishing Group, 1995.

Houston, Walter. *Contending for Justice: Ideologies and Theologies of Social Justice in the Old Testament.* London, England: T & T Clark, 2006.

Jackson, Bernard S. "'Law' and 'Justice' in the Bible." *Journal of Jewish Studies* XLIX.1 (1998), 218-229

Janzen, J. Gerald. *Job. Interpretation: A Bible Commentary for Teaching and Preaching*, edited by James Luther Mays. Louisville, KY: John Knox Press, 1985.

Jenni, Ernst, and Claus Westermann, eds. *Theological Lexicon of the Old Testament*. Peabody, MA: Hendrickson Publishers, 1997.

Johnson, B. "Sādaq." In vol. 12 of *Theological Dictionary of the Old Testament*, edited by G. Johannes Botterweck, Helmer Ringgren, and Heinz-Josef Fabry. Translated by David E. Green. Grand Rapids: William B. Eerdmans Publishing Company, 1998.

Johnson, B. "Mišpāt." In vol. 9 of *Theological Dictionary of the Old Testament*, edited by G. Johannes Botterweck, Helmer Ringgren and Heinz-Josef Fabry. Translated by David E. Green. Grand Rapids: William B. Eerdmans Publishing Company, 1998.

Keil, Carl Friedrich, and Franz Delitzsch. *Commentary on the Old Testament*. Peabody, MA: Hendrickson, 1996.

Keller, Timothy. *Generous Justice: How God's Grace Makes Us Just*. New York, NY: Dutton, Penguin Group USA, 2010.

King, Martin Luther, Jr. "Letter from a Birmingham Jail." Birmingham, AL, 1963 Accessed February 1, 2016. http://okra.stanford.edu/transcription/document_images/undecided/630416-019.pdf.

Kittel, Gerhard, and Gerhard Friedrich, eds. *Abridged Theological Dictionary of the New Testament: Abridged in One Volume*. Grand Rapids, MI: William B. Eerdmans Publishing Company, 1985.

Kittel, Gerhard, Geoffrey William Bromiley, and Gerhard Friedrich, eds. *Theological Dictionary of the New Testament*. 10 vols. Grand Rapids, MI: William B. Eerdmans Publishing Company, 1964.

Knierim, Rolf P. *The Task of Old Testament Theology: Substance, Method, and Cases: Essays*. Grand Rapids, MI: Eerdmans, 1995.

Kselman, John S. "Grace (OT)." In vol. 2 of *Anchor Bible Dictionary*, edited by David Noel Freedman et al. New York, NY: Doubleday, 1992.

Ladd, George Eldon. *Jesus and the Kingdom: The Eschatology of Biblical Realism*. New York, NY: Harper & Row, 1964.

Ladd, George Eldon. *The Gospel of the Kingdom: Scriptural Studies in the Kingdom of God*. Grand Rapids, MI: William B. Eerdmans Publishing Company, 1959.

Lange, John Peter. *A Commentary on the Holy Scriptures: Job*. Edited and translated by Philip Schaff. Grand Rapids, MI: Zondervan, 1950.

Lange, John Peter. *A Commentary on the Holy Scriptures: Matthew*. Edited and translated by Philip Schaff. Bellingham, WA: Logos Bible Software, 2008.

Lau, Peter. " Redemption." In *Lexham Bible Dictionary*. Edited by John D. Barry. Bellingham, WA: Lexham Press, 2015.

Leclerc, Thomas. *Yahweh Is Exalted in Justice: Solidarity and Conflict in*

Isaiah. Minneapolis, MN: Fortress Press, 2001.

Lloyd-Jones, D. Martyn. *Studies in the Sermon on the Mount.* 2nd ed. Grand Rapids, MI: William B. Eerdmans Publishing Company, 1976.

Mafico, Temba L. "Just, Justice." In vol. 3 of *Anchor Bible Dictionary*, edited by David Noel Freedman et al. New York City: Doubleday, 1992.

Marshall, Christopher D. *Beyond Retribution: A New Testament Vision for Justice, Crime, and Punishment.* Grand Rapids, MI: William B. Eerdmans Publishing Company, 2001.

Martin, D. Michael. *1, 2 Thessalonians.* The New American Commentary Series, edited by E. Ray Clendenen et al. Nashville, TN: B&H Publishing Group, 1995.

Mason, T.W. *The Teaching of Jesus.* Cambridge, MA: Cambridge University Press, 1935.

Mathews, Kenneth A. *Genesis 11:27-50:26.* The New American Commentary Series, edited by E. Ray Clendenen et al. Nashville, TN: B&H Publishing Group, 2005.

Melvin, David P. "History of Israel, Post Monarchic Period." In *Lexham Bible Dictionary.* Edited by John D. Barry. Bellingham, WA: Lexham Press, 2015.

Mieder, Wolfgang. *"Making a Way out of No Way": Martin Luther King's Sermonic Proverbial Rhetoric.* New York, NY: Peter Lang, 2010.

Miller, Jeffery E. "Tax Collector." In *Lexham Bible Dictionary.* Edited by John D. Barry. Bellingham, WA: Lexham Press, 2015.

Miller, Patrick D. *Israelite Religion and Biblical Theology: Collected Essays.* Sheffield: Sheffield Academic, 2000.

Millikin, Jimmy A. "Grace." In *Holman Illustrated Bible Dictionary*. Edited by Chad Brand, Charles W. Draper, and Archie W. England. Nashville, TN: Holman Bible Publishers, 2003.

Morgan, Christopher, and Robert Peterson, eds. *The Kingdom of God.* Wheaton, IL: Crossway, 2012.

Morris, Leon. *The Biblical Doctrine of Judgment.* Grand Rapids, MI: William B. Eerdmans Publishing Company, 1960.

Mott, Stephen Charles. "Justice." In *Holman Illustrated Bible Dictionary*. Edited by Chad Brand, Charles W. Draper, and Archie W. England. Nashville: Holman Bible Publishers, 2003.

Muraoka, T. *A Greek-English Lexicon of the Septuagint.* Leuven, Belgium: Peeters, 2009.

Neusner, Jacob. *Theological Dictionary of Rabbinic Judaism. Part One: Principle Theological Categories.* Lanham, MD: University Press of America, 2005.

Newman, Barclay Moon, and Philip C. Stine. *A Handbook on the Gospel of Matthew.* UBS Handbook Series. New York, NY: United

BIBLIOGRAPHY

Bible Societies, 1992.

Niehr, H. "*Šāpaṭ.*" In vol. 15 of *Theological Dictionary of the Old Testament*, edited by G. Johannes Botterweck, Helmer Ringgren and Heinz-Josef Fabry. Translated by David E. Green. Grand Rapids, MI: William B. Eerdmans Publishing Company, 1998.

Nightingale, Florence. *Florence Nightingale's Spiritual Journey: Biblical Annotations, Sermons and Journal Notes*. Vol. 2 of *Collected Works of Florence Nightingale*, edited by Lynn McDonald. Waterloo, Ont.: Wilfrid Laurier UP, 2001.

Osborn, Noel D., and Howard A. Hatton. *A Handbook on Exodus*. UBS Handbook Series. New York, NY: United Bible Societies, 1999.

Oswalt, John N. *Isaiah*. The NIV Application Commentary series, edited by Terry Muck et al. Grand Rapids, MI: Zondervan, 2003.

Oswalt, John N. "Justice and Righteousness." In *Dictionary of the Old Testament: Historical Books*. Edited by Bill T. Arnold and H. G. M. Williamson. Downers Grove, IL: InterVarsity Press, 2005.

Perkins, John. *With Justice for All*. Ventura, CA: Regal, 1982.

Pliens, J. David. "Poor, Poverty (OT)." In vol. 5 of *Anchor Bible Dictionary*, edited by David Noel Freedman et al. New York, NY: Doubleday, 1992.

Pinheiro, P. S. *World Report on Violence against Children*, UNICEF: New York, NY. 2006.

Rad, Gerhard Von. *Old Testament Theology. Volume 1: The Theology of Israel's Historical Traditions*. Louisville, KY: Westminster John Knox, 2001.

Rengstorf, K. H., II "Doulos" In *Abridged Theological Dictionary of the New Testament: Abridged in One Volume*. Edited by Gerhard Kittel and Gerhard Friedrich. 1985. Reprint, Grand Rapids, MI: William B. Eerdmans Publishing Company, 2008.

Reumann, John. "Just, Justice, Justification, Justify, Righteous, Righteousness." In *Westminster Theological Wordbook of the Bible*. Edited by Donald E. Gowan. Louisville, KY: Westminster John Knox, 2003.

Reyburn, William David. *A Handbook on the Book of Job*. UBS Handbook Series. New York, NY: United Bible Societies, 1992.

Rieder, Jonathan. *Gospel of Freedom: Martin Luther King, Jr.'s Letter from Birmingham Jail and the Struggle That Changed a Nation*. New York, NY: Bloomsbury, 2013.

Runesson, Anders. "Judgment." In vol. 3 of *The New Interpreter's Dictionary of the Bible: I-Ma*. Edited by Katharine Doob Sakenfeld. Nashville, TN: Abingdon Press, 2008.

Sacks, Jonathan, trans. *The Koren Siddur*. Jerusalem, Israel: Koren

Publishers, 2009.

Sacks, Jonathan. *To Heal a Fractured World: The Ethics of Responsibility*. New York, NY: Schocken, 2005.

Sakenfeld, Katherine Doob. "Love (OT)." In vol. 4 of *Anchor Bible Dictionary*, edited by David Noel Freedman et al. New York, NY: Doubleday, 1992.

Sakenfeld, Katharine Doob, ed. *The New Interpreter's Dictionary of the Bible*. 5 vols. Nashville, TN: Abingdon Press, 2008.

Schneider, W. "Judgment." In vol. 2 of *The New International Dictionary of New Testament Theology*, edited by Colin Brown. Grand Rapids: Zondervan, 1986.

Schrenk, Gottlob. "δίκη, δίκαιος, δικαιοσύνη, δικαιόω, δικαίωμα, δικαίωσις, δικαιοκρισία." In vol. 2 of *Theological Dictionary of the New Testament*. Edited by Gerhard Kittel, Geoffrey William Bromiley, and Gerhard Friedrich. Grand Rapids, MI: William B. Eerdmans Publishing Company, 1964.

Schtemeier, E. R. "Righteousness in the Old Testament." Vol. 2 of *The New Interpreter's Dictionary of the Bible: E-J*, edited by Katharine Doob Sakenfeld. Nashville, TN: Abingdon Press, 2008.

Schultz, Richard. "*Mishpat*." Vol. 4 of *New International Dictionary of Old Testament Theology and Exegesis*, edited by Willem A. VanGemeren, Grand Rapids, MI: Zondervan, 1997.

Schunck, K. D. "Wanting and Desiring." Vol. 6 of *Anchor Bible Dictionary*, edited by David Noel Freedman et al. New York, NY: Doubleday, 1992.

Schwarzschild, Steven S. "Justice." Vol. 2 of *Encyclopedia Judaica*. 2nd ed., edited by Fred Skolnik. Jerusalem, Israel: The Jerusalem Publishing House/Thomson Gale, 2007.

Scullion, J. J. "Righteousness (OT)." Vol. 5 of *Anchor Bible Dictionary*, edited by David Noel Freedman et al. New York, NY: Doubleday, 1992.

Seebass, H. "Righteousness." Vol. 3 of *The New International Dictionary of New Testament Theology*, edited by Colin Brown. Grand Rapids, MI: Zondervan, 1986.

Sicker, Martin. *The Political Culture of Judaism*. Westport, CT: Praeger, 2001.

Skolnik, Fred, ed. *Encyclopedia Judaica*. 2nd ed. 22 vols. Jerusalem, Israel: The Jerusalem Publishing House/Thomson Gale, 2007.

Smith, Billy K., and Franklin S. Page. *Amos, Obadiah, Jonah*. The New American Commentary Series, edited by E. Ray Clendenen et al. Nashville, TN: B&H Publishing Group, 1995.

Smith, Gary V. *Isaiah 40-66*. The New American Commentary Series, edited by E. Ray Clendenen et al. Nashville, TN: B&H Publishing Group, 2009.

BIBLIOGRAPHY

Smith, Luther E., Jr. *Christian Spirituality: The Classics*. Edited by Arthur G. Holder. London, England: Routledge, 2009.

Smith, Luther E., Jr. "Howard Thurman." In *Christian Spirituality: The Classics*. Edited by Arthur G. Holder, 341-353. London, England: Routledge, 2009.

Spence-Jones, H. D. M., ed. *Job*. In *The Pulpit Commentary*. London, New York: Funk & Wagnalls Company, 1909.

Stoebe, H. J. *"rhm"* Vol. 3 of *Theological Lexicon of the Old Testament*, edited by Ernst Jenni and Claus Westermann. Peabody, MA: Hendrickson Publishers, 1997.

Stigers, Harold G. "Sadaq, Sedeq, Sedeqah, Saddiq." Vol. 2 of *Theological Wordbook of the Old Testament*, edited by R. Laird Harris. Chicago, IL: Moody Press, 1980.

Strong, James. *A Concise Dictionary of the Words in the Hebrew Bible*. Bellingham, WA: Logos Bible Software, 2008.

Strong, James. "Malkûwth, malkûth, malkûyâh." In *A Concise Dictionary of the Words in the Hebrew Bible*, 67. Bellingham, WA: Logos Bible Software, 2008.

Swanson, James A. *A Dictionary of Biblical Languages with Semantic Domains: Greek (NT)*. Oak Harbor, WA: Logos Research Systems, 1997.

Thurman, Howard. *Jesus and the Disinherited*. Boston, MA: Beacon, 1996.

Tolstoy, Leo. *Pamphlets. Translated from the Russian*. Christchurch, Hants: Free Age, 1900.

Van den Born, A., ed. *Encyclopedic Dictionary of the Bible*. New York, NY: McGraw-Hill. 1963.

Van Gemeren, Willem A., ed. *New International Dictionary of Old Testament Theology and Exegesis*. 5 vols. Grand Rapids, MI: Zondervan, 1997.

Von Rad, Gerhard. *Old Testament Theology*. Vol 1, *The Theology of Israel's Historical Traditions*. Louisville, KY: Westminster John Knox, 2001.

Vos, Howard. "History of Israel." In vol. 1 of *Baker Encyclopedia of the Bible*. Edited by Walter A. Elwell. Grand Rapids, MI: Baker Book House, 1988.

Waard, Jan de, and William Allen Smalley. *A Translator's Handbook on the Book of Amos*. UBS Handbook Series. Stuttgart: United Bible Societies, 1979.

Waltke, Bruce K. "Creation Account in Genesis 1:1-3, Part V: The Theology of Genesis 1—Continued." *Bibliotheca Sacra* 133 (1975).

Waltke, Bruce K. "The Kingdom of God in the Old Testament: Definitions and Stories." In *The Kingdom of God*. Edited by Christopher Morgan and Robert Peterson, 49-72. Wheaton, IL:

Crossway, 2012.
Zuck, Roy B. "Job." In vol. 1 of *The Bible Knowledge Commentary: An Exposition of the Scriptures by Dallas Seminary Faculty (Old Testament)*, edited by John F. Walvoord and Roy B. Zuck, 715-778. Wheaton, IL: Victor Books, 1983.
Weber, Stu. *Holman New Testament Commentary: Matthew*. Edited by Max Anders Nashville, TN: Broadman & Holman Publishers, 2000.
Weinfeld, Moshe. *Social Justice in Ancient Israel and in the Ancient Near East*. Minneapolis, MN: Fortress Press, 1995.
Wesley, John. *The Nature of the Kingdom: Wesley's Messages on the Sermon on the Mount*. Edited by Clare G. Weakley. Minneapolis, MN: Bethany House, 1986.
White, R. E. O. "Sin." In vol. 2 of *Baker Encyclopedia of the Bible,* edited by Walter A. Elwell. Grand Rapids, MI: Baker Book House, 1988.
Whybray, Norman. *Job*. Sheffield, England: Sheffield Academic Press, 1998.
Williams, Ronald J., and John C. Beckman. "Hendiadys." In *Williams' Hebrew Syntax*. Toronto, Canada: University of Toronto, 2007.
Wolterstorff, Nicholas. *Justice: Rights and Wrongs*. Princeton, NJ: Princeton University Press, 2008.
Wood, Fred. *Amos*. Minor Prophet Series. Bloomington, IN: CrossBooks Publishing, 2009.
Yarbrough, Robert W. "The Kingdom of God in the New Testament: Matthew and Revelation." In *The Kingdom of God*. Edited by Christopher Morgan and Robert Peterson, 95-124. Wheaton, IL: Crossway, 2012.
Young, Norman H. "Paidagogos: The Social Setting of a Pauline Metaphor." *Novum Testamentum* XXIX, no. 2 (1987): 150-76.
Young, Warren C. "Redeemer, Redemption." In vol. 2 of *Baker Encyclopedia of the Bible,* edited by Walter A. Elwell. Grand Rapids, MI: Baker Book House, 1988.

GOD LOVES JUSTICE

A USER-FRIENDLY GUIDE TO BIBLICAL JUSTICE AND RIGHTEOUSNESS

Jessica Nicholas

BOOK@GODLOVESJUSTICE.COM
WWW.GODLOVESJUSTICE.COM

Printed in Great Britain
by Amazon